THE **boat electrics** BIBLE

THE boat electrics BIBLE

A PRACTICAL GUIDE TO REPAIRS, INSTALLATIONS AND MAINTENANCE ON YACHTS AND MOTORBOATS

Andy Johnson

ADLARD COLES NAUTICAL
BLOOMSBURY
LONDON · NEW DELHI · NEW YORK · SYDNEY

Adlard Coles Nautical

An imprint of Bloomsbury Publishing Plc

50 Bedford Square   1385 Broadway
London   New York
WC1B 3DP   NY 10018
UK   USA

www.bloomsbury.com

ADLARD COLES, ADLARD COLES NAUTICAL and the Buoy
logo are trademarks of Bloomsbury Publishing Plc

First published 2015

British Library Cataloguing-in-Publication Data
A catalogue record for this book is available from the British
Library. Library of Congress Cataloguing-in-Publication data
has been applied for.

ISBN: HB: 978-1-4081-8779-1
ePDF: 978-1-4729-2205-2
ePub: 978-1-4729-2204-5

2 4 6 8 10 9 7 5 3 1

Typeset in Antenna, Veljovic Book and Bliss
Colour origination by Ivy Press Reprographics
Printed and bound in China by C&C Offset Printing Co., Ltd

Produced for Adlard Coles Nautical by Ivy Contract
MANAGING EDITOR: Judith Chamberlain-Webber
COMMISSIONING EDITOR: Sarah Doughty
PROJECT DESIGNER: Kevin Knight
CONSULTANT: Andrew Simpson

Note: while all reasonable care has been taken in the
publication of this book, the publisher takes no responsibility
for the use of the methods or products described in the book.

Bloomsbury Publishing Plc makes every effort to ensure that
the papers used in the manufacture of our books are natural,
recyclable products made from wood grown in well-managed
forests. Our manufacturing processes conform to the
environmental regulations of the country of origin.

To find out more about our authors and books visit
www.bloomsbury.com. Here you will find extracts, author
interviews, details of forthcoming events and the option
to sign up for our newsletters.

Contents

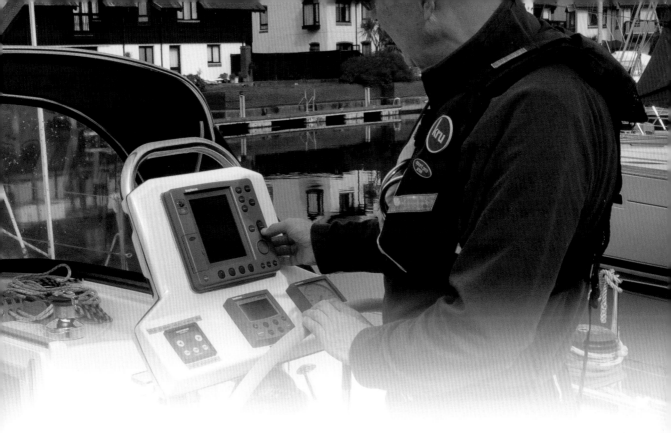

Welcome to boat electrics

If you have never attempted electrical work on a boat, or are reluctant to try, this book takes the mystery out of the wires, switches, fuses and other parts associated with a boat's battery powered, low voltage electrical equipment. Where necessary, the detailed explanations will enable you to gain a good insight into how it all works.

Many boatowners may feel unsure about tackling any electrical problems on their boat. However, with some basic knowledge and understanding, most aspects of the battery based, low voltage electrics that you are likely to find on your boat can be tackled.

It is not necessary to have a lot of complicated tools and equipment – a few basic items including a multimeter should be enough. The main focuses are to understand what is necessary to install a new piece of equipment and how to find and rectify problems or faults in existing systems.

Below **The distribution panel can take any format but is essentially a collection of switches and indicators controlling the power distribution to the boat's electrical equipment. It often also includes the fusing arrangements.**

Safety is always paramount and all aspects of working on boats have potential dangers. The low voltage battery based (12 volt and 24 volt) electrical systems are inherently safe but care is necessary because the batteries store a substantial amount of energy. Although mains electricity on board is discussed, working on high voltage systems is not covered in as much detail.

Key concepts

The concepts of voltage, current, resistance and power are all fundamental to the functioning of electrical systems. This is because:

❂ Without sufficient voltage, the equipment may not operate correctly.
❂ The correct wire size and most

Above **The multimeter is arguably the most useful tool. It measures voltage and current as well as resistance and continuity. Without one you are very limited in the electrical work and fault finding you can do.**

appropriate fusing arrangements, to protect the wiring, can be established based on the operating current consumed by the equipment.
❂ The operating current can be derived either by measurement or from the power consumption printed on the equipment itself or in its operating manual.

Since the whole low voltage system depends on the batteries, a thorough understanding of the different types available, how many you might need and how they work is important. Although they are low maintenance items, the way in which they are used and recharged will influence their performance and lifespan.

From the batteries, individual circuits feed electrical power to the many pieces of equipment on the vessel. Between the batteries and

Above Wire cutters are available in several sizes depending on the wire diameter to be cut.

Above The crimping tool attaches a range of connectors onto the wire.

Above The batteries are the heart of the electrical system on boats. They store the energy, making it available when required.

the equipment is an arrangement of switches, fuses, distribution panels, indicator lights and, of course, a mass of wire. There may be only one means of recharging the batteries on board – your engine (or at least the alternator attached to the engine) – or a whole raft of sources including shore power, solar power, wind power and water power. The management and regulation of these is worth knowing about as it will improve your boat's functioning.

Electronics and instrument systems

Nowadays, communication between instruments, radar, AIS and other aids to navigation and systems monitoring is a fundamental part of operating a boat. To understand how to get the best out of the various networks available, particularly NMEA0183 and NMEA2000 (or manufacturer's equivalents), it is important to look at both the theory

and practical examples. Instruments from different manufacturers can be linked together using both types of network either separately or simultaneously.

Once you are familiar with the concepts and have an understanding of what your objectives are, the low voltage electrical systems on your boat should present no more difficulty than anything else.

Above Having cut the wire, self-adjusting wire strippers remove the plastic insulation without damaging the wire itself.

Above A wide selection of connectors is available, along with cable ties to secure the wiring.

Left Wind generators are a popular source of power to help keep the batteries charged.

The basics

What is electricity?

Electricity is the flow of electrical charge and occurs naturally in events such as lightning and static electricity. However, when the flow can be controlled, it becomes the useful force that governs much of our lives. On a boat, electricity is important for comfort and, increasingly, safety.

Electricity is a form of energy that results from the existence of charged particles. All matter is made up of atoms, which have a nucleus surrounded by negatively charged electrons in a number of orbits. This is similar to the way satellites orbit the Earth. Electrical current is the result of the movement or flow of these charged particles.

In materials that conduct electricity, the electrons in the outer orbits are unstable and jump from one atom to the next, provided there is an electro-motive force (voltage) to encourage it. The electrons, being negatively charged, are attracted towards anything more positive (such as a positive battery terminal).

When an electron jumps from its orbit to the orbit of another atom,

it leaves a hole, which makes the original atom slightly more positive than it was. This means that it is more attractive to another electron en route to the positive battery terminal.

The new electron, filling the vacant hole, leaves a hole in the atom it has just come from and so on. As the electrons migrate towards the positive terminal, the holes they leave behind go the other way, to the negative terminal. It is this movement that defines current flow.

Direction convention

Early scientists understood the direction of current to be from a positive potential to a lesser, or negative, potential. Current is

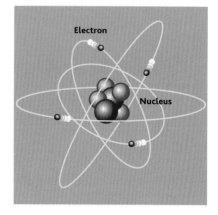

Above Atoms are the building blocks of all substances. Materials that are good conductors of electricity have spare electrons in their outer orbits which are free to move when coaxed by an electrical potential difference, or voltage.

Below Lightning is a natural form of the flow of electrical charge.

therefore defined as the movement of holes flowing from the positive terminal of the battery through the wire and, of course, the rest of the circuit, back to the negative terminal and is indicated on a circuit diagram by an arrow.

The direction of voltage can be indicated in a similar way with an arrow between two points of the circuit, pointing towards the higher potential. In the case of a battery, it would point from the negative terminal to the positive one.

Below **Negatively charged electrons are attracted to and move towards a positive potential. The 'holes' they leave behind migrate the other way to the negative terminal.**

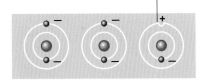

Vacant space or hole. The atom is missing an electron.

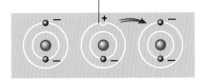

The electron, attracted to the '+' hole, leaves a new hole behind it...

...and so the process continues.

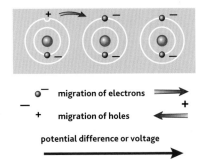

○⁻ migration of electrons ⟶

+ migration of holes ⟵

potential difference or voltage ⟶

Versatile form of energy

Electricity is not readily visible in its raw form, which explains some of the mysticism that surrounds it. You can't see it flowing in a conductor like you can water in a clear pipe but you can see the results of converting electrical energy into other forms of energy such as heat, light, motion and so on.

Electricity is an exceptionally versatile form of energy and, when put to work, can be used for most tasks. Almost all electrical energy ends up as heat, but in getting there, it can do some useful work. From integrated circuits using a few millionths of a volt (or microvolts (μV)), to houses with hundreds of volts and transmission of electricity around the country at tens of thousands of volts, it is all the same basic electricity, just converted to the most appropriate form.

The aim of this book is to examine how you are able to use the benefits of electricity on boats to have an enjoyable and safe life at sea.

Below **Electricity is converted into the most appropriate voltage level according to the requirements of the system. On smaller boats, this is typically 12 or 24V. Further conversion from these levels is often required for specific jobs such as LED lighting.**

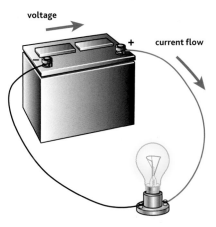

voltage

current flow

Above **The voltage arrow shows the potential difference between the two terminals and points to the more positive one. The current arrow describes the flow from the positive terminal of the battery, through the circuit and back to the negative one.**

Volts, amps, resistance and power

Fortunately there is very little theory involved in boat electrics from the user's point of view. All the hard work is done in initial engineering design and electrical system installation. However, being aware of the key terminology will give you a better understanding.

Voltage (V)

Voltage is the potential difference between two points in a circuit, measured in volts (V). If you think about a household water system, pressure is created in the pipes by fixing the water tank higher up in the house, so the higher the tank the greater the pressure. In a similar way, the potential difference between the two terminals of a fully charged battery is 12.7V, with one of them, labelled '+' (positive), being higher in potential relative to the other, labelled '-' (negative). On the circuit diagram this is indicated by an arrow pointing towards the higher potential (voltage) point – for a battery this would be from the negative terminal pointing towards the positive terminal (see page 13).

Current (I)

Current is the rate of flow of electrical charge through a material such as copper wire and is measured in amps (A). In the household analogy, current is equivalent to the flow of water through the pipes. Negatively charged electrons are attracted to the positive potential of the '+' battery terminal. They leave behind them 'holes' which move towards the '-' terminal. It is this movement of holes that constitutes the current, so the current flows from the positive battery terminal around the circuit returning to the negative terminal.

Below Voltage is the 'potential to do work' and current is the flow of electrical charge en route to doing the work.

constriction or 'resistance'

Above A material's resistance opposes the free movement of the electrons, reducing the rate at which they flow and hence reducing the current.

Resistance (R)

Resistance, measured in ohms (Ω), is the opposition to the flow of current through the material caused by the properties of the material itself. Good conductors have a very low resistance, allowing current to flow freely – copper is most commonly used as it is affordable and very versatile.

Materials that have a very high resistance through which no current can flow, like certain plastics, are known as insulators and are used to cover the copper wire to protect it from other wires and, of course, to protect us from getting electric shocks. Resistance manifests itself in terms of losses within a circuit, wasting battery energy in the form of heat.

Power (P)

Power is basically the rate at which electrical energy is consumed in an electrical circuit and is measured in watts (W). Being aware of the power consumption of on-board equipment is of great use in estimating cable sizes, battery capacities and the need for additional charging.

Every piece of equipment has a power rating which is usually stated on a label, in the documentation or on the packaging. Knowing the power rating will enable calculation of the current that is required by the equipment.

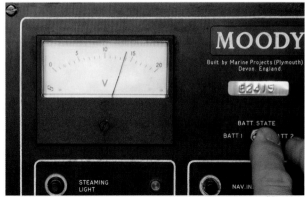

TIP

Many boats have a voltmeter in the distribution panel. On their own these are of limited use. However, they will tell you at a glance if charging is taking place. On a 12V system, measured battery voltage roughly between 13V to 14V indicates charging of some degree is occurring (or 26V-28V for a 24V system).

Top and above The value of the voltage is determined by the job it is intended to do. The voltmeter is showing a charging voltage of 13.8V to recharge a 12V battery bank. Current (6A in this case) can also be displayed. The polarity (+ /–) of the current shows whether current is flowing into or out of the battery.

Above left The power consumption of each piece of equipment is usually shown on a label or will be specified in the handbook.

Basic laws

If you think of electricity in terms of energy flowing around a particular circuit, you can use measurement and calculations to understand what is happening. Some of the laws of electricity were developed centuries ago, but it's worth looking at how these laws apply to on-board electrics.

Kirchhoff's Current Law

The German physicist Gustav Kirchhoff developed two laws in the mid-19th century relating to the flow of electricity, both of which are very useful in boat electrics. The Current Law states that the sum of currents flowing into a node, or junction, is equal to the sum of currents flowing out. In terms of an on-board DC system, this means that where cables are collected together, such as a bus bar, the current in the cable supplying the bus bar equals the sum of the currents in the cables taking current from the bus bar.

If you assume that current going into the bus bar is positive and currents going out are negative, then the sum of all of these currents into and out of the bus bars equals zero. Generally speaking, the cable feeding the current to the bus bar will have to be large enough to supply the total of all the currents going out to the equipment such as lights, chart plotter, water pump and so on. This is particularly important when adding new equipment to an existing system – you must consider if the cable supplying the current is sufficient to take the extra load.

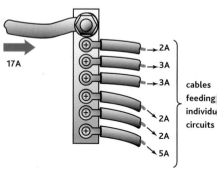

17A
2A
3A
3A
2A
2A
5A

cables feeding individu circuits

Above Incoming cable must be able to handle the sum of all the outgoing current.

Below A bus bar: the larger (red) wire comes from the battery and, according to Kirchhoff's Current Law, will supply the total current consumed by all the equipment connected to that bus bar.

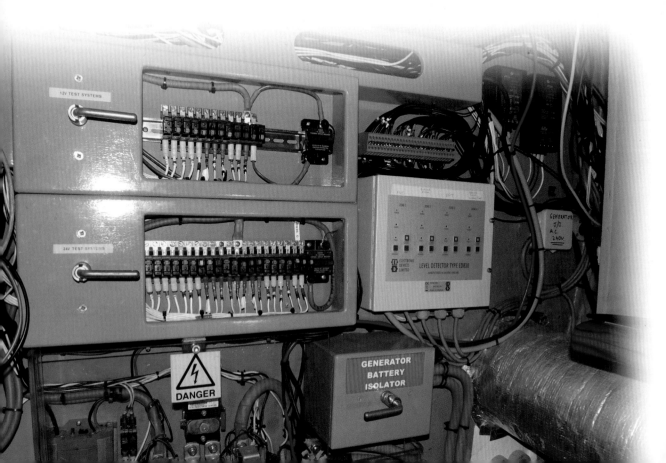

Kirchhoff's Voltage Law

Any circuit starts at the battery positive terminal and ends at its negative terminal. Kirchhoff's Voltage Law says that the voltage of the battery will be fully distributed across all the elements of the circuit, primarily the piece of equipment you want to power up. If positive voltages point clockwise around the circuit and anti-clockwise ones are negative, then the sum of these voltages, according to Kirchhoff's second law, equals zero.

This law forms the basis of fault finding in electrical circuits in that any difference between the voltage across the equipment and, the voltage across the battery terminals supplying it, is being lost elsewhere in the circuit.

Joule's First Law

The English physicist James Prescott Joule described the relationship between power, voltage and current in his first law. The resulting equation is:

Power (in watts) = volts x amps

Rearranging the equation, for practical use, into amps = power divided by volts, a 10-watt bulb, assuming a measured battery voltage of 12.5 volts, will consume a current of 0.8 amps (10 watts /12.5 volts). As most of the energy ultimately turns to heat, it gives an indication of whether ventilation is required.

Power of 10 watts is not that significant (although the bulb will be hot) but equipment consuming 50–100 watts of power will need some air flow to dissipate the heat. Secondly, as you now know what the current is, the cable size can be determined.

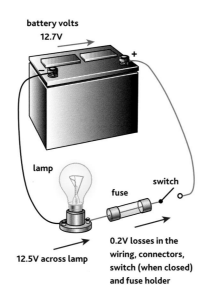

battery volts
12.7V

lamp

fuse

switch

0.2V losses in the wiring, connectors, switch (when closed) and fuse holder

12.5V across lamp

+V (battery) – V (lamp) – V (losses) = 0
+12.7V – 12.5V – 0.2V = 0
(or 12.7V = 12.5V + 0.2V)

Above According to Kirchhoff's Voltage Law, all the battery volts will appear at the lamp minus any lost across the connectors due to loose fit, corrosion etc. If the lost voltage across the connector is significant, the bulb will appear dim.

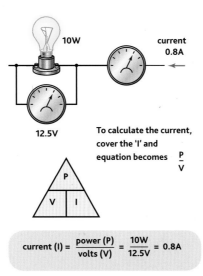

10W

current 0.8A

12.5V

To calculate the current, cover the 'I' and equation becomes $\frac{P}{V}$

P
V I

$$\text{current (I)} = \frac{\text{power (P)}}{\text{volts (V)}} = \frac{10W}{12.5V} = 0.8A$$

Above Knowing the current helps you to appreciate the impact on battery life, discussed in detail on page 42.

Ohm's Law

The other fundamental law of electricity is that of 19th-century German physicist Georg Ohm. This states that the voltage (V) across an element of a circuit is equal to the current (I) flowing through the element multiplied by its resistance (R). Ohm's Law tells us that the resistance of, say, a connector will appear as a voltage drop across it when current is flowing through it.

Kirchhoff's Voltage Law says if some of the available battery voltage is dropping across a resistive connection, there will be less voltage available at the bulb, so it will not be as bright as it should be. Joule's First Law says that because of its resistance, heat (in watts) will be generated in the connector.

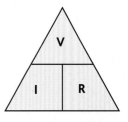

V

I R

volts = current x resistance
V = I x R

Above Cover the measurement you want and the triangle will show the equation. For example, if you want to work out the resistance, cover the 'R' and it leaves V/I (volts divided by amps).

AC and DC electricity

Generated electricity comes in two forms, alternating current (AC) produced by rotating machines such as alternators, or direct current (DC) produced by a dynamo, chemical or other types of reaction such as batteries, solar panels and fuel cells. It is possible to convert from one form to another, but first we need to find out how these different types are generated.

Alternating current

Rotating machines such as alternators have a magnet held within a frame, around which a long insulated wire is wound to form a coil. As the North Pole end of the magnet passes over the coil, it induces a current in one direction and when the South Pole passes in the second half of the revolution, it induces the current in the other direction, with the process repeated on each rotation.

The voltage this produces is in the form of a sine wave with a frequency (measured in Hertz or Hz) equal to the number of repetitions per second, which is determined by the speed of rotation of the machine. Worldwide, domestic electricity has a frequency of either 50 or 60Hz and a voltage of between 110 and 240V AC. There are many advantages to having electricity produced as AC, but a big limitation is that it cannot be stored in this form, hence the need for conversion.

Direct current

Power emanating from batteries and solar panels produces DC electricity at a particular voltage that remains constant over time (nominally 12 or 24V for boating applications). Unlike

Below **Batteries produce a constant DC output voltage over time.**

the photovoltaic process of the solar panel (which uses energy from sunlight to release electrons in the photovoltaic material, creating a current flow), the chemical reaction in a battery is reversible. The battery can be recharged by forcing energy back in from an external source, such as a charger. This versatility gives the battery pride of place on our boats and creates the potential for endless hours of discussion.

Conversion

Converting from one form of electricity to another, or indeed from one voltage to another, is not too difficult and voltage conversion is carried out on most boats. A good example is the mains-powered battery charger which accepts input voltages ranging from 110V–240V AC, converts this to DC and then steps it down to around 14V (or 28V) before presenting the power to the batteries.

The alternator also generates AC as a raw output, which is converted to DC by the rectifier pack fitted within the alternator. So as far as you are concerned, the output of the alternator is DC and can go straight into the battery.

Left The boat's alternator actually produces AC due to its rotating nature. This is converted to DC by the internal rectifier pack and can pass straight to the batteries.

VENTILATION

Conversion from one voltage to another is not 100 per cent efficient. The losses, which can be as high as 30 per cent, will be in the form of heat so equipment like chargers and regulators will need adequate ventilation. It may be important how the equipment is mounted as you want to maximise the airflow for improved cooling. It is therefore advisable to follow the installation instructions.

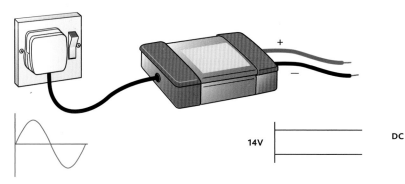

mains AC (input)   **14V**   **DC**   **charger output (DC volts to battery)**

Above The charger's mains AC input is converted to a DC voltage suitable for charging the batteries.

Below The boat's alternator actually produces three separate 14V AC phases due to its rotating nature. These are combined and converted to DC by the internal rectifier pack and can pass straight to the batteries.

The left hand edge (above) has fins of aluminium to increase the dissipation of any heat produced..

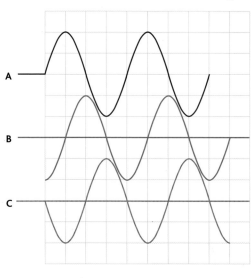

A

B

C

alternator

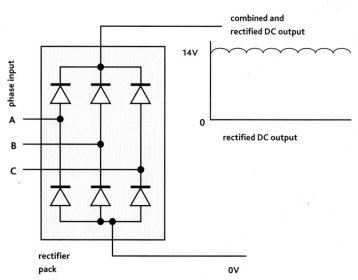

phase input

A

B

C

rectifier pack

combined and rectified DC output

14V

0

rectified DC output

0V

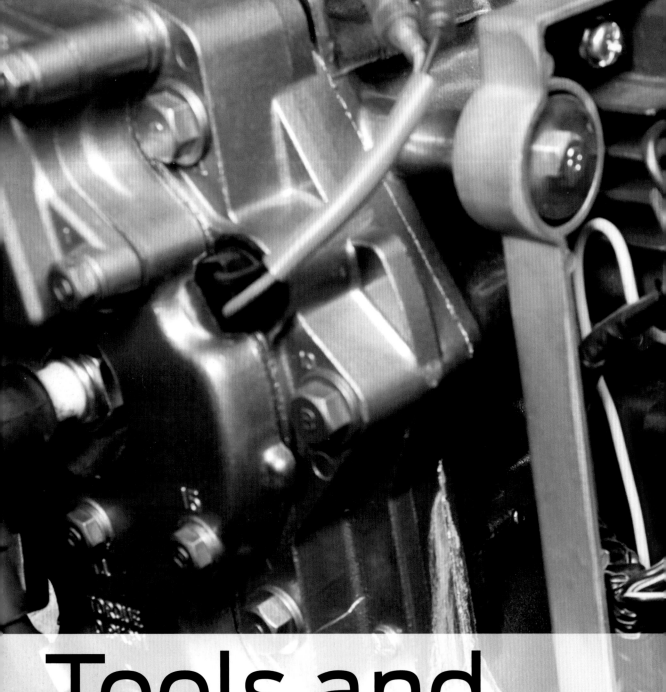

Tools and measuring

Tools for electrical work

You should always carry an assortment of basic electrical tools on board so that you can troubleshoot and make repairs. It's best to get cables carrying larger currents from batteries and alternators made by specialist suppliers, but nearly all other low voltage DC system work can be done with these tools.

The multimeter
Perhaps the most important tool in the toolbox, this instrument is used to take various electrical measurements such as voltage, current and resistance.

Crimping tool
This is used to attach the cable connector or crimp to the wire. The ratchet-type tools are the best of the cheaper ones. They cater for the red, blue and yellow crimps, for different wire sizes, and have a release lever should they become jammed. American and European crimps differ in size so you will need to check you get the right tool.

Wire strippers
Wire strippers are hand tools used to remove the insulation from the cut end of the wire.
- Self-adjusting wire strippers are the best as they tend not to damage the strands of wire whilst removing the insulation.

Wire (side) cutters
It is worth having two or three different sizes. For example, 6mm^2 wire is quite tough to cut cleanly with lightweight cutters.

Wire chasers
These are flexible fibreglass interconnecting rods, which can be used for pulling cables through from behind panels, and under floors and roof linings.

Screwdrivers
These come in all shapes and sizes, and a good assortment, including the very smallest, is invaluable. A small, rechargeable battery-operated electric screwdriver (with light) is also very useful.

Heat gun
Electric or butane hot air guns are needed for use with heat-shrink tubing to seal the connection and avoid moisture getting in.

Below **A long extension wire for the probe in the COM socket allows access right back to the battery negative terminal from anywhere on the boat.**

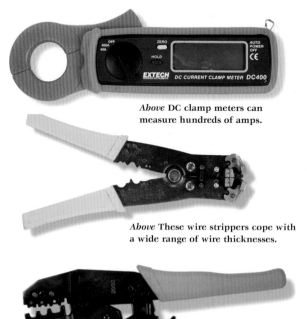

Above **DC clamp meters can measure hundreds of amps.**

Above **These wire strippers cope with a wide range of wire thicknesses.**

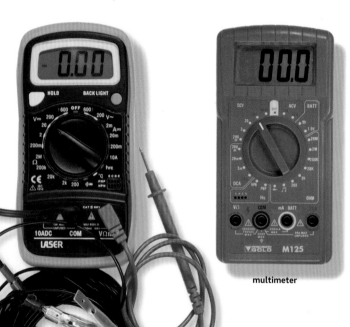

multimeter

crimping tool

Soldering iron

Generally, soldering is not recommended. If you do have an electric soldering iron, it needs to be reasonably powerful, at around 100W. This will generate enough heat to ensure good solder flow in between the wire strands. Gas versions are also useful and, again, they generate plenty of heat.

Tweezers and a mirror

Not necessarily used together in electrics, but they definitely have a place in the tool kit.

Other useful kit

- Hand drill
- Horizontal axis electric drill
- Hole cutter set

- Socket set (up to around 15mm)
- Hobby/craft knife
- Small hack saw
- Large lump of Blu Tack®
- Electrical tape
- Self-amalgamating tape
- Small tin of Vaseline® (for battery and other high current terminals).

Consumables

- Cable ties, of different widths and lengths, for collecting wires together and securing them to attachment points.
- Heat-shrink tubing of various diameters and colours.
- A reasonably wide range of crimps and other connectors (this is discussed in detail in the next chapter).

Above **A small mirror is very useful to have in your toolbox.**

Above **Keep a reasonable stock of different connectors and cable ties.**

Above **Different end pieces make this into a butane gas powered soldering iron or heat gun.**

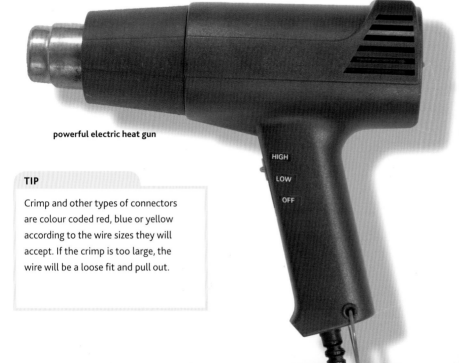

powerful electric heat gun

HIGH
LOW
OFF

Below **The chaser can be made up to the correct length.**

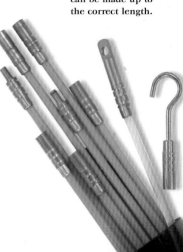

TIP

Crimp and other types of connectors are colour coded red, blue or yellow according to the wire sizes they will accept. If the crimp is too large, the wire will be a loose fit and pull out.

Safety first

Great care needs to be taken when working on wiring systems. The boat's low voltage (12V or 24V DC) system is inherently safe, but the batteries store an enormous amount of energy and can easily result in a fire if this is released in an uncontrolled manner. Unless you are experienced you should certainly leave the mains power system to a qualified electrician. Think SAFETY all the time.

Hand tools
- In general the tools you need are not difficult to use and should not present a problem but it is always worth reading the instructions before you start.
- A sharp blade is invaluable when working on electrics. The most suitable knives have fully retractable blades. Get into the habit of retracting the blade, especially when you return it to the toolbox.
- Screwdrivers should have plastic insulation along the length of the shaft to prevent making electrical contact with things that might cause a shock or short circuit.

Electric tools
Ensure the mains supply has a Residual Current Device, or RCD (also called a Residual Current Circuit Breaker or RCCB) to protect you from a fault with the equipment. If you use long extension cables, a portable RCD is a good safety precaution. On board, your mains system will have a permanent RCD near where the shore power is plugged into your boat.

Soldering irons
- For small electric and gas irons, use a holder with a piece of damp high temperature foam. Cover the immediate surface with a heat resistant mat to protect the woodwork. Wipe the tip on the foam each time to clean off excess solder.
- Larger electric irons have a trigger and they are turned off when you are not soldering, but they have enough power to heat up quickly when required.
- Solder gives off a fair bit of smoke, so make sure you have plenty of ventilation.
- When you have finished, allow enough time for the tip to cool down before touching it or putting the iron away.

Left Take care when wielding a screwdriver in amongst the DC panel – positive and negative terminals are often close together. If you touch both, that is a direct short circuit and will result in a big spark.

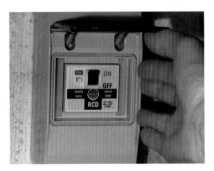

Above Because of the long extension lead, the shore power protection may not be as effective as you expect so always use a RCD on board. Otherwise, you can use a portable RCD plugged into your end of the extension lead.

Above Heat guns get very hot! Watch you do not melt something close by the intended target.

Below Portable RCDs plug in to the on-board end of an extension lead.

Above Be aware of any exposed mains connections. Make sure they are covered, or better still, disconnect the shore power completely.

Heat guns

 These are very useful but, as the name suggests, they get extremely hot. Never touch the end to test for temperature; it will become hot after only a few seconds of use.

 Always start with the gun some distance away and gradually move it closer to the item you're working on, until you see the effects you are looking for. Gently oscillate the gun to spread the heat instead of concentrating it on one spot.

 As you move the gun away from the area you are working on, be aware of where you subsequently point it.

 As with the soldering iron, allow plenty of time for cooling once you have finished.

Reaching in...

Take great care when reaching into a cavity through a bunch of wires, as there may also be exposed mains voltage contacts in there. It is worth disconnecting the mains and your battery terminals before you start – be doubly careful if this is not possible.

Short circuits on the 12V/24V system

A short circuit is a direct connection across the battery terminals, either at the battery or at some point in the wiring system, caused by touching a positive connection to a negative (0V) one. The only thing limiting the current is the resistance of the wire between you and the battery – tens if not hundreds of amps and a big spark will be the result. If you are working on a battery terminal with a spanner or screwdriver, protect the other terminal from accidental contact occurring.

RE-CONNECTING

When re-connecting the battery terminal, hold the clamp onto the terminal first. If there is a problem you can instantly remove it. You often get a small spark as you initially touch the two together. Once you are satisfied everything is okay, you can clamp it up. Cover the other terminal so as to insulate it.

The multimeter

The standard piece of test equipment is the multimeter, which is variously known as the DVM (digital voltmeter), or colloquially as a voltmeter. All multimeters have different ranges for each parameter they measure. On some types this is automatically done (auto ranging), but on others the appropriate range is manually selected. Most have digital displays but analogue versions are also available.

The multimeter is a multi-purpose, battery-powered instrument capable of measuring AC and DC voltage, DC current and resistance, as well as testing diodes and torch batteries. On the auto-ranging versions you have only to select the main function, for instance DC volts, and the meter will set up the appropriate range once you start measuring. Most types require you to rotate the central selector to the appropriate function and range, while all have several sockets into which the probe leads are plugged, depending on what you are measuring.

Additional features

✪ 'Auto turn off' is a useful feature to prolong the multimeter's battery life (although it can be mildly irritating at times).

✪ A display backlight will facilitate reading the display deep in the darker regions of your boat when you are trying to make a measurement.

✪ 'Measurement HOLD', when selected, will hold or retain the measured reading. Many models include this feature, but it can cause confusion if you forget to turn it off.

✪ Some models also include a temperature measurement capability and supply a thermocouple for measuring surface temperatures. You simply plug it in, select the function and touch the surface that you wish to measure.

Voltage ranges

For DC voltage, the multimeter will have several ranges, the smallest being 0–200mV (0.2V) and the largest at least 0–600V on full scale. Most are also capable of the same AC voltage over three or four different ranges.

Current measurement

There are two sets of current ranges. The first bank will cover quite low values up to 1A and the second will be a single range for higher current, normally 10A or on some models 20A. The probe leads will use different sockets depending on which range you want to use.

Resistance and continuity

A number of ranges for resistances up to 10MΩ (10 million ohms) is normal.

Diode testing

A diode (or rectifier) is an electrical one-way valve through which current will only flow in one direction. The multimeter can determine whether the diode is functioning properly.

Below These are some common types of multimeter, including a Fluke auto-ranging version.

SETTING UP

Set the multimeter up for the type of measurement you are taking. Here the 200V voltage range has been selected as this vessel has a 24V battery system. The probe leads are plugged into the 'VΩ' and 'COM' sockets for measuring voltage.

Set to measure current, the 20A range is used and the leads plugged into the '20A' and 'COM' sockets. The multimeter is reading 3.68A.

Above Testing a diode on the alternator. A working one will give a reading of around 0.7V.

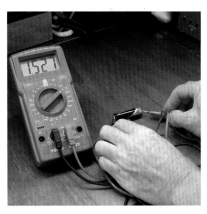

Above The battery test function is for checking the state of 1.5V and 9V batteries. A battery that is depleted will show around 1.2V.

The most common example on boats is found in the alternator, where six diodes (the rectifier pack) convert the raw AC output to DC that can be connected directly to the boat's batteries.

Pen torch battery tester

This allows you to test the state of small 1.5V and 9V batteries that are commonly used in a wide range of equipment.

Leads and probes

The multimeter will come with a basic set of leads and probes, but the addition of a few different end fittings will be well worthwhile. In particular, croc clips and spring-loaded hooks are very useful as they free up your hands.

TIP

You may have to press the probe end onto the point you are measuring quite hard. Over time, metal tarnishes, forming an oxide layer preventing an electrical connection. You may even have to scratch through it to get a reading.

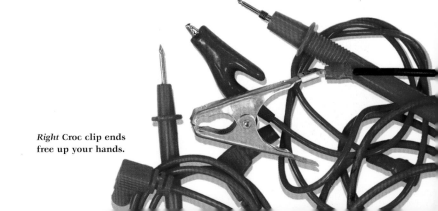

Right Croc clip ends free up your hands.

Making measurements in-circuit

Measuring voltages and currents require the systems to be powered up, so before you start diving in with the probes you will need to set up the multimeter in preparation. Multimeters are fairly robust instruments and have in-built protection.

Plug in the probes

Study your particular multimeter manual as there are differences. In general the black lead plugs into the socket marked 'COM', while there are a number of options for the red lead, depending on what you are measuring:

- For AC or DC volts it will be 'VΩ'.
- For DC current up to 200mA use the 'mA' socket.
- For DC current up to 10A (or 20A) it will be the '10A' (or '20A') one.

Selecting the range

Each function will have an absolute maximum value that the multimeter can measure – in the case of DC volts this is usually 600V or 1000V. By splitting this into a number of ranges, the meter optimises the resolution. Select the range that covers the voltage you are measuring so, for 12V, it will be the 20V range but for 24V battery systems you will have to go to the next range up, usually 200V. Attempting to measure a voltage in excess of the selected range will not damage the meter.

Voltage measurement

Multimeters measure the voltage difference between the red and black

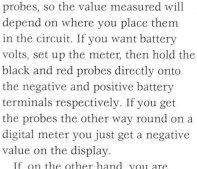

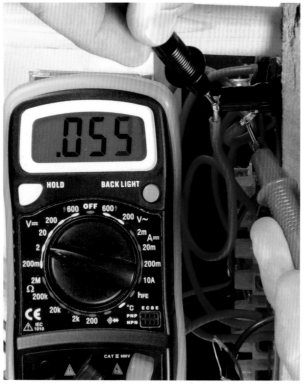

Left **Measuring voltage drop across a fuse. The multimeter is set to the (2V) scale, as you would be expecting a small voltage across the fuse holder when several amps are flowing through it. The multimeter will not be damaged if the voltage exceeds the scale setting.**

probes, so the value measured will depend on where you place them in the circuit. If you want battery volts, set up the meter, then hold the black and red probes directly onto the negative and positive battery terminals respectively. If you get the probes the other way round on a digital meter you just get a negative value on the display.

If, on the other hand, you are measuring the voltage drop across a fuse holder, then you would expect this to be a lot less, as any drop here constitutes a loss so select the 200mV or 2VDC range. To get the correct polarity, the red probe should be on the point where the current enters the fuse holder (the battery side) and the black probe where it exits.

Current measurement

To measure current, you need to break the circuit and include the multimeter in the circuit. As the same current flows around the whole circuit you can open it at any convenient point. Plug the black probe into the 'COM' socket and the red into the '10A' socket on the multimeter, select the '10A' scale and attach the probes to the wires.

For a positive reading, current should flow into the '10A' socket via the red probe and out of the black probe. Within a particular circuit, you can achieve this without having to remove any wires if you probe the switch terminals. When the switch is set to OFF, it breaks the circuit so no current can flow. If you now attach the probes to the switch terminals, current can flow through the meter, completing the circuit once again and making the measurement easy to obtain.

Internal fuse

To protect the multimeter from damage from excessive current there is an internal fuse. You should also bear in mind that the leads and probes are not rated for handling high current for any period of time and will get hot, so just do short duration tests to get the measurement you need.

Above **Multimeters are self protected to a large extent. To get at the internal fuse, the back will have to be removed.**

TIP

When measuring current, remember that the probe leads can only handle a limited amount without getting hot and even melting. They will withstand the maximum (say 20A) but only for a few seconds, so do a quick test, get the reading you want and then remove the leads.

MEASURING CURRENT

Because the higher current range is used, the probe leads are plugged into the '10A' (on this multimeter) and 'COM' sockets.

To measure current in the lighting circuit (for the LED down lighter only), set the panel switch to OFF then probe across the two switch terminals. The multimeter completes the circuit whilst measuring the current.

PROBING DIRECTLY

Voltage probes have sharp ends that can be pushed through the insulation to touch the wire. This can be useful in low-voltage systems in which a conveniently located connector is not available, thus making it difficult to obtain a voltage measurement. Place a piece of wood behind the wire (not your finger) and never do this on a mains cable.

Measuring high currents

It's very useful to be able to measure currents from the alternator and batteries – with the engine running you can then immediately see how much current the alternator is generating. However, these currents, and those from wind or solar power, are too large for the multimeter, so an alternative instrument is required.

DC clamp meters

Measuring current in the main battery, starter motor and alternator leads will not be possible with the multimeter. DC clamp meters have a different sensor technology and are ideal for this job. Whenever a current flows in a wire, it produces a magnetic field directly proportional to the amount of current, and the sensor in the clamp meters make use of this property to measure the current. Simply clamp the jaws over the cable.

There are a number of clamp meters on the market, but make sure you buy one that can measure DC

Below **Measuring the starter motor current (127.5A) is straightforward with the DC current clamp. Current flowing in the direction of the arrow will register as positive on the display, in this case, into the starter motor.**

current; as a bonus, they often have integral voltmeters. Clamp meters will measure much smaller currents as well, but tend to be less accurate at low values. However, this may not be an issue and the ease of making a measurement often outweighs two decimal places of accuracy.

Where are the currents going?

Boats with two or three battery banks and multiple sources of power generation inevitably have complex systems. Being able to trace the entire cabling, from the largest battery cable to the smaller lighting wires, will help you to get to know your boat. This is particularly beneficial if you have newly acquired your vessel.

✪ The beauty of the clamps is you do not disturb the

wiring to measure current. Do observe the 'positive direction arrow' on the meter that tells you which direction will give a positive current reading. It does not matter to the meter itself, but it will help you to understand what is going on. Stick to a convention – for instance, the current going IN to the battery is the + (positive) direction.

✪ Confirm which batteries make up the domestic bank. Turn on some lights and place the clamp meter over each of the positive battery

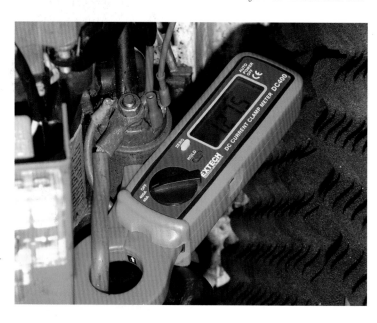

Left **This clamp meter has an integral voltmeter which means amps and volts can be simultaneously measured and power calculated.**

CURRENT FLOW

With the charger on, the clamp meter shows the current going into the battery (2.47A).

Without the charger on, there is a net flow of -4.21A out of the battery.

Above Understanding a switch and cable arrangement is greatly simplified once you can see which cable is carrying the current while operating the switches. In this case, the red cable with black tape around it was in fact a 0V cable, not a 12V one. The direction of the current (flowing back to the batteries) confirmed this.

cables in turn. Those associated with the domestic bank will show a negative current flow, or discharge, assuming you follow the convention above.

- Confirm alternator charging by clamping over the domestic battery bank positive cable and turning some lights on to get a discharge current flow (negative reading on the meter). Start the engine and see the current become a positive higher reading as alternator current begins to flow. As the lights are still on, some of that current is going to them, so remember you are measuring the remainder going into the batteries.

- Mains chargers can be checked in the same way by switching on the chargers instead of starting the engine. The more lights you switch on, the less current is available for the batteries (so charging will take longer).

Checking the alternator

You can get a good idea of the characteristics of your alternator by watching the rise in current as you increase engine speed. If the batteries are in a state of low charge, or if you turn on lots of electrical systems, the alternator should produce a much higher current, showing that it's in good order. On the other hand, you will probably see that running the engine at idling speed produces little, if any, charging current for the batteries.

TIP

Each time you use a clamp meter it needs to be 'zeroed' by turning it on, closing the jaws (without a cable running through them) and pressing the 'auto zero' button, or rotating the zero control.

ALTERNATOR OUTPUT

At idle revs the current generated by the alternator will be small (a respectable 9A here) but may actually be zero if the regulator is not performing correctly.

As engine revs increase so the alternator output will increase (to 17A) until the battery volts get nearer 14V.

Continuity, resistance and diode testing

To use the multimeter functions, the circuit must be disconnected – the multimeter provides the small voltage needed to carry out the test. In most cases both ends of the item or wire being tested must be disconnected. To check whether a fuse has blown, you must first remove it from its holder.

Continuity

Continuity determines whether two things are connected electrically (irrespective of whether they should be) and the multimeter incorporates a buzzer to indicate this. It does not matter which way round the probes are and it is a good idea to touch the probes together first to check the meter's buzzer is working.

Break in a circuit

There will always be connections in a circuit and, unfortunately, these are the weak link. A wire will not break of its own accord, but whenever it is crimped or soldered to a terminal the copper becomes more brittle and is therefore prone to damage from repeated movement such as vibration. Corrosion can also cause breaks or high resistance in wires as well as in connectors.

Tracing a wire and reverse engineering

Once a wire leaves the distribution panel it invariably goes into a bundle of all the other wires, then disappears behind a bulkhead. Using the multimeter with an extension lead you can trace where any particular wire emerges at the other end of the boat.

You can also check whether one wire is connected (correctly or otherwise) to a number of others, for example, in a lighting circuit, where several sub-circuits are collected together onto one switch. This technique is called reverse engineering and can be used to build up a wiring diagram of your systems.

Understanding switches

The continuity tester is helpful in determining which contacts are connected together on a switch. It is quite common to have six spade terminals on a switch base and the function of each terminal may not be immediately obvious from the diagram on the side of the unit.

Resistance

It is very rare that you will need to measure actual values of resistance but if you do, you must completely electrically isolate the device before making a measurement. Power

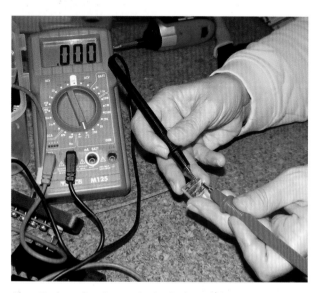

Above Testing a fuse for continuity, ie determining has it blown or not. It will have to be removed from the fuse holder first.

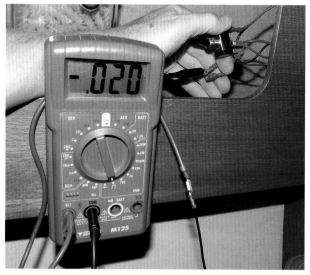

Above Checking the continuity of the supply wire to a lamp. Remove the bulb, switch OFF the lamp circuit at the panel. Use the 'extension' lead clipped to one end and the probe at the other.

management systems need to know the resistance of the current shunt, which is too small to measure with the multi meter. The only way to get an accurate figure is by applying Ohm's law in that if you pass a current through the shunt and measure the voltage drop across its terminals, the resistance is the voltage drop/the current. Typical values for these shunts are 0.00025 and 0.0005 Ohms.

Diodes

The most likely (but rare) occasion where you will need to test a diode is if you suspect a fault with the six separate diodes in the alternator rectifier pack. Set the multimeter to the 'Diode Test' function, which may be combined with the continuity feature on some models, plug the black probe lead into the 'COM' socket and the red lead into the 'VΩ' sockets and probe the two ends of the diode, one way then the other.

Right As diodes only conduct electricity in one direction, the probes need to be the correct way round. As this is often difficult to determine, try one way first, then the other. A working diode will show a value on the multimeter of around 0.7V with the probes correctly positioned, and simply a figure '1' if not.

Above Calculating the very low resistance of a current shunt. Measure the current flowing through it and the voltage drop across its terminals. Applying Ohm's Law, the resistance = voltage drop (2.7mV) / Current (10.94A). This gives a result of 0.00025 Ohms.

Above You can use the continuity function to establish the switch contact arrangement.

TIP

When testing continuity, test the multimeter's 'beeper' by touching the probe ends together once you have set the meter up. Once testing, make sure the probes get a good contact to the item you are testing. Scrape through any oxidation on metal surfaces.

Fault finding in low voltage systems

Fault finding is essentially a process of elimination. You may find yourself spending many hours puzzling over the seemingly implausible. However, a methodical approach to fault finding should lead to a solution to the problem.

In general terms equipment either stops working, or works intermittently, and since everything electrical depends on a supply, it makes sense to start there. It is useful to know the voltage at the battery in order to compare with the measurements you take elsewhere.

It also helps to have a wiring diagram to hand, although on some boats you may have to create this yourself. Every piece of equipment from a bulb to a multi-function display can be considered in the same way – as a 'box' with positive and negative supply wires.

It's simply not working

If the equipment has stopped working, either the equipment itself or the supply has failed, so look for the obvious solution first – has the bulb gone, has a wire come off, or has the fuse blown? If the failure doesn't appear to be due to an obvious problem the next step is to investigate the supply.

✪ With the system powered up as normal, check for any evidence (sight or smell) of burn marks or discolouring of wires and connectors. Also, touch connectors to see if they are warm.

✪ If there is no evidence of the supply (ie battery) voltage at the equipment terminals, the fault could be in the positive or negative parts of the circuit.

Below If the equipment is not working, it may be the 0V return path at fault. Remove the 0V connection from the back of the switch and continuity check right back to the battery negative terminal (-), using the extension wire.

Checking the positive side

To check this part of the system in isolation you need to disconnect the positive wire from the equipment and measure the voltage between this wire and the battery negative terminal (0V), using an extension wire. Going back to the negative battery terminal eliminates any other possible 0V return path issues that might affect your measurements.

Set the multimeter to read DC voltage on the appropriate scale and clip the black probe (plugged into the 'COM' socket) to the extension wire, the other end of which is clipped on to the battery negative terminal. The red probe is clipped onto the positive wire to obtain the voltage reading – if all is well, this will be the same as the battery terminal volts that you have already measured.

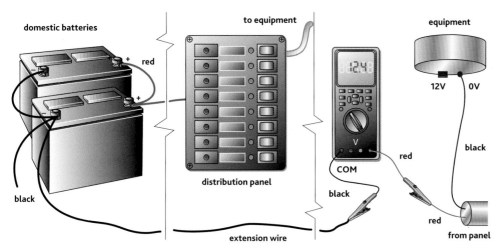

domestic batteries

red

+

+

black

to equipment

distribution panel

extension wire

COM

black

red

black

equipment

12V   0V

black

red

from panel

Left Testing for positive supply at various points around the circuit needs a good 0V connection to the multimeter. Again the extension lead can be taken right back to the battery to provide this.

Supply, return paths and fuses

- If there is no voltage at the equipment end of the wire (tested above), then the source at the distribution panel is next in line. Leaving the black probe attached to a known 0V point as above, probe the switch and fuse terminals. If you see battery volts here, the problem is in the wire itself.

- To check the return path (negative side), disconnect the negative wire from the equipment and do a continuity test back to the battery negative terminal. If this is also all good then the equipment is becoming increasingly suspect.

- Fuses rarely blow without a reason, so the cause needs to be identified. The usual culprits are a fault in the equipment or chafed wiring – either way the same methodical approach will find the problem.

Equipment not performing

Excessive voltage drops in the wiring or connections will result in the voltage available at the equipment itself being less than required for correct operation. For a lamp this just means it's less bright, but for some equipment it will result in intermittent operation or the unit being unable to power up beyond standby mode.

Measure the voltage at the equipment's switch, firstly with the equipment off, then as you power it up and let it run. Losses elsewhere in the circuit mean a lower voltage is available at the unit's terminals.

MEASURING LOSSES

With the equipment turned off, the positive voltage at its switch terminal is the same as the battery volts, 13.52V.

Once the equipment is turned on and drawing its current (say a couple of amps), the voltage drops by half a volt. This is being lost in the circuit due to resistance somewhere. Any more than this would be worth investigation.

TIP

A long length of thin wire (about the length of your boat) with croc clips at either end, will work as an extension to the multimeter probe. This enables voltage drops in the supply cables to equipment remote from the batteries to be measured. It will also be useful for testing long cable runs for continuity.

Batteries

Battery basics

Batteries are the heart of the electrical system, which includes the consumption of power and the all-important restoration of charge so that an energy balance is achieved over time. A thorough understanding of how batteries work enables us to get the best performance and lifespan from them, as well as improving reliability.

Above 'Gel' batteries have the electrolyte as a gel. These are very rugged, can operate in any position and have the best characteristics of any type of lead-acid battery.

Chemical generators

All batteries produce electricity through a chemical reaction. In so-called 'primary cells', this is a one-way street and once exhausted the batteries are disposed of. In 'secondary cells', the reaction is fully reversible and offers enormous flexibility in that the charge/discharge cycle can be repeated thousands of times over a few years, so long as a few simple guidelines are followed.

Lead-acid battery technology still leads the way as the lowest cost per amp, although as electric vehicles become more widespread, other technologies will begin to look more attractive. The lead-acid battery

has been around for over 150 years, so it's a well tried and tested technology. A 12V battery is made up of six 2.1 volt cells in series, which are placed in a strong, vibration-resistant case.

The reaction

If two plates of dissimilar metals are immersed in a fluid, or electrolyte, a voltage potential will be developed between them. In the lead-acid battery, the negative plate is made of lead (chemical symbol Pb) and the positive plate from lead dioxide

Below Batteries can be charged and discharged many times because the chemical reaction is reversible.

(PbO_2). The electrolyte is a dilute solution of sulphuric acid (H_2SO_4). As current is drawn from the battery, electrons are moved around, gradually converting both plates into lead sulphate ($PbSO_4$) and the electrolyte to pure water (H_2O). At the extreme, you would end up with two electrodes of the same metal

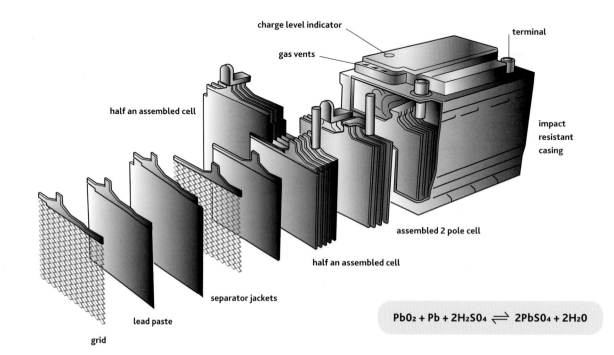

charge level indicator

gas vents

terminal

half an assembled cell

impact resistant casing

assembled 2 pole cell

half an assembled cell

separator jackets

lead paste

grid

$$PbO_2 + Pb + 2H_2SO_4 \rightleftharpoons 2PbSO_4 + 2H_2O$$

Above These batteries need periodic checking for electrolyte levels in each cell. Do not overfill them.

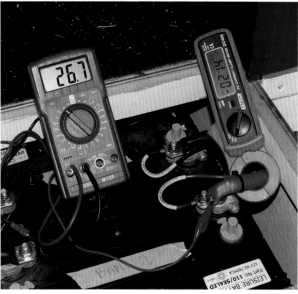

Above Sealed batteries are often called 'low maintenance'. There is no access to the cells so no topping up is required.

and water – a combination no longer able to produce electricity or, in other words, a flat battery.

Fortunately the reaction can be reversed from an external source (a charger) restoring the plates back to lead and lead dioxide and the electrolyte solution to its correct concentration. Once this is achieved the battery is fully charged again.

The perfect solution – nearly

On the face of it this reversible reaction looks perfect, but there are some secondary effects to consider:

✪ Over time some of the pure water is lost to evaporation (especially if the batteries are overcharged). This will need topping up with distilled or de-ionised water to keep the sulphuric acid at the correct concentration. Tap water or water from dehumidifiers should not be used because of impurities. If you are using sealed or 'maintenance-free' batteries, the evaporation is contained so no topping up is required, but it is even more important to prevent overcharging occurring.

✪ If the batteries are not fully recharged then the plates will retain a thin coating of lead sulphate as it won't all have been converted back. If allowed to remain over time this goes hard (a process known as sulphation) and can no longer be broken down, irrespective of how much you charge at a later

date. This means the capacity is permanently reduced. Because of this process it is beneficial to keep the batteries fully charged for as much of their life as possible. (Standard alternators only achieve about 85 per cent of charge capacity so if they are the only means of charging, a small amount of capacity will be lost over time.)

Types of batteries

Outwardly batteries look very similar; however, their internal construction differs according to the function they were designed for and it's important to appreciate the strengths and weaknesses of each one. The type of vessel and the way it is used should determine battery choice – paying more is not always necessary.

Internal plate structure

The plates are immersed in the electrolyte and the greater the surface area of the plates, the faster the chemical reaction can occur, enabling the battery to deliver higher currents.

The trade off, however, is that the penetration of lead sulphate in a heavily discharged battery is also much higher and more difficult to dislodge on charging. Batteries

Below **The type of vessel and your on-board equipment should determine which are the best batteries for you.**

designed for short bursts of very high current do not cope well with deep discharge cycling.

To achieve that goal, a smaller number of thicker and more robust plates are used with less surface area, so reducing the maximum current, but markedly improving the re-conversion of lead sulphate on charging. This results in an increase of several hundredfold in the number of heavy discharge cycles that the battery is capable of delivering.

Engine start, deep cycle or leisure battery

It is common practice to have a separate battery dedicated to starting the engine which will be excluded from any other duties (via the battery switch or switches) and this should be an 'engine start' type. Although the current will be very high, it will normally only be demanded for 10 or 15 seconds until the engine starts, so the percentage discharge of the battery is small and it is immediately followed by charging from the alternator.

For all the other, so-called domestic, equipment on board the amount of current required at any one time is much less, but it is drawn for significantly longer periods. This results in a deeper discharge between charging opportunities, so for this role a 'deep cycle' type of battery should be selected.

Finally, there is the 'leisure' type, which is a compromise between the engine start and deep cycle batteries, giving respectably high starting current but highly tolerant of deep cycles of charge. These should be used on boats that do not have separate engine start batteries, instead relying on a bank of two or three leisure batteries wired in parallel. With this configuration you must be particularly vigilant against running the batteries down, as you are also reliant on them for starting the engine.

Below **The structure of the plates is different according to the type of battery. The 'engine start' has more as well as thinner plates than the 'deep cycle' type.**

Wet, sealed or gel?

The electrolyte is sulphuric acid, a particularly nasty substance when slopping around the boat so containment within the battery case is essential.

- The 'wet' battery has the electrolyte in liquid form and provides access to each cell for both topping up and testing for state of charge using a hydrometer via screw caps. The big disadvantage here, of course, is that wet batteries are not leak proof so there is a likelihood of spillage.

- Sealed or 'low maintenance' batteries still have liquid electrolyte but the case is sealed to prevent any leakage. A pressure relief valve is incorporated to allow gasses to vent should the battery be heavily overcharged.

- Absorbed Glass Mat (AGM) batteries have improved performance, are truly sealed, accept faster rates of charge and are more tolerant of deep cycling. With a small increase in size, they

Above Sealed batteries give no access to the individual cells so the electrolyte cannot be topped up. This also means no access for a hydrometer to test the state of charge.

Above Gel batteries are very high quality and can withstand many repeated deep cycles.

offer a considerable improvement in capacity.

- 'Gel-Cell' or 'dry' batteries have the sulphuric acid in gel form so preventing any leakage, and with a sealed case these become very rugged. Although more expensive, their tolerance of deep discharge is better and when left in a state of discharge they are less prone to permanent sulphation. They do require a slightly different charging strategy compared to wet cells but most modern chargers incorporate this.

> **TIP**
>
> The different battery technologies have subtly different charging requirements. Within one battery bank only one type of technology should be used, and your chargers set accordingly. If you do need to mix battery types for any reason, set all the chargers to the battery technology with the lowest float voltage.

Above This physically small AGM battery can deliver up to 650A to start the engine. It is designed to tolerate deeper discharge cycling but still having a high starting current, making it more versatile for vessels with a single battery bank.

Above Innovation in battery design extends the performance. Absorbent Glass Mat technology is virtually spill proof and is not affected when at high angles of heel.

Above Absorbent Glass Mat batteries achieve very high values of cold cranking amps in a relatively small space outline, ideal for engine starting.

Specification, testing and maintenance

Understanding how batteries are specified is important when it comes to replacement, and having a good idea of the state of your existing batteries will help get the timing of replacement right. As with most things on a boat, a little maintenance will give you the best serviceable lifespan.

How batteries are specified

To give a degree of standardisation across the industry, typical parameters are used to define the performance depending on the type of battery:

- 'Cold Cranking Amps' (CCA) is quoted for engine start batteries. The value defines the amount of available current from the battery to start the engine, sustained for at least 30 seconds and in an outside air temperature down to -18°C.

- 'Marine Cranking Amps' (MCA) defines this at 0°C and is arguably more relevant to boats. Even the smaller of the 12V engine start batteries will achieve a CCA of 350–400A and an MCA in excess of 500A, easily supplying the typical small boat starter motor current of around 200A.

- 'Amp-hour rating' (Ah) is the specification for deep cycle batteries. It is quoted either over a period of 10 hours – the 'C/10' value – or the more common 20-hour 'C/20' rating. It specifies the number of amps discharged for 10 or 20 hours so as to fully flatten the battery. Here lies the rub though: fully flattening a battery damages it beyond recovery, so considerable amendment needs to be made to the value quoted, but at least the specification is consistent across manufacturers (see pages 48–49).

- Leisure batteries will quote CCA, MCA and Amp-hour rating as they are intended for engine start and deep cycle use. Being a compromise, their performance on each parameter will be slightly less than those designed specifically for each job.

Testing for state of charge

Knowing the state of charge at any point indicates how long the batteries have left before charging becomes necessary. Unfortunately measuring this is far from straightforward.

- Battery terminal voltage is the simplest method, but it is essential to allow the battery to 'rest' (everything, including any charger, turned off) for at least three hours before measuring, otherwise the reading will not be accurate. For a rough estimate though, one hour is sufficient.

Left **Where you have access to the cells, the hydrometer gives an accurate reading of battery charge by measuring the specific gravity of the electrolyte. Allow the battery to 'rest' for a while before measuring.**

○ The second method is measuring the 'specific gravity' of the electrolyte using a hydrometer to determine the strength of the sulphuric acid, indicating the state of charge. For this, you need to have access to the electrolyte, so that rules out sealed and gel-type batteries. Again you need to allow a shorter, half-hour rest period before measuring. Also remember you are now handling sulphuric acid so wear gloves and eye protection and have a bucket of water and sponge handy.

Maintenance

In an ideal situation all your batteries should be the same age, otherwise the whole bank of batteries will be dragged down by the weakest one. As much as is practically possible they should be kept fully charged.

○ Wet, unsealed batteries will need periodic checking for electrolyte level and should be topped up with de-ionised or distilled water to 2–3mm above the plates – there is usually a marker to show the correct level. Sealed, AGM and gel batteries do not need this of course.

○ Visually inspect the batteries for cracks in the case and the battery compartment for evidence of electrolyte leakage.

○ Keep the top of the battery case clean to stop the build up of dust. When dust gets moist, it can allow a very small but continuous leakage current to pass between the terminals, discharging the battery over time.

Above Sealed wet batteries have an internal hydrometer in one of the cells which gives a general indication of charge state.

BATTERY STATE OF CHARGE

'Rested' battery voltage (volts)	State of charge (%)
12.7	100
12.6	90
12.5	80
12.3	70
12.2	60
12.1	50
12.0	40
11.8	30
11.7	20
11.6	10

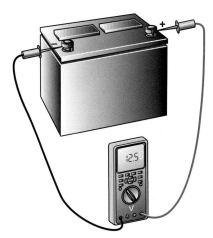

Middle Top up the cell to the mark with de-ionised water. Avoid overfilling so there is no spillage.

Above For an accurate state of charge, the batteries must have 'rested' for three hours or more. However, a reasonable indication can be gained after an hour or so.

TIP

There are many myths and legends about batteries, some true, some false. One of the (slightly unfortunate) truths is that it is much better to replace all the batteries in a bank at the same time. Having old ones in amongst several new batteries will drag the new ones down prematurely.

Charging the batteries

Charging is a chemical process that reverses the reaction producing the electrical energy consumed from the battery. It's arguably the most important aspect of battery management, and paying attention to a long-term charging strategy will extend battery life and reliability. How this can be achieved will depend on the way in which the boat is used.

What batteries need

To achieve maximum lifetime and capacity, as much as is practically possible, certain requirements need to be met:

- Batteries should ideally not be discharged below 70 per cent of their full capacity and certainly never below 50 per cent. This requires a full understanding of the typical energy consumption between charging opportunities and that sufficient capacity (ie the number and total size of batteries in the bank) has been made available in the first place.
- Batteries should not be left partially or heavily discharged for long periods of time – it's far better to leave them fully charged.
- To recharge the batteries to full capacity, a so-called 'multi-stage' charging plan is needed, which requires you to have a fair degree of electronic control.

Charge regulators

A regulator is an electronic device that controls the input of energy into the batteries from one or more sources. In some cases, the regulator will control the amount of energy made available according to the needs of the batteries (typical of alternators) or, as in most wind generators, it will divert excess energy away from the batteries. A simple regulator will at least ensure the batteries do not get overcharged and more complex ones will achieve multi-stage charging control as well. Looking at each source in isolation:

- Most modern **mains chargers** are excellent multi-stage controllers and can charge several battery banks independently to full capacity given enough time. They can be left switched on when mains power is available and, for boats that are based in marinas, can be used as the prime source of charging, with the alternator doing the work when out on the water.

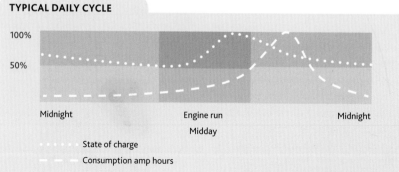

TYPICAL DAILY CYCLE

100%

50%

Midnight   Engine run   Midnight

Midday

· · · · · State of charge

– – – Consumption amp hours

Below **The main consumption tends to be in the evening, when the lights go on. The engine will have to go on for a suitable period each day to fully recharge the batteries.**

Above **So long as the same amp-hours of charge are put back into the batteries as was consumed in the period, energy balance is achieved and they will not go flat.**

- **Alternators** have built-in regulators, varying the amount of current produced to maintain a constant battery voltage of around 13.8V. In its standard form, the alternator will not replenish much more than 80 per cent of the battery capacity.
- **Wind generators** normally need an additional, external regulator. It is quite common for a wind generator regulator to also manage power from solar panels.
- For **solar panels**, there is a rule of thumb that if their maximum output power is less than 10 per cent of the battery capacity they are charging, no external regulator is required.
- **Fuel cells** have more advanced multi-stage regulators built-in, allowing them to be left switched on for long periods, charging as and when required.

Smart chargers

If there are a number of charging sources on a boat, things become more complicated and attention needs to be paid to controlling all the power. Combined or 'smart' charge controllers will take several sources of power into one regulator unit and electronically control the energy transferred to the batteries.

One of these sources could be the alternator itself, although this typically involves a small modification or replacing the regulator completely with an external one. The overriding advantage is that you now have a multi-stage charging system tailored to the needs of the batteries, ensuring they are recharged to 100 per cent of capacity whenever that is possible.

Above The total power capability is shared between the three outputs, giving smart charging for up to three banks.

Above The usual alternator regulator is 'machine sensing', as it measures (and regulates) the output voltage at the alternator itself. Losses in the cabling between the alternator and batteries are not accounted for so they may not get all the available voltage, but it is rarely a major issue.

Left An external multi-stage alternator regulator replaces the internal one completely but will transform the alternator performance, recharging the batteries to 100 per cent capacity.

Below and below right So long as the combined power is within the capability of the regulator, this one regulator controls both the wind generator and the solar panels. The hydrogen fuel cell has a smart regulator built in.

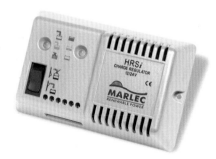

How many batteries?

Over time it is necessary to try to achieve an energy balance between consumption and charging. Batteries are the store of energy providing the electrical current to the boat's equipment in the period between charging opportunities. Battery capacity, and therefore the number and type of batteries required, is determined by the amount of equipment you have on board and the length of time the items are typically used between charges.

A detailed study of the electrical equipment on board and its typical usage will establish whether the existing capacity is matched to the way in which the boat is normally used. If the nature of use changes, say for an extended cruise instead of weekend sailing, going through the same process will forewarn you of any likely capacity shortfall so you can plan ways to tackle it.

Electrical audit

This is a simple process of listing all the electrical equipment on board, working out the current each item consumes (in amps) and estimating within a set period, say 24 hours, how many hours it is likely to be used. Multiplying the current consumption by the estimated hours of usage results in an 'Amp hour' (Ah) figure for each item. This is the same measure you use for battery capacity and is therefore directly comparable. Once the list is complete, add up the total amp-hours used in the period. Appendix 2 has a typical example.

Real capacity required

Having calculated the typical daily consumption, you now have the number of amp hours that will be taken out of the batteries. In order to protect them, it is essential to set a limit on the acceptable amount of drain that will result (as a percentage of the fully charged, C/20 Ah value) before charging. So:

☼ Boats with a single battery bank serving both domestic and engine starting should not use more than 40 per cent of the maximum available, on the basis that you should allow an additional 10 per cent safety margin to ensure you can always start the engine.

☼ Boats with a dedicated engine start battery can allow the domestic bank to discharge down to the 50 per cent level because starting the engine is protected by the separate battery.

☼ Allowance also needs to be made for the fact that standard alternators can only recharge up to around 80 per cent of maximum amp hour capacity. If a modified alternator with a so-called 'smart' regulator is fitted then this figure can be increased to at least 95 per cent.

☼ A further 10 per cent of capacity needs to be allowed for batteries getting older and their natural decrease in capacity.

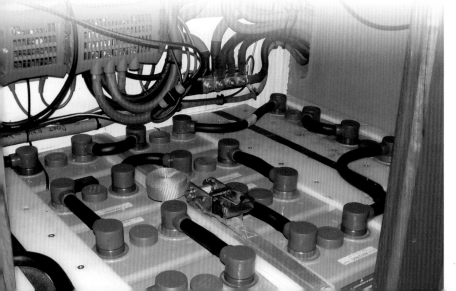

Left The total battery capacity you need depends entirely on the way your vessel is used. In this case, even the on-board mains is generated (via inverters) from the batteries so the loading is very high, hence the massive battery banks.

WORKED EXAMPLE

From the electrical audit example in Appendix 2, the estimated daily consumption came to 70Ah. The total C/20 designated capacity needed to ensure you do not discharge below 50 per cent can now be calculated and then further modified depending on the boat's system.

$$C = \frac{Ah}{D}$$

C = Calculated C/20 capacity requirement.
Ah = Daily consumption from the electrical audit.
D = The maximum allowable discharge percentage, divided by 100.

• With 70Ah consumption using a single battery bank system, hence a 40 per cent drain limit, from the equation the total C/20 available capacity (C) required would be 70/0.4 = 175Ah.

• For standard alternators this would represent only 80 per cent of the battery capacity because of the charging limitation, so the modified total becomes 175/0.8 = 219Ah.

• Allow a further 10 per cent for ageing, 219 x 1.1 = 241Ah.

From this example you need to have in place about 240Ah of C/20 designated capacity (two 120Ah batteries wired in parallel) allowing the 70Ah daily consumption without using more than 40 per cent of the total capacity. To maintain the energy balance, the engine would have to be run for a sufficient time each day to replace that consumption.

In summary, allow for maximum discharge, the deficiencies of the standard alternator's regulator and a bit for ageing.

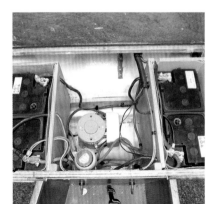

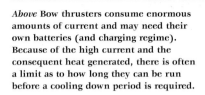

Above Bow thrusters consume enormous amounts of current and may need their own batteries (and charging regime). Because of the high current and the consequent heat generated, there is often a limit as to how long they can be run before a cooling down period is required.

Below Understanding the daily demands you intend to place on the batteries is the first step in working out your requirements.

Above Electric windlasses also fall into the high current category although do not consume as much current as the bow thrusters.

	10.3m sail			11m sail			11.4m sail			10.7m sail		
	Hallberg Rassy 34			Hallberg Rassy 36			JeanneauS/Odd 37			Moody 35		
Typical usage category	Charter			Charter			School/Charter			Charter		
Average voltage	12.5V			12.5 V			12.5 V			12.5V		
Domestic battery usable Ah capacity	180Ah			160 Ah			120Ah			100Ah		
Diesel tank capacity (litres)	155L			345L			136L			186L		
	Amps	Hrs	WHrs/Day	Amps	Hrs	WHrs/Day	Amps	Hrs	WHrs/Day	Amps	Hrs	WHrs/Day
Solar panels			0			0			0			0
Wind generator			0			0			0			0
Diesel/petrol generator			0			0			0			0
Towing generator			0			0			0			0
Fuel cells			0			0			0			0
Engine (alternators)	20	4	1000	30	3	1125	20	5	1250	20	4	1000
Mains charger			0			0			0			0
Daily generation capacity			1000			1125			1250			1000
Daily consumption (total from below)			1228			1443			1550			1230
BALANCE converted to AMPS HRS...		-18	Ah		-25	Ah		-32	Ah		-18	Ah
Equipment	Amps	Hrs	WHrs/Day	Amps	Hrs	WHrs/Day	Amps	Hrs	WHrs/Day	Amps	Hrs	WHrs/Day
Navigation related equipment												
Multi-function display	1	4	50	1	4	50	1.2	4	60	1.8	4	90
MFD repeater			0			0	0.8	3	30			0
Radar	2.5	3	94	2.5	3	94	2.5	3	94	2.5	3	94
Fish finder			0			0			0			0
AIS			0			0			0			0

Increasing capacity

Adding new equipment increases average daily consumption, eventually resulting in the need for increased battery capacity. The modified installation is likely to involve a new housing, cables, switches and, as the additional capacity will need charging, possibly (although not necessarily) a higher output alternator system. The way in which the boat is typically used will also influence the outcome.

Adding an engine start battery

⚙ To increase the capacity of a single battery bank system, it may be easier to install a dedicated engine start battery rather than simply adding another domestic battery.

⚙ In calculating the new available capacity, the now separate domestic bank can be discharged from 40 per cent down to 50 per cent of its C/20 capacity. Using the example shown on page 47, this will increase the usable capacity of the domestic bank to 87Ah.

⚙ The new engine start battery will need a connection to the alternator and the battery switch. The switch arrangement may have to be altered to give independence from the domestic bank. This will involve some new cables but, with luck, little else.

⚙ It is worth adding an emergency transfer switch between the engine start and the domestic bank so that the domestic bank could be used to start the engine in an emergency.

⚙ The additional battery will need to be safely secured in a new housing away from any fuel tanks, filters and pipes. A vented top cover should also be fitted to ensure no objects can come into contact with the terminals.

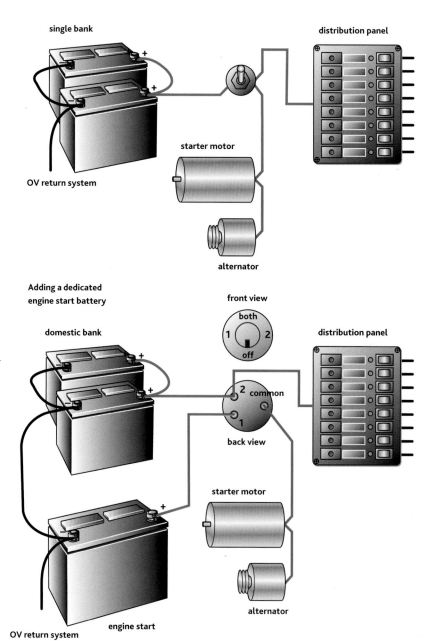

single bank

distribution panel

starter motor

OV return system

alternator

Adding a dedicated engine start battery

front view

both

1   2

off

domestic bank

distribution panel

2   common

1

back view

starter motor

alternator

engine start

OV return system

Increasing domestic bank capacity

This can be achieved by adding batteries, changing battery technology, improving elements of your charging system or a combination of all three.

- Adding an additional battery of the same type will involve the construction of a new housing and a small amount of extra cabling, but will result in a 50 per cent capacity increase if going from two to three batteries.
- Keeping the same number of batteries, but moving up a notch in technology, assuming they will fit into your existing housings, can achieve a similar increase in capacity. The increase in cost of AGM batteries compared to wet or leisure types may well be offset by the fact that no installation, wiring or switch modifications should be required.
- Existing battery capacity can also be increased by up to 20 per cent with a change to a smart, multi-stage regulator, allowing the alternator to achieve much nearer full charging.

12V DEEP CYCLE BATTERIES

	C/20 amp hours	CCA amps	MCA amps	Typical dimensions (mm) L x W x H
Flooded				
	110		650	348 x 173 x 228
	135		900	345 x 175 x 275
Sealed (leisure)				
	125	900		330 x 175 x 242
	180	950		513 x 220 x 225
AGM				
	145			341 x 173 x 309
	230	1300		513 x 273 x 242
	260			521 x 269 x 224
Gel	120	950		408 x 175 x 209

Impact on charging

The impact of the extra capacity on charging depends on the way the boat is used. Staying with the existing arrangements means it will simply take longer to recharge the batteries. If, however, charging time is limited, then the amount of charging current will have to be increased.

Upgrading the alternator to a higher output version will achieve this, and generally it will not be necessary to modify the mechanical mountings to take the new alternator, apart from fitting a larger cable to handle the extra current, so this is a simple solution. As a guide the maximum output of the alternator should be around 25 per cent of the total C/20 capacity for wet and leisure types but this can be much higher for AGM batteries as they accept greater rates of charge.

Above Moving up a notch in technology may give the extra capacity without adding batteries. AGM batteries have the added advantage of accepting much faster charging rates, while gel batteries can tolerate a higher percentage discharge.

Below A higher output version (130A) of a standard alternator will mean the larger capacity can still be charged in roughly the same time.

Above and left This is the back view of the typical 4 position rotary battery switch used in two bank systems. The diagram to the left illustrates how it can be used to direct the alternator charging current.

Make the connection

Wire and wire size

Cables comes in all shapes, sizes and colours and it is important to buy the correct type, particularly considering its use in the marine environment. Fortunately it is easy to narrow the field down, based predominantly on the current the cable will be required to carry and its length.

Type of wire

Assuming the wire material is copper, multi-strand cable made from many strands of much thinner wire is the preferred choice (battery cables, for instance, will have more than 100 strands). Solid core, such as is used in house mains electrical wiring, does not survive vibration well and is not recommended for marine use.

The next choice is whether to use tinned copper wire, where each strand is coated with a thin layer of tin. While this is more expensive, it is much more resistant to corrosion and should certainly be considered for any external wiring, for example navigation lights and mast electrics.

When ordering cable there can be confusion over terminology, with suppliers talking in terms of single- or multi-core cable. Single-core means one wire made up of multiple strands, coated overall in PVC insulation, whereas multi-core refers to two or more single-core wires collected together with a second outer PVC coating.

Selecting the size

All wire exhibits resistance when conducting current and Ohm's Law dictates the voltage loss, or drop, along the length of wire as its resistance multiplied by the current being conducted through it ($V = IR$). Although the resistance will be too small to measure easily, it can be calculated based on the electrical properties of copper, its 'resistivity', its cross-sectional area and the length of cable:

$$R = \rho \times \frac{L}{A}$$

R is the resistance (Ω)
ρ is the resistivity of copper, 0.0168 at 20°C
L is the length of the cable in metres to the equipment and back
A is the cross-sectional area of the copper in the cable (mm^2)

These losses are important to quantify because volts dropped in the cabling are wasted as heat. As a guide, these losses should not exceed 3 per cent of the available battery voltage for 'critical' equipment such as auto pilots and navigation lights, and or no more than 5–10 per cent for applications such as lighting. Appendix 1 shows the minimum wire size in cross sectional area to be used according to the amount of current being conducted and the total length of the cable for the 3 per cent and 10 per cent cases.

How to choose wire

Your choice of wire will be based on cross-sectional area because you are concerned about its resistance and

Below left **Main battery cables need high quality terminal attachment. Most battery suppliers and some chandlers will also provide this service at minimal cost.**

Below **All cables (for marine use at least) are made up of many small diameter wires surrounded by an insulating outer covering, usually PVC material. The thinner the individual strands, the more flexible is the cable.**

Below left Tin plating of each strand gives excellent corrosion resistance.

Below right This 150A battery cable is remarkably flexible because of the large number of very thin strands.

the consequent voltage drop when current is flowing. The cross-sectional area is, of course, a function of its diameter which can be described as American Wire Gauge (AWG) or (more typically in Europe) 'mm' diameter.

Wire is made by drawing rods of the material (copper) through a die, progressively stretching its length and reducing the diameter. The diameter of the die is referred to as its gauge and, today, it is the American Wire Gauge standard which prevails, still in wide use for describing wire diameter. Because thin wire will have been drawn through successively smaller die many times, it has a larger number, so 12AWG is thinner wire than 6AWG and so on.

The concept of wire gauge relates to a single strand of solid wire. Multi-strand marine cables will have a very slightly smaller equivalent cross-sectional area because of the minute air gaps between each strand. Generally speaking though, this is of no consequence. A conversion table between the various ways of describing the cross-sectional area is also included in Appendix 1.

WORKED EXAMPLE

To install a fridge compressor on a 12V system, the worst case continuous current needs to be established, for the purposes of wire sizing.

- From the user manual the power rating is quoted as 45W. Assuming a battery voltage of 12.2V this equates to 3.7A.

- Once the location of the compressor has been determined, the total cable run of positive and negative cables from the electrical distribution panel to the compressor is measured at, for this example, 15m (49ft).

- As the fridge function is important, the lower cable loss value of 3 per cent should be used. At 12.2V this equates to around 0.4V, and from Ohm's Law the cable resistance that would create at 3.7A is 0.4/3.7 = 0.108Ω. From the equation above the minimum cross-sectional area of the cable needed is calculated as 2.3mm^2.

- Using the table of wire size in Appendix 1, and taking 4A as the nearest current with a cable run of 15m (49ft), the cross-sectional area is shown as 2.7mm^2, which is perfectly acceptable. If you fall between two options on cable size, choose the larger one. The appendix also shows a conversion to AWG; for this example you would use 12AWG.

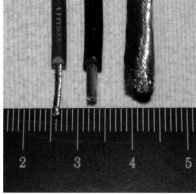

Above Some cables have the size printed on the outer insulation material. Usually both the AWG and mm diameter figures are shown.

Above right If the cable is not marked, measure the diameter (Dia) of the copper. The cross section area is then = (3.142 x Dia x Dia /4)mm^2. These are (from left) 18AWG, 14AWG and 5AWG (1.0, 1.6 and 4.5mm^2).

Left Instrumentation, multi-core cable has a layer of screening to minimise interference from other nearby wires. Break off the foil and (if possible) connect one end of the screening wire to 0V.

TIP

If you need to increase the current handling capability of a cable, for instance between the battery switch and the distribution panel, rather than replacing the cable you could fit a second one alongside the existing one. Even if not the same wire size, the two cables will contribute an overall increase in capacity.

Connections and connectors

Having installed new equipment, sorted out the wiring diagram and sized the cables, you will soon realise just how many connections are needed. Unfortunately, connections are the weak link in the system – they can corrode, break or come loose, so it's worth investing in the right type for each job you undertake.

Above Connecting a 'new' wire into an existing one using a Scotchlok™. The blade can cut through the insulation without cutting the wire.

Type of connection

There is a massive array of connectors on the market but that is partly because there are many ways wires can be joined and many different sizes of wire to accommodate. Fortunately the options can be rapidly whittled down. The type of connections essentially boil down to:

- Extending a wire or joining two wires.
- 'Tapping in' a new wire to an existing one, a bit like a T piece.
- Attaching a wire to the terminal of a piece of equipment. The choice is easy here as your connector simply needs to be compatible with the equipment.
- Joining many wires to one, such as for cabin lights, where the power for all the lights come from just one point on the distribution panel.
- High-current connections like battery cable terminals or equipment that needs to be connected directly to the battery, for example, a diesel heater.
- Connecting a fuse and switch into the circuit.

Make the connection

- **A crimp connector** is one where the wire fits into an appropriate diameter tube which is then compressed onto the wire, either by a hand crimp tool or, for much larger crimps (like battery terminals), by a hydraulic version.
- **A bus bar** is a bar of copper with many screws fitted along it which allows one or even two wires (with the appropriate end connector) to be secured by each screw. The bus bar therefore connects many wires together in one place.
- **A stud** is a piece of copper with two or three bolts secured into it for joining much larger high-current cables. They often also have smaller screws fitted to attach smaller cables to the same point. Avoid using stainless steel washers as they are surprisingly resistive, causing unwanted voltage drops.
- **Scotchlok™**, a trade mark of 3M, connects wires by forcing a blade through the insulation without cutting the wire itself. These are designed for tapping a new wire into an existing one or joining two wires together.
- **Terminal blocks** allow a number of pairs of wires to be joined by screw terminals, with each pair insulated from its neighbour. One type has the screws on the top face and you need to crimp the appropriate connector onto both wires. With the other type, the bare wires go into a tube and the screws tighten onto the wires.
- **Soldering** is not normally recommended (other than connecting thin wires) as it creates a hard spot that's liable to vibration-induced fracture. In addition, unless the solder has properly flowed in between each of the wire strands a dry joint may result, and this can compromise the quality of the electrical connection.

Choosing the right one

The connector should be the right size to fit the cable. Crimps suitable

Left Heat-shrink tubing is ideal for sealing connectors. Remember to slide it on the wire before you crimp the connector.

CRIMP CONNECTORS

The cutter blades are in the centre of these self-adjusting wire strippers.

Strip back the insulation by about 5mm (0.2in).

Choose the correct size of crimp. Twisting the strands makes insertion easier.

The bare wire should not be visible out of the end of the crimp.

The crimping tool has three sizes of die according to the colour (and hence size) of crimp used.

You can rub some grease into the top of the crimp, around the wire entry, to discourage moisture.

Above There are many connectors available but these types are very useful, carry a handful of each in your spares box. Also have a load of the appropriate crimp connectors to go with them, both red and blue versions.

Above Several wires can be joined together using a variety of terminal blocks according to the wire sizes.

TIP

It's good practice to prevent moisture getting into connections between wires and there are several ways to achieve this:

• For standard crimp terminals, rub some petroleum jelly into the ends.
• Use connectors with heat-shrink tube ends.
• Cover the whole connection with heat-shrink tubing.

for use with the ratchet-style hand crimp tool come in three colours according to the wire sizes that will fit: red is the smallest (22–16AWG, 0.5–1.5mm²); blue the intermediate (16–14AWG, 1.5–2.5mm²); and yellow the larger style (12–10AWG, 4.0–6.0mm²). These three types should be suitable for the vast majority of wiring.

Connecting thin wires

Very thin, multi-strand wire is difficult to connect reliably which makes it important to use connectors designed for the job. Electronics manufacturers now tend to have bespoke connection systems linking pieces of their equipment together using robust and watertight connectors. However, even some of the most widely used interfaces still require thin wires to be joined together.

Why thin wire?

Multi-core, multi-strand wire is used between instruments to pass data and, as the current involved is very small, the wire can be very thin. The most important thing is to support the wire (using cable ties for instance) so that there is no strain on the connection itself. If using connectors they should be of an indirect bearing type, where a flat plate clamps the wire, the clamping force being applied either by a spring mechanism or a screw. Alternatively, soldering wires together can also be considered, along with heat-shrink tubing to insulate and seal against moisture.

Suitable connectors

The connectors described here are designed specifically for thin wire and will accept the bare end of the wire (with the strands twisted together) without any need for soldering.

- **Terminal blocks** are a very convenient way of joining together up to four wires. The clamping (or spreader) plate under the screw grips with an even load, preventing damage to the wire strands. These are considered a professional standard and are generally only available in small quantities through specialist marine electronics dealers or installers.
- **Crimp terminals** of many styles can be considered, although even the smallest red size may be too large for the wire to be clamped effectively. Ideally you should aim to only ever have one wire per crimp.
- **Butt and heat-shrink** crimp connectors are very good for joining two wires and sealing against moisture. Again the red style is the smallest, with the same limitation on wire size.

Soldering two wires together

Generally it is not advisable to solder two wires together, although the thinner the wire, the better the joint you will achieve, so this option should not be ruled out. However, don't be tempted to twist several wires together and solder over the bundle.

- For each wire, strip off 5–6mm (0.2in) of insulation and twist the strands.
- Slide the heat-shrink tubing over one of the wires, keeping it at least 10cm (4in) away from the joint when applying the solder to prevent it starting to shrink before you are ready.

Left Although these connectors are overkill for the thin signal wires, they do make a good, secure connection. When you crimp on the terminal to the wire, give it a pull to check it has crimped effectively.

- Melt solder into the bare end of each wire separately (so-called tinning the ends), ensuring a good flow between the strands.
- Hold the soldered ends alongside each other. With the iron, fully re-melt the solder on both.
- Slide the heat-shrink tubing over the joint and apply heat to shrink it down. Take care not to apply too much heat as you may melt the solder again and the joint will fall apart.

The solder butt

Used to connect two wires together end to end, these have a band of solder within heat-shrink tubing. The two wires are stripped back, inserted from each end and crimped. The crimp action holds the wires in place then, using a heat gun, the solder band is melted into the wires and, at the same time, the heat-shrink tube then shrinks over the joint producing a moisture seal. As with crimps, these come in the three sizes denoted by colour.

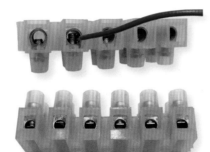

Top If the connector block is too large, the wire tends to go up the side of the screw.

Above Terminal blocks can be used – they are not ideal but choose the smallest hole size to accept the wire. Always ask for the type with spreader plate if available, and 'tin' the wire end if you can.

TIP

Soldering the end of the wire, called 'tinning', will improve the connection. Standard terminal blocks, of the smallest size that will take the wire, can be used as the wires will not get damaged by the screw. Make sure the cables are fully supported so that there's no strain on the connection.

CRIMP TERMINALS ON THIN WIRE

To improve attachment of a crimp terminal onto thin wire, it is useful to 'tin' the wire end with solder. This 'bulks' up the wire with the softer solder and allows the crimp to dig in a little when it is compressed by the crimping tool.

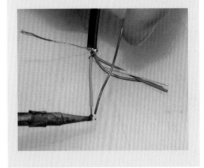

MAKING A SOLDER BUTT

The solder butt is a neat solution but takes some practice. The stripped ends overlie each other in the central solder ring.

Using the crimping tool, compress the solder ring , clamping the wires in place.

Using a heat gun, gently heat until the solder has melted and the heat-shrink tubing has shrunk, sealing the joint.

Power management

5

Alternators

The alternator is an inherently reliable workhorse and is the principal source of charging in most, if not all, marine systems. Its beauty is in its simplicity and the few limitations can be resolved to give an efficient battery-charging machine. Used in isolation, or with other arguably less flexible sources of power, battery charging can be successfully managed irrespective of your style of boating.

What is it?

The alternator is a rotating machine attached to your engine and driven by a flexible belt (flat or V shaped) from a pulley mounted on the engine's crankshaft. It must rotate quite a bit faster than your engine, so the pulley on the alternator is about half the size of the one on the engine, increasing its speed by a factor of two.

The rotation generates electricity that, with a simple conversion, can go straight into your batteries (for charging) and to all your 12V equipment. 24V systems will need a 24V alternator and battery bank.

How it works

Michael Faraday, an English scientist, is generally credited with discovering the relationship between electricity and magnetism in the mid-nineteenth century. Two of his many discoveries were:

- If a length of wire is passed through a magnetic field, then a voltage will be induced in the wire. The faster this happens the greater the induced voltage – in other words, it has become a generator.
- If, on the other hand, a current is passed down a length of wire then a magnetic field will be produced around the wire. If the field is concentrated or focused, then it has become an electro-magnet.

The alternator uses both of these qualities, turning the first on its head slightly in that it holds the wire stationary and rotates the magnetic field, and using the second to create the magnetic field itself.

- The 'rotor' (the inner rotating part) is the electro-magnet, made up of a coil of wire, through which a current is passed, surrounded by a cage that concentrates the created field.
- The 'stator' (the stationary outer part) has three separate long pieces of wire wound in coils over which the rotating magnetic field (from the rotor) passes, inducing voltage in the stator windings.
- The amount of power generated in the stator is a function of both the amount of magnetic field created in the rotor and the speed at which it rotates.

The remaining elements

- **The rectifier pack:** Because the magnetic field is rotating, it generates an AC voltage in the stator windings, so a conversion to DC is required to make it compatible with the boat's electrical system. This is the job of a bunch of six internal diodes known as the rectifier pack.

Left The alternator is an integral part of the engine and driven from the main crankshaft by a flexible belt, which also drives the water pump. The belt has to have the correct amount of tension, to prevent slipping.

Above The rotor (on the right) concentrates the magnetic field, which then 'washes' over the stator windings, inducing current in them. The rotor current (controlling the amount of magnetic field) is passed from the regulator via the slip rings.

⚙ **The regulator:** To control the power delivered by the alternator, the regulator monitors the battery voltage and supplies current to the rotor winding to generate the appropriate amount of magnetic field. The lower the voltage at the battery volts, the greater the magnetic field that is required, and so more current is supplied from the regulator.

⚙ **Slip rings and brushes:** These convey the regulator current to the rotor windings. The brushes, which are held against the slip rings, eventually wear and may need replacing after many thousands of hours of use. The slip rings are part of the rotor itself.

⚙ **Indication:** A connection is made to a charge warning light, usually mounted on the engine control panel, which goes out when power is being generated.

⚙ **Rev counter:** The final connection from the alternator is to the rev counter.

Above right The standard alternator unit has an internal regulator, which picks up its reference voltage within the alternator, so-called 'machine sensed'.

Right The rectifier pack is made up of six separate diodes pressed into the casing.

Bottom right Most alternators have four connections:
• B + : for the 12V (battery positive) terminal
• B - : for the 0V (battery negative) terminal
• W : for the rev counter
• D + : for the ignition warning light circuit.

TIP

A permanently installed voltmeter will immediately indicate whether the alternator is charging the batteries. Once the engine has started, if all is well, the volts will go up to around 14V (28V for a 24V system). If you have a current measuring system fitted then you will see a positive current reading, signifying current is flowing into the batteries, as long as the switches are set correctly!

Care, maintenance and fault finding

The alternator is a mostly maintenance-free, fit-and-forget device, requiring just a little care to get the best out of it. Limited repairs can be carried out in the rare event of failure, but a replacement unit is generally the easiest option. There are some key points about alternator use that we'll highlight here.

The Achilles heel

Alternators are hardy machines but the vast majority of boat installations have diesel engines and rely on the user to protect the alternator from two very distinct scenarios:

- **Stopping a diesel engine** must always be done via the pull cord or designated stop button (which interrupts the fuel supply). The key switch or power button only supplies power to the regulator. Turning this off with the engine still running means the alternator loses its controller and the output voltage will rise rapidly, damaging the regulator itself as well as risking total destruction of the rectifier pack.

- **Battery switch 'OFF'** position must never be selected with the engine running because it disconnects the alternator.

Below **The alternator is usually the primary source of power for recharging the batteries, irrespective of the style of boat.**

The current flow, which now has nowhere to go, forces the voltage at the output to rise rapidly. This can result in damage or destruction of the diodes and regulator. Most battery isolation switches have a warning note as a reminder of this.

Periodic/annual maintenance

The alternator has a direct connection to the battery and starter motor so it is strongly recommended that you remove the battery positive terminal before working on the alternator and its associated connections.

- There are several connections on the back of the alternator. Stud and nut types need to be checked for tightness and cleanliness – at least one of these carries the high charging current. There may well be spade terminals where a visual inspection will suffice, checking

they are secure and that the wire is not damaged or frayed.

- The charging circuit, even in the simplest system, starts at the alternator, goes to the starter motor then to the battery switch. These connections should be checked in the same way. Finally, the last connection will be to the battery positive terminal which, for the moment, you will have removed for the purposes of doing these checks.

- The drive belt is equally important. Consult your engine manual and check for correct tightness but also look for signs of black dust or belt wear due to slippage on the pulleys.

- The alternator's integral fan provides the airflow to cool the windings. This is a foolproof arrangement, but beware of any modifications you make in the engine compartment that might restrict the airflow.

Above **The 'notice' serves as a reminder to make sure you have a battery linked to the alternator when the engine is running.**

THE POWER CONNECTIONS

The alternator positive output is usually joined to the battery cable at the starter motor.

0V connection to the engine.

Positive output from the alternator.

Fault finding

A few indicators that will warn you of problems with the alternator are:

- With the engine running, battery volts are around 12.6V. Normally, they should be close to 14V.
- The battery charge light does not go out after the engine has started up. The alternator voltage must exceed battery voltage for this light to go out completely. The first check is belt tension – remember to stop the engine before checking! If that is correct then the rectifier pack is the next suspect.
- Always check that the battery charge, oil warning and over temperature lights come on as you begin turning the 'start' key. The battery light is actually part of the alternator control circuit so the bulb must be working for the alternator to function.

Right The formed metal on the front of the alternator acts as the cooling fan forcing air through the unit.

Right All the lights come on when the ignition switch is initially turned, to confirm the bulbs and sensors are working. When the engine starts they should all go out.

If you do find a fault, it is unlikely that you will be able to repair the alternator, particularly at sea. Long-distance sailors should consider carrying a complete replacement unit. Coastal cruisers, on the other hand, are likely to be able to buy an exchange unit at the nearest port. Ask in the marina office or the local chandlers for advice on local repair and exchange centres.

TIP

Much focus is given to the positive 12V (or 24V) side of circuits, but the negative cables and connections are equally important. Most alternators rely on their mountings to provide the return path for the alternator current, or have a short cable to the engine block. It is also acceptable to add a second 0V cable direct to one of the battery negative terminals, as they are all connected together.

Sizing and upgrading

Deciding whether to upgrade your alternator system depends on many factors, so start with an electrical audit. You can then estimate how long the engine will need to be run each day to power all your equipment. If this is excessive, work out ways to reduce your usage. Start small and think how the existing system could be improved before making any big changes.

Estimate what is needed

From the previous electrical audit (see pages 46–47), the daily consumption was estimated to be 70Ah from a single battery bank of 240Ah total capacity and a standard alternator.

For small to mid-sized boats, the alternator will have 50–60A output capability at around 1500 rpm (engine revs). However, to allow for losses and heating effects, this figure should be reduced to 45A, which has to supply the batteries and any equipment.

Estimating the daily engine run time needed to recharge the batteries depends on several different factors:

- Turn off as much equipment as possible to reduce the total amount of current being fed by the alternator to the batteries.
- The alternator's maximum current will flow into the batteries only at first. Once they are 75 per cent charged, the current will have dropped down to less than half this amount (as determined by the battery's internal resistance).
- For 70Ah of charge to be supplied at 35A, between two and three hours of engine running time per day is needed. This would also need to be at reasonably high engine revs – the alternator will only generate maximum charge at high speeds.

Charge acceptance rate

There is a limit to how fast charge can be returned to the batteries. This is known as the 'charge acceptance rate', and higher rates will heat the battery up significantly. Fast chargers have a temperature sensor attached to the battery, backing off the current if necessary to prevent overheating.

The battery type and its state of charge both influence charge acceptance rate. Working between 50 and 70 per cent of capacity (the bulk charge region), then:

- Flooded lead acid batteries can accept around 25 per cent of C/20 capacity (see pages 42–43). Here, 240Ah x 25 per cent = 60A.

Above A smart regulator is probably the first port of call to improve your system.

Right Harnessing alternative energy sources means you can reduce your engine hours.

Far right Solar panels may be the easiest additional power source to install. They can be brought out when required if a permanent installation is impractical.

Left and below The second alternator gives you a spare unit as well as more power. Dual smart regulators are also available.

- Gel-type batteries accept around 50 per cent (120A).
- AGM batteries can take much higher rates, the value varying between different manufacturers.

Need more power?

The figures above are suggesting, for a sailing boat at least, that more charging current is needed to reduce the daily engine running time. But, there are other routes to improving charging efficiency:

- **Smart regulators** bypass the original regulator, increasing the alternator output voltage during the initial stage. This maintains maximum current for much longer, while making sure overcharging doesn't take place. In addition, they are multi-stage chargers that will get your batteries charged back up to 95 per cent of the C/20 capacity.
- **Other sources** like solar panels, a wind generator or fuel cells can contribute a portion of the requirement throughout the day.

- **Exchange your existing alternator** for a larger version. Standard alternators usually have more powerful relatives with the same mountings.
- **Do both!** Exchange to a larger alternator and then also fit a smart regulator.
- **Fit a second alternator.** This is a fairly major undertaking, but is advocated by some long-distance cruisers as you have a back-up unit if one fails.

Squeezing the most out

The alternator circuit handles high current for long periods of time and is the most susceptible to losses in the cabling. If you are upgrading the system then you will also need to fit larger positive and negative cables. These should be sized for full alternator current, allowing for 3 per cent maximum losses, plus a larger size to allow for the elevated temperature that occurs inside the engine compartment.

As an example, for charging at 85A, with a 6m (20ft) length of cable, 3 per cent maximum losses and allowing for raised temperatures, the table in Appendix 1 shows AWG1 or 42mm² wire is appropriate (it's good for 90A over this length of cable).

Left The uprated unit has about 40 per cent increase in power output and will usually fit on the same mounting points (and should fit in the same space, but it's worth checking first).

Intelligent chargers

A good charger will get the very best out of your batteries. It incorporates quite complex electronic control systems to continually monitor the state of the batteries and adapt the charging characteristics accordingly, even catering for the different battery technologies available. Many chargers can also manage multiple sources of power automatically, thus ensuring batteries are not overcharged.

Three- or four-stage charging

When being charged, batteries will behave very differently depending on their state of charge at any point in the charge cycle. Although the stages are common to most battery technologies, there are subtle differences, so you need to set the charger for the appropriate battery type when it's installed, or after changing to a new type of battery. The process may be referred to as either three-stage or four-stage charging – depending on whether you count the reset stage as a distinct stage.

- **Bulk charge (1)** takes place when the battery state of charge is roughly 50–75 per cent of its capacity. During this phase the charger outputs as much current as possible, limited only by the battery's internal temperature rise, which is monitored by an external sensor. As the battery progressively absorbs more charge its voltage will rise and when this reaches a certain value, depending on the type of battery, the charger switches to stage 2.
- **Absorption (2)** maintains the charger output and battery at a constant voltage for a set period of time. For unsealed lead acid batteries this will be 14.8V, but it will be a little lower for sealed leisure, AGM and gel types. During this period the current will gradually fall off and the time

(which is set by the charger) allows the charge to distribute itself around the structure of the cells.
- **Float charge (3)** stage takes over once the time period is complete and the charger output voltage drops down to the float value appropriate to the battery type. The charger can be left in this mode, as achieving near 100 per cent charge may take many hours.
- **Reset (4)** occurs if the battery voltage drops below about 11.5V. This is interpreted by the charger as a significant battery usage to a point worthy of starting the process over again, so it resets to the bulk charge mode.

Chargers can also supply current (typically around 10A or 20A) to your boat equipment without interfering in any way with the charging process.

Managing multiple sources

A wide range of products is available to manage multiple charging inputs. If anything, the biggest problem is deciding which one is the best approach to take.
- **Mains chargers** convert mains electricity into the four-stage

Below Four-stage charging graph. Three- or four-stage chargers are the same. The so-called fourth stage is actually a reset to the first stage when the batteries have become discharged below the reset threshold.

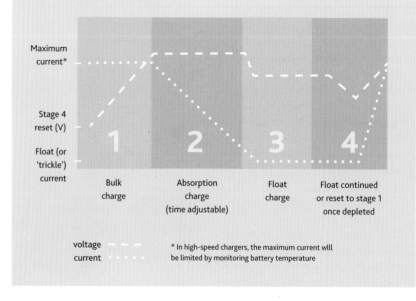

4-STAGE CHARGING PROCESS

Maximum current*

Stage 4 reset (V)

Float (or 'trickle') current

| 1 | 2 | 3 | 4 |

Bulk charge

Absorption charge (time adjustable)

Float charge

Float continued or reset to stage 1 once depleted

voltage – – –
current ·······

* In high-speed chargers, the maximum current will be limited by monitoring battery temperature

Left **With a 12V and 24V system, two mains chargers will be necessary.**

SMART REGULATORS

By replacing the alternator's internal regulator with an external smart regulator, much better performance can be extracted from the alternator.

This regulator takes in both the wind generator and energy from solar panels. It is important not to overload the unit with too much power.

battery charging process. Nowadays, most have a so-called 'universal input', accepting between 110V to 240V AC.

⚙ **Alternator to battery (or boost) chargers** take power from one or two alternators into the charger and manage the distribution of charging to the engine start battery (which is given priority) and the domestic battery bank. Once the engine start battery is charged, the voltage from the alternator is directed to the domestic bank but is boosted to a higher value by the charger so that it can achieve the four-stage charging process.

⚙ **Battery to battery chargers** are installed between the engine start battery and the domestic bank. With the engine running they take power from the alternator (feeding the engine start battery) and boost it to provide four-stage charging for the domestic battery

bank. By drawing current from the alternator to feed the domestic batteries it 'fools' the alternator into working harder, while ensuring that the engine start battery still remains sufficiently charged.

TIP

Fully recharging the batteries requires a long time in stage 3 (float charge). On sailing boats, a smart or fast charge regulator will get through stage 1 (bulk charge) much faster, leaving more of your engine running time devoted to stages 2 and 3. This will help get your batteries up to an 80 or 85 per cent charge state in a reasonable time. Realistically, you are looking at many further hours of engine running to get above 90 per cent charge.

Above **If you stay with the standard alternator, accepting the fact that the engine start battery will suffer a small amount, you can boost its output (with a battery to battery charger) to give four-stage charging to the domestic bank.**

Wind and water

A wind generator is essentially a second alternator with a propeller on the front. When mounted high in the rigging, the wind is the driving force, or if it's mounted on the transom with a propeller in the water, the boat's movement through the water can be the driving force. Some units are convertible between both types.

Here, the alternator differs from the standard engine type in that the rotor is a permanent magnet, giving a constant rotor magnetic field. Also, there is usually no internal regulator so the power generated is purely a function of the speed of rotation.

Performance

The amount of power generated is described by a graph of amps (or power in watts) against wind or boat speed. The smaller units produce a maximum of 100W; larger versions achieve up to 700W.

The Watt&Sea Hydrogenerator is a transom-mounted, water-powered device that promises an impressive 125W at just 5 knots of boat speed, rising to 500W at 8 knots. Some very exotic magnetic materials are used to achieve this, making the unit expensive but, in performance terms, impressive.

At the other end of the cost scale, the Aquair 100 generator quotes around 7A at 12.7V with a boat speed of 8 knots. When operated as a wind generator, it achieves 5A in 25 knots of wind, making it a versatile cruising companion.

Wind generator regulators

Generators will continue to produce energy so long as there is wind and there will come a time when you simply don't need any more. Unlike engine alternators, there is no means of controlling the power output.

Wind generator regulators work by diverting excess power away from the batteries and converting it to heat via large dump resistors (supplied with the regulator). The regulator will control this process whilst keeping the batteries topped up.

To get the best degree of regulation the battery terminal voltage needs to be monitored via a sense wire from the regulator (which allows for voltage drops in the cable). Regulators are available that will accept additional power input from solar panels, with the combined power from both sources managed by a single unit.

Water-powered generator regulation

Using the Aquair 100 in water mode (unlike in wind mode) does not require a regulator, as the output voltage will not rise high enough to overcharge the battery.

Other manufacturers, however, recommend that regulators are always used in conjunction with their generators.

Below **Use a realistic average boat speed to estimate the amount of power generated. For a 24-hour period at 5 knots you would put around 130Ah back into the batteries. A similar figure is achieved with an average of 18 knots of wind.**

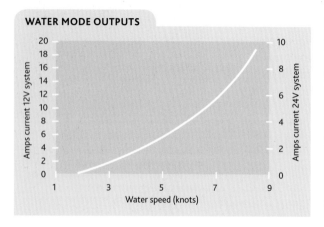

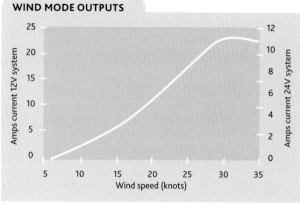

Stopping a wind generator

Wind generators will withstand storm force winds but, as with the rest of your boat, it should be shut down in advance of a severe storm. Clearly you have to stop the propeller turning and manufacturers always describe how best to do this. It is not an easy task in strong winds and care should be taken to avoid the blades inflicting injury. There are two common methods:

- The electrical way is to use a switch that disconnects the generator from the batteries, and directly connects the 12V (or 24V) output to the 0V terminal, forming a direct short within the unit. This produces so much electrical loading that it stalls and the propeller slows down almost to a stop. This method is not recommended in very high winds, so...

- The manual way is to approach from downwind, wearing thick gloves, grab the tail vane of the generator with a boat hook and turn it side on to the wind. Once the blades have stopped turning you bag them or tie them off. Take care not to manhandle the blades too much, as they are precisely balanced and a little fragile in this respect.

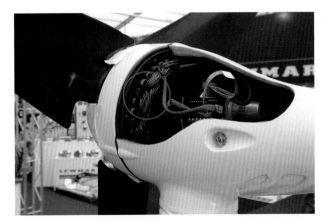

Left A look inside the wind generator shows the alternator windings.

Below left Solid shafts to the propeller are more convenient than the older rope type but are vulnerable if hit by floating objects.

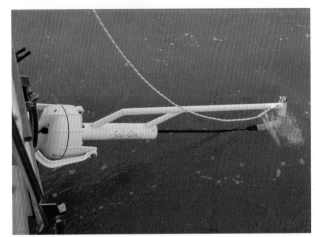

Above Wind generators must be sited above head height to prevent the possibility of a head injury.

Above For small to medium-sized boats, water-powered generators produce a very useful amount of electricity.

TIP

The contribution made by a wind generator should be estimated based on average wind speeds of 10–15 knots. If installation cost is spread over ten years, the annual cost of generation is far less than running the engine to generate the same power.

Solar panels

Solar panels produce DC electricity by converting energy from the sun. Their output is low compared to other generators and may not provide all the power needed, but they make a useful contribution. They are particularly good at keeping batteries topped up if the boat is unused for long periods. They are maintenance free and are available as rigid, semi-rigid and fully flexible panels.

Solar panels are made from two layers of silicon, each 'doped' with different impurities. As photons of sunlight energy collide with the top layer, electrons are released and a voltage potential is produced across the junction of the two layers.

The panel is made up of an array of cells giving a typical output voltage of around 20V. There are three general types, each with their own characteristics:

- **Monocrystalline cells** consist of single large crystals of near perfect form and have the highest efficiency, at 14–17 per cent.
- **Polycrystalline silicon** is formed from molten silicon, which forms smaller crystals when cooled. These have many defects and the panels are less efficient, at around 13–15 per cent.
- **Amorphous silicon** is a less expensive process, depositing vaporised silicon onto a backing material. They have the lowest efficiency at around 5–7 per cent, but have the most flexibility, even allowing the panel to be rolled up.

Electrical characteristics

- **Open circuit voltage** is the voltage at the output of the panel with no current flowing and is typically around 20V. This will be a lot higher than you might expect because the output voltage drops rapidly as you draw current.
- **Peak power (watts)** is the maximum power the panel can produce in perfect conditions. Again, this falls off rapidly if there is cloud, shading or if the panel is not at right angles to the sun.
- **Voltage at peak power** sets the optimum operating point for the panel. By controlling the voltage output, the maximum power (output voltage x current) can be extracted from the panel

according to the amount of sunlight available.
- **Current at peak power** is the maximum current that can be produced by the panel when optimally aligned.
- **System voltage** is the system voltage the panel is intended for use with, for example 12 or 24V.

Regulation

As a rule of thumb, if the maximum power from all panels is less than 10 per cent of the total C/20 battery capacity, no regulator is required. Otherwise, three types are available:

- **Simple regulators** switch the panels through to the batteries when the battery voltage falls below a certain value (typically 12.9V for a 12V system or 25.8V for a 24V system) and switch them off at 14V or 28V respectively. These are low cost and ideal for lower output panels used to float charge over long periods. However, this will not allow the panels to operate at their optimum output.
- **Pulse Width Modulated (PWM) regulators** control the current that is drawn from the panels maintaining the output voltage at a pre-set value, extracting the

Left Semi flexible panels can be adjusted to the shape of the coach roof.

Right Fully flexible panels can (literally) be rolled up and put away. Technology in these types is improving rapidly and these panels are rated at 45W.

Right For long-distance cruising, solar panels offer a useful source of energy, though a small array will not produce the same output as wind or water generators.

available power more efficiently than the simple regulator. As the batteries become fully charged, the PWM regulator reduces the charging current down to the float level.

⚙ **Maximum Power Point Tracking (MPPT)** is the ultimate regulator control that gets the very best from your panels. It uses the same techniques as PWM regulation for four-stage charging. The output power is maximised by controlling the output voltage at the 'critical' value, often around 17V. This is then converted down to the appropriate level for charging the batteries.

The solar panel's maximum power rating assumes perfect conditions with bright sunlight perpendicular to the panel. For practical purposes, assume near full power output for four to five hours per day in sunny climates, and a little less for northern latitudes.

Left MPPT (Maximum Power Point Tracking) regulators wring every last drop of energy from the panels.

Below By controlling the panel output voltage at the 'critical' value, the maximum power from the photovoltaic (PV) panels is maintained. As 17V is too high for the batteries, it is converted to the correct voltage. For 24V systems, you would pair the 12V panels in series.

TIP

Studies have shown that panels mounted horizontally give, on average, the best overall daily power generation. For optimum performance, there are motorised controllers that will 'follow the sun', tilting the panels to maintain a perpendicular aspect to it all day.

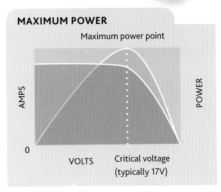

MAXIMUM POWER

Maximum power point

AMPS

POWER

0

VOLTS   Critical voltage
(typically 17V)

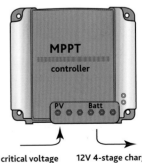

MPPT
controller

PV   Batt

critical voltage
(typically 17V)

12V 4-stage charging
voltage O/P

Installing a mains charger

Modern mains chargers are extremely versatile. Mid-range units support single or multiple battery banks and independent four-stage charging, with the output tailored for different battery technologies. All but the lowest cost units also incorporate a power supply, so energy not required by the battery is available for other purposes on board. But the biggest advantage is they can be left running indefinitely, keeping the batteries fully charged and prolonging their life.

Common terminology
- **Universal input** means the charger can be plugged in anywhere in the world, with acceptable mains inputs ranging from 80–250V and 40–70Hz. Some slightly older units may be switchable between US and European mains.
- **Power factor correction** is an additional front-end circuit in the charger which improves the efficiency of the power conversion from the mains. New regulations in Europe in particular are demanding this. From the user's point of view this gives a truly universal mains input.
- **Charger and power supply** in one unit is common for all but the lowest cost chargers. The batteries get priority, but when their current requirement is low the balance is made available through the power supply. Any connected loads on your boat such as lights and fridge can be used without disturbing the charging process.

Below **Mains chargers are complex electronic systems and generally give long, reliable service.**

Isolated outputs
Most mid- and top-range chargers have three outputs, which are usually described as 'isolated outputs'. This means each output is independently controlled by the charger, allowing separate battery banks to be charged. In addition, some models can be configured to charge 12V and 24V battery banks simultaneously.

Installation procedure
- Select a position in a ventilated area to allow good airflow. Check whether the unit must be mounted vertically or horizontally to improve air cooling – some are specific on this.
- The input mains voltage (110V or 220V) may have to be selected, although this will not be necessary on chargers with universal input.
- Cable runs and size need to be established. Measure the total distance from charger to each battery bank and back, then use the cable size chart in Appendix 1. Typically for a 10m (33ft) total

cable run, 20A chargers should
have a minimum of 8–6AWG
(9mm^2) and 30A units should
have 6AWG (13mm^2).

○ Select battery type using switches
or 'cable jumpers'. This will only
need to be changed in the future
if the battery type changes.
Ideally do not mix types but if
you do, use the setting that gives
the lower absorption and float
voltages of the types used.

○ Set absorption time according to
the total battery bank capacity.
Divide the batteries' total C/20
capacity by the maximum current
from the charger and use this
ratio as a guide. The smaller
the ratio the less absorption
time required – there should
be guidance on this in the
manual (although it may also
be taken care of automatically).
In general ratios of:
• 1–4 require one hour
of absorption charge
• 5–9 need two hours
• 10–13 need three hours
• 14–18 and gel batteries
should have four hours.

○ Unused outputs may have to be
connected in parallel. If you have
a three output charger, for instance,
and are only charging one or two
battery banks, some manufacturers
will ask you to link the unused
outputs to one that's connected to
the batteries. This will be clearly
stated in the manual.

Above Some manufacturers require unused
outputs to be connected to an active one,
so check the installation instructions.

Above The charger needs to know what
type of batteries are attached so that the
right charging profile is implemented.

MEASURING CURRENT

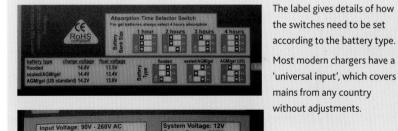

The label gives details of how
the switches need to be set
according to the battery type.

Most modern chargers have a
'universal input', which covers
mains from any country
without adjustments.

○ Connect the cables to the charger
first, then to the batteries. Be
ready for a small spark when you
connect the final cable.

○ A fuse should also be installed in
the positive wire going to each
battery bank. The manual will
advise on the appropriate rating.

TIP

There are subtle differences between
manufacturers on installation
requirements for their mains chargers.
You should follow their instructions 'to
the letter' particularly with regard to
ventilation, what to do with unused
outputs, and settings for the type of
batteries. If you change the type of
batteries (eg leisure to AGM) remember
to change the settings on the charger.

Hydrogen fuel cells

Fuel cells offer an instant source of electricity to support power generated by the wind, sun or an engine. While not as powerful as diesel generators, their advantages are quietness, the lack of any exhaust (apart from an occasional cup of water) and that they are largely maintenance free. The DC output can be fed directly to the batteries and integral voltage monitors will turn the fuel cell off when other sources of charging are active.

How is power generated?

Fuel cells use the chemical reaction between hydrogen and oxygen (producing water) to generate electricity. As there is no combustion, they are clean and very quiet. In addition they are versatile and simple to use, whether switched on and off manually or whether they are left in automatic mode.

Generators of this type tend to differ only in the way the hydrogen is stored – it may be in the liquefied form of methanol or a cylinder of pure hydrogen gas. In both cases the oxygen needed is drawn from the air.

Are the fuels a problem?

The storage and use of all energy-rich fuels needs careful consideration, particularly with regard to handling a substantial leakage. Methanol is flammable but it does mix with water so a leak into the bilge can be diluted with water and pumped out. As it is naturally occurring anyway, there are no real environmental issues. It's sold in 5 or 10 litre containers, with distributors able to ship supplies to pretty much anywhere in the world.

Below **With a maximum capability of around 160W, (12A at 14V), fuel cells are a useful source of back-up power.**

Hydrogen gas is 14 times lighter than air, so a permanent installation with appropriate ventilation at the highest point is the best solution. Leakage therefore does not linger on the vessel and would present no environmental issue. Hydrogen is supplied in purpose-designed cylinders and major suppliers such as BOC have worldwide supply networks for all their gasses, so marinas would be able to order your supplies just as they do with gas for cooking.

Electrical performance

Fuel cells are not yet as powerful as petrol or diesel generators and are currently available with continuous outputs of 40–150W. Fuel consumption depends a little on how they are used, but both types are similar in terms of consumption and running costs.

- ✿ 1 litre of methanol produces 1.1 kilowatt hours (KWh) of electricity. As an example, a daily average contribution to power requirements of 20Ah per day equates to 280 watt hours (Wh) per day. As one 5 litre container generates 5.5KWh, each container will last around 20 days at 280Wh per day.
- ✿ The 10 litre container weighs 8.4kg (18.5lb) and measures approximately 230 x 190 x 320mm (9 x 7.5 x 12.5in).
- ✿ The hydrogen cylinder produces 7KWh and, following the same

Left Once permanently installed, fuel cells can give reasonable amounts of power at the flick of a switch.

Below The heart of the fuel cell is where the hydrogen is combined with the oxygen. It is only how the hydrogen is stored that varies.

TIP

For smaller boats at least, the running costs compared to diesel generators are slightly less for the fuel cell, with the added bonus of virtual silence, very low maintenance and no exhaust.

example, the cylinder would last 25 days. Hydrogen cylinders are heavier at 16kg (35lb) with a diameter of 320mm (12½in) and a height of 520mm (20½in).

Operation and limitations

Smart control electronics give fuel cells a four-stage charging capability and in manual mode they can supply up to 14A if required. There is a limit on the angle of heel that a fuel cell can be subjected to – this is typically 35 degrees, with up to 45 degrees allowable for ten minutes. If this figure is exceeded, the unit simply switches off until the heel angle returns to these limits.

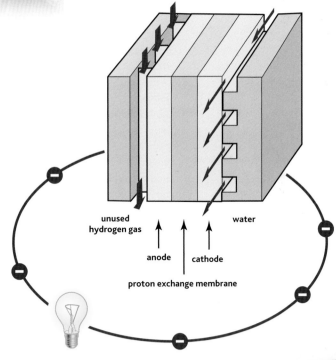

hydrogen gas   air (oxygen)

unused hydrogen gas   water

anode   cathode

proton exchange membrane

Right 10 litres of methanol will produce around 10KWh of electricity.

Far right Controls on this model are on the front of the unit or via a remote panel which is plugged into the serial port socket.

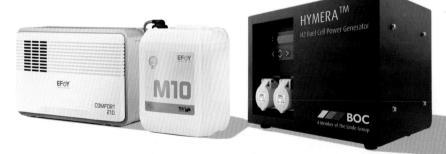

DC to DC converters

DC to DC converters change one DC voltage into another and are often the simplest way to power equipment that runs at a different DC voltage to the boat's electrical system. Such converters are very efficient, have inbuilt overload protection and are easy to install. If both voltage systems have their own batteries. the secondary system can be charged from the primary one by a DC to DC converter/charger.

Buck converters

These reduce the voltage to a lower level, for instance from 24V down to 12V. They are the most efficient converter, often exceeding 90 per cent. A boat with a 24V electrical system that also has a couple of pieces of 12V equipment will benefit from this type of converter, which eliminates the need for a 12V battery and charging system. Lower power versions are available with different fixed outputs, or with user adjustable settings.

Below **For a predominantly 24V system, it is often easier to DC to DC convert down to 12V (from the 24V) for the small amount of kit that can only run on 12V. You won't need separate battery banks or charging systems.**

Boost converters

This type converts from a lower voltage to a higher one. They tend to be lower power than buck converters, ranging from a few watts up to 600–700W. The most common equipment requiring this type of DC to DC conversion is laptops. They typically need between 16V and 19V DC (from 12VDC). This approach is simpler and more efficient than using the mains charger through an inverter.

Isolated or un-isolated

Both types are available, the former being more expensive and slightly less efficient but offering the advantage of electrical protection. Thus, if you get a major fault on the output side, it will not compromise the input side.

This protection, along with inbuilt monitoring circuits that shut down in the event of over-current or over-temperature faults, make the unit as bullet proof as you can get. Models without isolators can only rely on the monitoring circuits and fuses, but are still inherently reliable – they just lack the belt and braces feature of electrical isolation.

Battery to battery chargers

These are DC to DC converters with inbuilt, four-stage battery charger controllers. They operate when the engine is running, taking power from the alternator. They are available as both buck and boost types.

◆ Consider a boat that has 12V engine start and domestic battery banks and an alternator with a smart regulator to provide four-stage charging. A bow thruster and electric windlass are also installed and powered from an additional, separate 12V battery remotely positioned from the main batteries near the bow.
◆ The alternator is the source of power and priority is given to engine start and the domestic bank charging.
◆ Once those batteries are catered for, the battery to battery charger siphons off alternator power and starts charging the thruster and windlass battery. These chargers boost the input from the alternator a little to give the

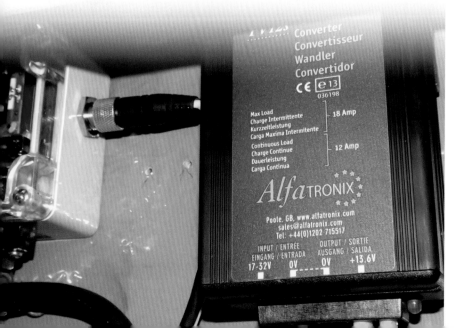

voltage the headroom required for the four-stage charging of the remote battery.

Another common scenario is a predominantly 24V system.

⚙ The high power consumers like thrusters, windlass, electric autopilots and water makers are powered from the main 24V battery banks. Alongside is a 12V system and batteries for lighting, radios and so on.

⚙ The battery to battery charger would be a 24V to 12V converter providing four-stage charging for the 12V battery bank from the main 24V banks.

⚙ With this set up, only one alternator (24V) is required to take care of the main 24V battery bank and the 24V engine start battery bank.

The other advantage of this approach is that only one mains charger is required, taking care of the main battery bank, while the battery to battery charger looks after the lower voltage secondary system.

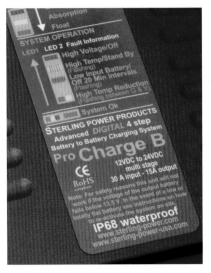

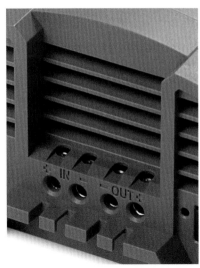

Top **Various DC to DC converter power ratings are available.**

Above **DC to DC converters can be used to charge one battery bank from another. This removes the need for a separate charging regime for both the 12V and 24V batteries and includes the battery switching functions, so automating the management as well.**

Above right **Wiring up is straightforward.**

TIP

Like all equipment, a DC to DC converter consumes a small amount of current when in standby mode, 0.3 to 0.5A is typical. On a small boat this becomes significant if the converter is left on continuously so establish the standby current (from the manual or by measurement) and decide whether you need to turn it off when not required.

Regulating multiple sources

Preventing over-charging while still getting the best out of the batteries is the job of the regulator. This chapter has examined many of the different ways power can be generated. Ultimately all the power needs to be controlled before it reaches the batteries. As each manufacturer recommends its own regulators, how can you safely connect them all together?

A regulator, by way of an analogy, is like a ball cock or float valve at the end of a water pipe filling up a household water tank. The valve progressively closes as the water level rises towards a full tank. The valve is effectively monitoring the water level and adjusting the flow of water into the tank as required to keep it full. A large outflow of water (to run a bath for instance) will drop the level in the tank and the float will fall with it, opening the valve fully to start refilling.

Now consider five pipes supplying the one tank, each with their own float valve. Because the valves can never be perfectly matched as to the water level at which each one closes, they will begin to shut off one at a time until the fifth one finally shuts and the tank is full. The question is, does it matter which one shuts off last? The answer is no, water is water whichever pipe it comes from.

In a similar way the electronic regulators, whether a mains charger, an alternator or a wind and solar regulator will all be monitoring the battery voltage and adjusting the current flow from their respective source accordingly. As they are all supplying the same batteries, they will start to switch off as the voltage gets to the level required.

Some will do this before others but it doesn't matter, current is current whichever source it is coming from. Even if they are all four-stage charging regulators – which is the best approach – the outcome will be the same. Theoretically, there should be no problem!

Mixing battery technologies

Within a particular battery bank, it is far better to stay with a single type of battery technology. If you have to mix, then all the regulators supplying that bank need to be set to the type of battery technology with the lowest absorption and float voltages. While one of the batteries will not get all the charge it would ideally need, the trade off is that the other batteries do not get over-charged, which would shorten their life considerably.

It is possible to have different technologies in different battery banks so long as each has an independent charging regime set to the appropriate type. This would be a good application for a battery to battery boost charger dedicated to one particular bank and set to the correct technology type.

Regulator protection

One of the many ways regulators look after themselves is by having an output or blocking diode. If another regulator is pushing out a higher voltage, the blocking diode prevents current going back into the output terminal of those regulators that have already backed off.

Solar panels also (usually) have these fitted internally for the same reason, especially where their output power is small enough not to need a regulator at all. Beware of using a solar panel regulator with a wind generator, as the output voltage can go much higher than the solar regulator components can stand, causing failure.

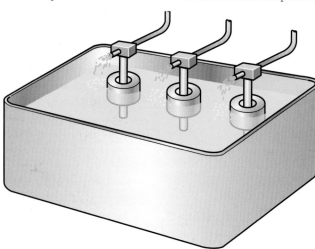

Left **The water level in the tank is measured and sent to each of the flow regulators. When the level is low, each regulator will supply whatever it can. As the level approaches the top, the regulators begin to shut off to prevent overfilling.**

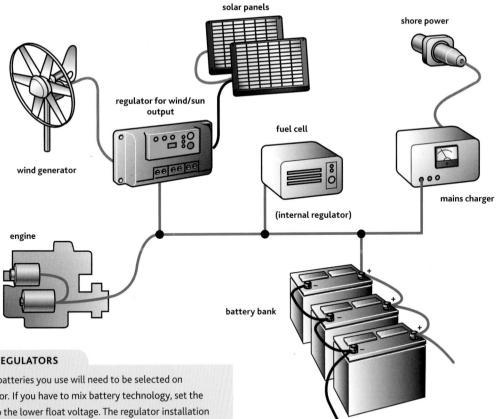

solar panels

shore power

regulator for wind/sun output

fuel cell

wind generator

mains charger

(internal regulator)

engine

battery bank

TYPES OF REGULATORS

The type of batteries you use will need to be selected on each regulator. If you have to mix battery technology, set the regulators to the lower float voltage. The regulator installation manual will indicate the appropriate values.

solar panel regulator

external smart alternator regulators

Above Each of the regulators will measure the battery terminal voltage and regulate the current flow accordingly. If the batteries are heavily discharged, each regulator will supply all it can from its source of power.

Below The 'blocking' diode prevents current from another source going back into the charger and damaging the electronics.

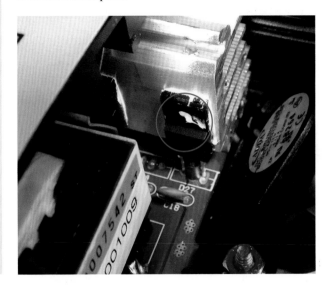

Monitoring battery and alternator currents

There is value in knowing the amount of current flowing around the DC system. It is useful to know how much is going in or out of the battery banks and the amount being generated by the various sources of power, particularly the alternator. These currents can be very large – way beyond the scope of a multimeter – so different measuring techniques need to be employed.

One of the main considerations when measuring anything is the effect the measurement itself has on the system being measured. Each of the options has good and bad points:

- **Moving coil ammeters** need the current being measured to pass through the meter itself. This may involve extending the battery cable run (increasing the

cable voltage drops), particularly if the meter is positioned some distance from the batteries. They are simple to fit, but probably not the best choice for alternator or battery currents, because of the large cables. They are better suited for monitoring lower currents from mains chargers, solar panels and wind generators.

- **Resistive or current shunts** are precision, very low-value resistors. The current passing through creates a voltage drop (according to Ohm's Law), which is measured by a suitably calibrated voltmeter. Some heat is generated and of course, there is a tiny voltage drop as a result of that, typically up to 50 or 100mV.

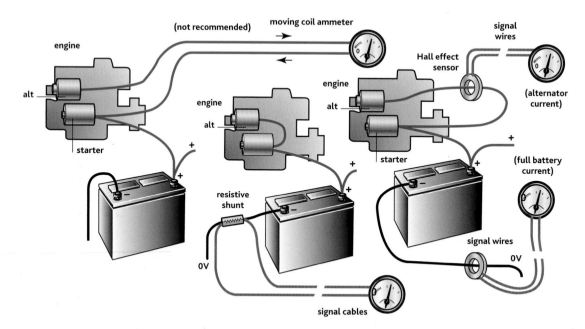

Above The cable carrying the current will have a longer run to wherever the ammeter is positioned. For the lower currents of solar and wind generators this will not be a major issue.

Above The resistive current shunt can be positioned near the battery bank (minimising the cable run), but in the 0V return cable (low side measurement). A very small voltage loss will occur according to Ohm's Law 'V = IR' where 'R' is the resistance of the shunt.

Above The Hall effect sensor does not create any voltage drop (unlike the resistive sensor). The Hall effect sensor is the best device for measuring the alternator current as you only have to pass the positive output cable through the centre of the sensor.

⚙ **Hall effect sensors** detect the magnetic field around the cable, which is directly proportional to the amount of current flowing. The cable passes through the sensor housing which produces a small signal voltage, proportional to the current. The remote meter head (a volt meter) converts this to a calibrated reading fed to the display. The sensor will need a 12V supply, but that will come from the meter head itself.

Sizing resistive current shunts

Shunts come in two common ratings, 50mV and 100mV. This is the voltage drop across the shunt at full rated current, which will typically be 100A up to 500A. The 100mV type improves the sensitivity as there is twice the volt drop for a given current.

You must select the current rating to cover all eventualities within the particular DC system. For example, it is possible that the domestic battery bank could be used to start the engine (via an emergency transfer switch). The current shunt must therefore be rated to handle the starter motor current as well as the normal currents associated with the domestic system. The resistor element at its heart will heat up slightly anyway but, given enough excessive current it could melt, acting like a fuse.

Installation

The shunts tend to be positioned in the negative (return) cable, referred to as the low side, because measuring the voltage drop is much easier and less prone to interference. Shunts can be positioned in the positive cable, or high side, but the meter used to measure the shunt's

MEASURING CURRENT

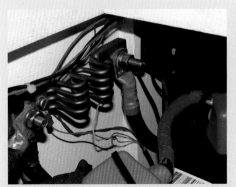

A resistive current shunt measuring the main battery bank current. It is in the 0V return cable, requiring it to be cut and appropriate terminations to be fitted to connect to the shunt. Two signal wires (green and yellow) go to the calibrated meter.

The Hall effect sensor requires no cable modification. The cable just has to be removed, passed through the hall effect sensor and re-attached. It can go in the positive or 0V return cable; you just have to get the meter connections the right way round.

voltage drop must be designed for this. The alternator output is a good example because its return path is through the engine block, which carries other currents including the starter motor, so high side measurement is easier.

The cable carrying the current being measured will need to be cut and connected to the shunt's two terminals. There will also be two small screws to attach the signal wires that go to the meter head and display unit. These wires can be as long as you want as they are only sensing the voltage drop across the shunt mounted close to the battery and therefore carry only a very small amount of current.

Above The meter 'head' for the current shunt (as with the Hall effect sensor) is actually a voltmeter measuring the voltage across the shunt. The display is suitably calibrated and marked up to display amps.

Below A typical 100mV resistive current shunt.

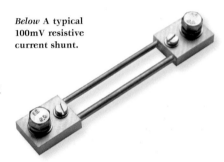

Power monitoring systems

'How full are the batteries?' This seems a simple enough question, but to give a reliable answer over a period of time is so difficult, it has spawned a whole industry dedicated to the task. In theory, if you measure the current going in and out of your batteries over a period of time, the net difference will tell you how full they are at any point. So, what are the problems?

Solutions using current sensing

The vast majority of the products on the market use resistive current shunts to measure the current. The panel meter, which is the brains of the monitoring system, will compute and display the following type of information:

⊙ **An amp hour meter,** which takes the current measurement from one of the shunts, normally the domestic battery bank, and accumulates the net current flow over time. If this is positive, showing current going into the battery bank, the meter will show an increasing state of charge.

⊙ **Current at other positions** in which shunts have been installed and battery bank voltages can be selected and displayed.

⊙ **Control of battery switches,** which can be activated from some units. The panel meter has all the information it needs and you can link this system to control voltage-sensing relays.

⊙ **Alarms,** which for a multitude of eventualities can be activated by the panel.

Below **Battery management systems usually only monitor amp hours into and out of one bank. The other current shunts will give spot readings of current but do not form part of the overall management. Once you are confident the bank is fully charged, the system can be synchronised to read 100 per cent.**

A few considerations

Generally, these systems are very helpful but they need to be used with a little care.

⊙ The amp hour meter computes the state of charge based on the net flow of current, comparing it to a known state from some time in the past. The only realistic one is when the batteries were last deemed to be fully charged.

⊙ This 'reset' or 'synchronisation' is automatic in some models, whereas others rely on manual synchronisation.

⊙ There will always be a small error in measurements, which will accumulate over time. If the unit is not synchronised for many

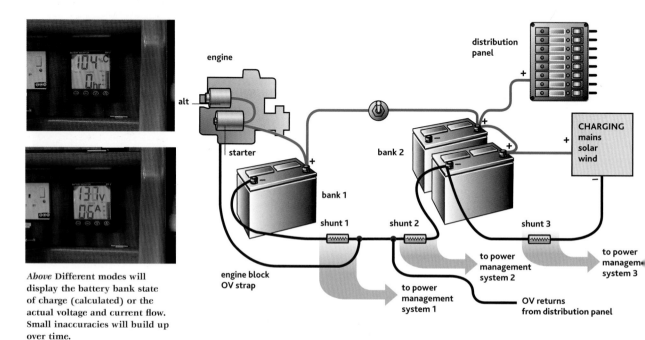

Above **Different modes will display the battery bank state of charge (calculated) or the actual voltage and current flow. Small inaccuracies will build up over time.**

days or weeks, the error will become significant.

- On long voyages the batteries may never achieve the level to give automatic synchronisation, so again, the display can become misleading.

As with many other monitoring systems, experience should guard against over-reliance on what the meter is telling you.

Installing the shunts

It is very important to follow the manufacturer's installation instructions, but different approaches are used throughout the industry.

- Shunts are most commonly installed in the low side, negative battery cable and a heavy duty bus bar is needed to connect all the return cables together. Additional cables then run from the bus bar to one side of the shunt and from the other side to the battery's negative terminal. No other connection can be made directly to the battery terminal as its current would bypass the shunt and not be included.
- A few manufacturers allow high side shunts in the positive cables, which can be more convenient and allows alternator current to be measured directly.
- The shunts should be sized according to whatever is recommended. In practice those measuring battery currents will be at least 200A, even for small boats.
- Two signal wires go from either end of the shunt to the panel meter. These have to be wired with correct polarity, because the direction of the current is fundamental.

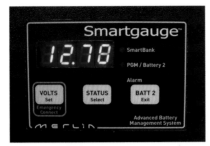

Above **The 'Smartgauge' does not require current to be measured. It only monitors one battery bank in detail.**

Other solutions

Power monitoring systems are available which only measure the battery bank voltages and do all the computing based on these. They are very easy to install, requiring only signal wires to go to the battery terminals and a supply to the panel meter. Highly intricate software algorithms effectively learn how your batteries behave and adapt over time to give a percentage charge reading. The advantages of this approach are that no synchronisation is required.

Right **All the 0V return cables (engine block strap, distribution panel returns, generator return etc) must be collected together on the one end of the resistive shunt. The other end goes direct to the 0V terminal of the battery.**

Below **The voltage across the current shunt represents the total current flow into or out of the battery bank. This can also be displayed by the power management system or a separate meter.**

MEASURING A SHUNT

The resistance of the current shunt needs to be programmed in to the power monitoring system. It is too small to measure accurately with a multimeter. Ohm's Law can be applied by passing a current through it and measuring the voltage across it R = V / I (ohms).

The voltage drop across the shunt will only be a few millivolts (mV). The 200mV range is selected on the multimeter. 10.94A are flowing through the shunt and 2.7mV (0.0027V) is being measured across it. From Ohm's Law, R = V / I (0.0027V/10.94A) so R = 250 micro ohms (0.000250 Ohms). At a maximum current of 200A, this makes this shunt a 50mV type.

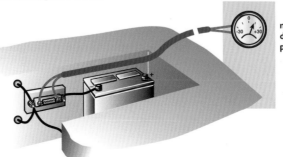

meter on distribution panel

Reducing consumption

The need to balance your power requirements can be approached from another angle, namely reducing consumption. Lighting has led the way, but many other pieces of equipment have low power modes which, on a long passage will make a big difference to power consumption – without compromising your quality of life on board.

There are two aspects to reducing the power you consume: what equipment you use, and how you use it.

○ **Lighting** is the best example. In terms of light output per watt, fluorescent tubes are the most efficient. The downside is that the quality of light may not be to your taste. LEDs have forged their way into second place in efficiency terms. Halogen types are next, with incandescent bulbs last.

○ **Navigation lights:** consumption can fall quite considerably by switching over to LED units.

○ **Fridges and freezers** consume significant power. The dilemma is whether to leave them on continuously, or power them intermittently. The best possible thermal insulation makes a big difference as well.

○ **Chart plotters** have improved a lot. Latest generations are 30–40 per cent less power hungry than their predecessors. People often leave them running all day, however, irrespective of whether they are being used.

○ **Navigation instruments** have also improved, but in general they are not big consumers. The benefit of having them on continuously while at sea will outweigh any saving.

○ **Autopilots** have different response levels that progressively maintain a better track, at the expense of working much harder. Choose the lowest response level

Below **The vast array of LED lighting products now available can allow you to reduce current consumption significantly.**

you feel comfortable with – over time you will still average the same course.

○ **Radars** often have timed operation modes in which you can set them to come out of standby into transmit mode for, say, 30 sweeps every five minutes, if visibility and traffic density permit.

○ **Audio systems and TVs** consume a lot of power even on low volume and tend to be left switched on for long periods.

○ **Standby and 'OFF'** modes for chart plotters and instruments rarely make any savings in power consumption, especially in networked systems. Turning an individual networked unit off usually only turns out the display backlight, but the processing electronics still has to continue working for the other equipment on the network. Check the manual to see if the manufacturer owns up!

Below **The LED replacement bulbs fit in the same socket but consume around one eighth of the power. The light output is slightly higher as well.**

Left Modern chart plotters consume much less current and often have a power save or standby mode, reducing the current still further. This chart plotter consumes 174mA when in power save mode compared to 250mA in full operation.

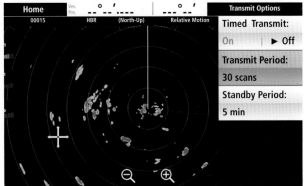

Left Operating the radar in 'timed period' mode reduces power consumption by about 30 per cent (from around 60W to 40W). Make sure you appreciate the effect this mode has on MARPA and safe zone alarms as this varies between manufacturers.

SAVING POWER

Lighting and refrigeration are two areas where energy consumption savings can easily be made. LED versions of most bulb types give up to 75 per cent power reduction. Many fridges have metal drain plugs and a pipe into the bilge – installing a trap in this, or sealing it off completely from inside the fridge, significantly reduces the power consumption.

On the face of it, a fridge drain seems a good idea. In reality, more cold air than water flows down the plughole.

LED lighting

LED (light emitting diode) lighting has developed to the point where it is usable in both the cabin and for navigation lights. Lighting manufacturers have finally recognised how important it is to protect the LED in a lamp design. The light-emitting element of the LED is incredibly small and the heat it generates has to be removed, otherwise its lifespan will be drastically reduced.

LEDs are also very intolerant of excessive voltages, requiring a degree of sophisticated electronics within the lamp to prevent damage. There are three things to look for in the sales information:

- A wide input voltage operating range. This shows electronic control is being used within the lamp.
- Some statement about how good the thermal management is.
- A commitment to a lifetime minimum of 50,000 hours is not unreasonable.

These design issues help explain why LEDs seem expensive, but the power saving will be between 60–80 per cent in many applications. A 10W incandescent bulb in a ceiling light, for instance, will typically consume just under 1A, but its LED bulb equivalent will use around 150–200mA, with the same brightness.

Below The LED array consumes 120mA compared to 800mA for the bulb, and the light output is slightly higher as well.

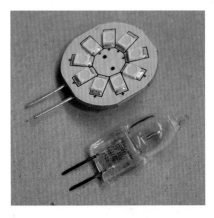

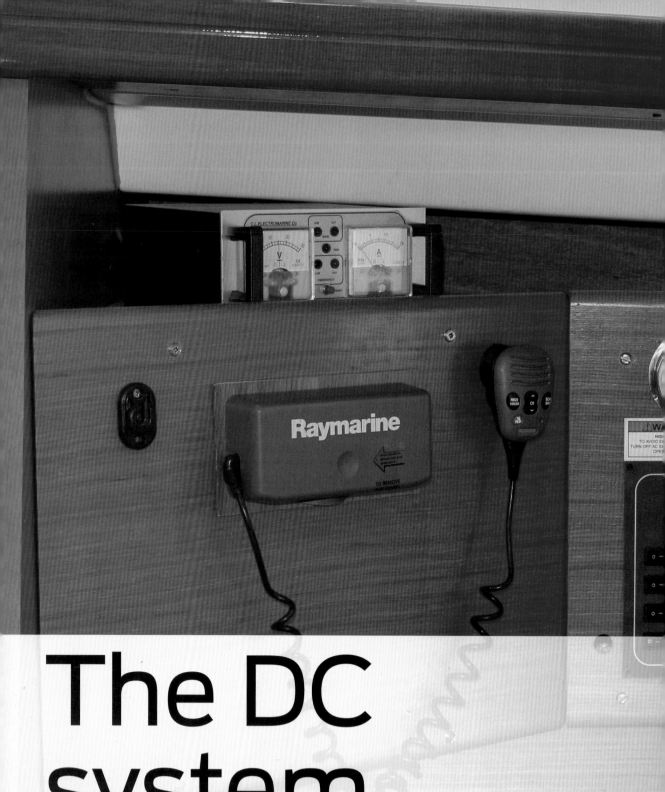

The DC system

Battery switches

Battery switches must be capable of handling very large currents and it is common to expect a switch to be rated up to 500A, with thousands of operations over many years. Switches are the main part of the battery management system and may be manually operated or controlled remotely.

A large array of switches are available, so the choice comes down to the type that is most appropriate to the function required.

Types of switches

All of the types that are available have to be capable of handling very high currents and have a secure means of attaching a number of large cables.

- **Mechanical switches** can be a single 'ON/OFF' type with a removable tab. Another common type is the multiple contact version in which the current can be directed to one of two battery banks, both banks or neither, depending on the position of the rotary knob. A warning notice is often included to remind you not to have it set to 'OFF' when the

engine is running to prevent damage to the alternator.
- **Diodes,** usually referred to as 'diode splitters', are electrical components that act as a one-way valve to the flow of current, allowing charging current into the battery but stopping it discharging back out beyond the diode. The 'splitter' part of the name refers to the way this feature is used on boats and has nothing to do with the diode as a component itself. Diode splitters automate the switching process, making life easier for the crew.
- **Relays or voltage sensing relays (VSR)** are mechanical switches requiring a small electronic 'command' signal to open or close the main high current contacts. The command

signal will come from an electronic circuit (usually internal) that monitors battery voltage and decides whether to open or close the switch, effectively making battery management automatic.
- **Solid state relays (SSR)** use an electronic power transistor, called a MOSFET (Metal Oxide Semiconductor Field Effect Transistor), that can handle large currents and allow a higher degree of electronic control. They are expensive but offer a very flexible type of switch when associated with more sophisticated electronics, again making battery management fully automatic. They also have the advantage of having no moving parts.

Left **Battery switches should always be easily accessible. Don't forget to explain to the crew how the switching system works.**

Below **Many boats have several single battery switches with removable keys.**

Which should I use?

The main consideration is the degree of automation you want, while a secondary factor is the voltage drop (or loss) across the switch. It is important that all the voltage generated by the source of charging reaches the battery, but losses in the switch arrangement will reduce the amount of charge the batteries receive.

Each approach has various aspects worth considering:

○ Mechanical switches have almost no voltage drop across the contacts. The only disadvantage is that the battery management system is totally manual, but you might also feel that, as there are no electronics involved, there is nothing to go wrong.

○ The diode, when allowing current through to the batteries, will cause a voltage drop of around 1V across the component – a very significant loss. In a 12V system, a standard alternator generates 14.2V at its output and the diode voltage drop means that only 13.2V will get to the battery, which is not enough for efficient charging. To counteract this, the alternator needs to have a different type of (battery sensing) internal regulator, or a smart regulator installed alongside the existing alternator.

○ Voltage sensing relays have the benefit of mechanical contacts with virtually zero voltage drop and electronic control, giving the possibility of a fully automated management system.

Above The solid state, MOSFET transistor type battery switch has very low losses and is fully automated with no moving parts.

Below VSRs are a good compromise as losses are negligible and control is easy to achieve, giving full automation.

TIP

With one or two battery bank systems, the amount of 'management' or intervention by the crew is minimal and mechanical switches are perfectly adequate. Once you introduce a third bank (for the bow thruster, for instance) then automating the system, with devices such as VSRs, is well worth considering

Below There is a notice to remind you to stop the engines before switching to the 'OFF' position. The same applies at start up so never start the engines with the switch in the 'OFF' position.

Below The back of the switch has the terminals clearly marked.

Below The diode switch takes away the need for manual intervention.

Battery switch configurations

The battery switching configuration directs charging current to the batteries, prioritising the order in which they receive it. This is straightforward with a single bank, but the order in which charging takes place can be important with multiple battery banks. The other function is to prevent the accidental discharge of the engine start battery when charging is not available.

The simplest arrangement is to have two or three batteries wired in parallel, with a master 'ON/OFF' switch to isolate them when you are not on board. With everything running off this one bank, you must be careful not to discharge them more than around 40 per cent, as you will also start the engine from these batteries.

The alternator, mains charger and any solar/wind power will all feed into the positive terminals. If you have a current-sensing battery management system, the shunt resistor may well be in the negative return to the batteries.

Once you separate the engine start battery (often referred to as battery 1) from the domestic bank (battery 2),

Below There is no ideal configuration. The best one for your boat is the one that works reliably.

you will need a switch arrangement that does two things:

- ✪ Directs charging from the alternator to the engine start battery. After a reasonable time (10–15 minutes), the domestic bank can be switched in to share the charging current. The battery bank with the lowest charge level will naturally take most of the alternator current.
- ✪ When the engine is stopped, the two banks need to be separated again. This ensures that only the domestic bank (battery 2) supplies the domestic equipment, leaving battery 1 unused, with its capacity kept for engine starting.

The arrangement can be achieved in three ways:
- ✪ A manually-operated switch with a number of options: 'Off', 'Battery 1',

'Battery 2' and 'Both'. The most common type is the single four-position rotary switch, but the same can be achieved with two 'ON/OFF' key type switches. Select 'Battery 1' position in preparation for starting the engine and 'Battery 2' when the motor is not running.

- ✪ A pair of high power 'diode splitters' automatically directs the charging current to both battery banks, while preventing a reverse flow of current that would deplete the engine start battery when the engine is off. This is not ideal, as it does not give the engine start battery absolute priority, but is generally seen as an acceptable solution and has the advantage of being fully automatic. This approach needs to compensate for the diode voltage drop, either by a (battery) voltage sensing alternator regulator, or by fitting an external smart alternator regulator that senses the battery voltage.
- ✪ The diode splitters can be replaced by a single voltage sensing relay (VSR). This has virtually no voltage drop, so no change is required to the alternator's regulator. They can also sense the engine start battery voltage, waiting until this has reached around 13.3V before switching in the domestic bank for charging. These often have an 'emergency battery combiner' button that allows manual activation of the main relay. Therefore, if the engine start battery fails you can use the domestic bank to start the engine.

Once you bring in to play a third battery bank, the switching arrangement needs extending, but

engine

alt

starter

distribution panel

back of battery switch

bank 1

common

mains charger

bank 2 (domestic)

operates in a similar fashion. The most common arrangement is:

- Battery bank 1 (one battery): Engine (and diesel generator) start.
- Battery bank 2 (two or three batteries): All domestic equipment via the distribution panel.
- Battery bank 3 (one or two batteries): The very high current consuming bow thruster and/or electric windlass. These will usually (but not always) only operate when the engine is running because of the current demand.

24V DC systems have twice the number of batteries described above, as a single '24V battery' consists of a pair of 12V batteries wired together in series.

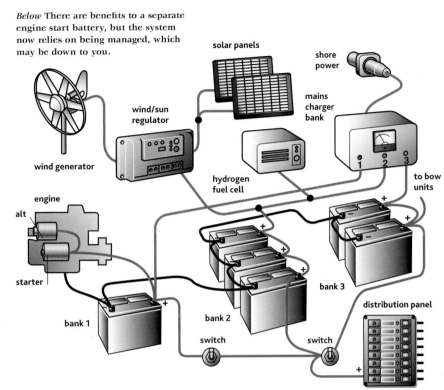

Below There are benefits to a separate engine start battery, but the system now relies on being managed, which may be down to you.

Below The assumption here is that the engine start battery is happy with the standard alternator output. The domestic bank, however, benefits from four-stage charging provided by the battery to battery charger, taking its power from the alternator/engine start battery.

Right The diode splitters automate the switching arrangement. If the regulator senses the voltage at the battery bank (voltage sensing) then the diode voltage drops and cable losses are compensated for, leaving the correct charging voltage at the batteries.

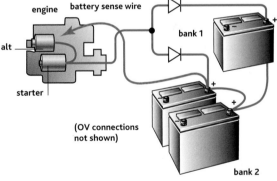

(OV connections not shown)

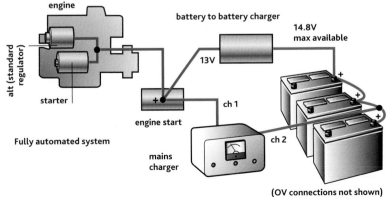

Fully automated system

(OV connections not shown)

Fitting a voltage sensing relay

Automating the charging process removes a burden from the skipper and avoids problems arising when manual battery switches are not operated. Voltage sensing relays (VSR) take control of the process as you start, run and stop the engine. VSRs can carry enormous currents with virtually no voltage drop.

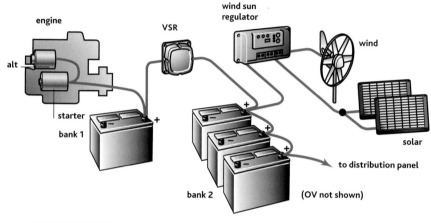

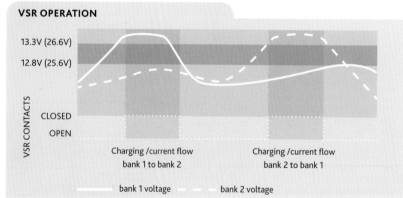

Voltage sensing relays (VSRs) sit between battery banks and are an 'intelligent' alternative to the splitter diode or mechanical battery switch options used with multiple banks. Their main features are:

⚙ Internal monitoring and timing circuits that also drive the solenoid, operating the main contacts. Some models allow external input from a battery management system, which will then control the VSR.

⚙ Usually the contacts close, allowing charge through to the secondary bank, when the measured battery volts rises to 13.3V and open again if this drops down to 12.8V, isolating the two banks.

⚙ A manual means of operating the contacts, acting as an emergency transfer switch, allowing the domestic bank to start the engine.

⚙ An 'ignition switch' interlock is offered on some versions so that the VSR can only function with the engine running.

⚙ Similarly, a 'starter engaged' interlock will open the contacts while you engage the starter motor. This ensures the starter motor current cannot pass through the contacts (which may not have a sufficiently high rating).

Above If bank 1 is higher than bank 2 (due to alternator charging) then, once the VSR contacts have closed, charging current flows from bank 1 to 2. If bank 2 has the higher voltage then, with closed contacts, charging current flows from bank 2 into bank 1.

Left A VSR only needs three terminals – two high-current battery cable studs (so the battery current passes through the VSR) and one spade terminal for the 0V connection, needed by the internal electronics.

Right The VSR's operating voltages are shown on the unit. The difference or gap between the cut in and drop out voltages helps to reduce contact 'chatter'.

⊙ As with the mechanical switches, there is no voltage drop, so a standard alternator can be used.

One-way or bi-directional charging

Different versions are available depending on the priorities you wish to give to your battery system.

⊙ **A one-way charging VSR** will monitor the battery volts on only one of its two terminals, with the one connected to the battery bank given priority. In most cases this is the engine start battery, and as the engine fires up the alternator begins charging it. The VSR remains 'open' until this battery reaches 13.3V. The internal solenoid will then close the main contacts, connecting the domestic bank in parallel, allowing the charging current to be split between the two banks.

⊙ **Bi-directional VSRs** monitor the battery volts on both terminals, so either bank can cause the VSR to operate. This type might be used where the domestic bank also receives charge from additional sources such as wind or solar. If the domestic bank

VOLTAGE SENSING RELAY (TYPICAL DATA)

System voltage	12V	24V
Continuous current	140A	100A
Intermittent current	170A	140A
Cut in voltage	13.3V	26.6V (contacts closed – pull in)
Drop out voltage	12.8V	25.6V (contacts open – drop out)

becomes well charged (above 13.3V), these inputs can be shared with the engine start battery.

Drawbacks of VSRs

VSRs are nearly perfect, but there are a few foibles to be aware of, including clicking (chatter) or cycling. This tends to happen when there's a huge disparity between battery bank capacities: when the engine start reaches 13.3V, the contacts will 'close', connecting the much larger capacity domestic bank. This may pull down the engine start battery to its level, potentially bringing it to below the 12.8V VSR 'open' threshold, opening the contacts again.

This cycle will keep repeating, resulting in clicking (or chatter) as the solenoid bangs in and out. To reduce this, once the contacts close, the electronics keep them closed for a minimum time (from one to four minutes). Between each cycle the domestic bank voltage gradually begins to rise and the cycling eventually stops.

Another drawback is the current needed to hold the contacts together. The solenoid has to be continuously energised for this, using as much as 250mA of current, which has to be provided from one of the battery banks. This will negate some of the charge from the solar panels or wind generator.

Some manufacturers offer 'latching' relays which hold the solenoid in position by a mechanical or permanent magnet latch so no hold-in current is required.

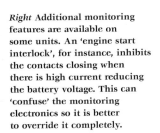

Right Additional monitoring features are available on some units. An 'engine start interlock', for instance, inhibits the contacts closing when there is high current reducing the battery voltage. This can 'confuse' the monitoring electronics so it is better to override it completely.

TIP

You may want to put a mechanical battery switch in parallel with the VSR as a 'belt and braces' option to override the VSR in the (very unlikely) event that the VSR fails.

DC distribution panels

The low-voltage DC distribution panel brings all the different electrical systems and circuits together in one location. It performs switching, protection and monitoring functions, focused on the positive (12V or 24V) portion of the wiring. It is supplied with power from the battery switch and breaks this up into the individual circuits around the vessel, each of which has a switch, fuse and indicator.

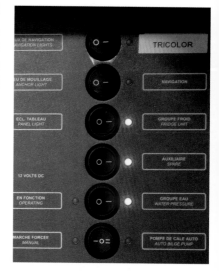

Switching groups

The individual circuits typically handle maximum currents of 10–15A. This limitation is governed by the spade connection to the switches. It is common to split the lighting into two circuits (port and starboard for instance) because the total current consumed by all the lights could be around 20A, even for mid-sized vessels.

Protection

Immediately to the side of the switch, or included as part of it, will be a fuse of some variety. The job of this device is to protect the wiring in the event of a short circuit fault in the equipment or elsewhere in the circuit. The protection device is rated to ensure it will not operate under normal conditions, but will blow, disconnecting the supply from the circuit in an overload or fault situation. In general, you should rate the fuse device at around 150 per cent of the maximum current the circuit will normally handle.

Above LED indicators consume the lowest current and are ideal for the job. They also seem to last for ever.

Indication

It is useful to know whether or not each circuit is powered up. Indication of this can be passive, indicated by a marker or the switch appearance when in the 'ON' position, or active, where an indicator light comes on. Lower cost panels tend to have incandescent bulb indicators which consume an appreciable current, while LED indicators consume only 10–15mA each, so are a better choice.

Meters and monitoring

It is logical to have displays that show system data at or near the switch panel. A permanently installed voltmeter, able to monitor each battery bank in turn, is extremely useful. A measure of current flowing at various strategic locations is also of interest, showing for example solar panel or wind generator charging current, total current into or out of the domestic battery bank and so on. Fuel and water gauges and other strategic

Below Neat, well planned panels put all the boat's controls at your fingertips.

data about your vessel can also be fed back. Many of the new generation chart plotters are able to collect all this sort of data and present it at the navigation station.

Maintained supplies

There are a few pieces of equipment that need to be left powered up and these may feature on the panel only to indicate that the circuit is live.

- Some equipment is turned on whenever you are on board, with items such as a Navtex receiver or VHF/DSC radio getting their power directly from the battery switch. They will therefore be turned off only when the battery switches are off. Such items are provided with an in-line fuse in the positive wire, and indication at the panel is not necessary.
- Other equipment, such as an automatic bilge pump, is switched on at all times. These items will have to be wired directly to the battery with their own fuse and will be independent of both battery switches and the distribution panel.

Remote panels

When adding new equipment it may be more convenient to install a small remote distribution panel nearer the equipment to simplify the wire routing, even though you will have to install a feed from the battery switch to the new panel. Generally there is nothing wrong with remote fuses and switches as long as you remember where they are.

Above Smaller boats are usually less complicated and can live with a little disorganisation.

Left Modern production boats leave little room for additional equipment.

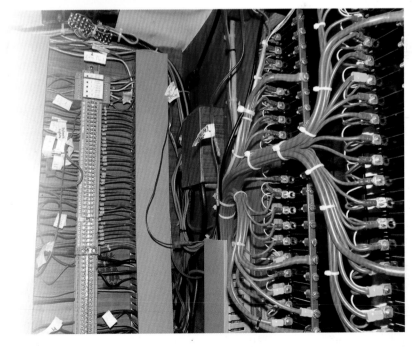

Right Once the complexity of the wiring system grows, neat layout and labelling become essential.

Protection

The fuse device is an integral part of the electrical circuit or system. It may spend its whole life doing nothing, but if called upon to act will prevent further damage and alert you to a potentially serious problem. The type of electrical equipment determines the fuse arrangement, but its function is always to protect the wiring.

Circuit protection options

There are many types of circuit protection device available; some of these are very specialised, while others are more general.

- A fuse, or protecting device, is a deliberate weak link placed in the positive wire of a circuit that will not be broken by the normal circuit current. However, if the current rises beyond a certain limit, for any reason, the device will 'blow' or 'trip', creating a break in the positive wire and isolating the circuit from the batteries.
- The device will have a continuous current rating, below which it is guaranteed not to blow or trip. There will also be a voltage rating, which must be either at or above the battery voltage you are using.
- Very high-current devices, such as the main battery fuse (if fitted) will have a 'rupture rating' as well as a continuous current rating. The rupture rating is the maximum fault current that the fuse can withstand (and safely blow) without catching fire, exploding or other nasty eventualities. This will be several thousand amps and certainly well above the current handling capacity of the cabling.

Selecting the continuous current rating

The fusing device protects the wiring, rather than the equipment, within each individual circuit. There are a number of factors that influence selection of the device:

- **Absolute maximum rating:** Irrespective of the equipment on the circuit, the resistance of the cable will limit the worst-case short circuit current. The fusing device rating should be less than half this value. From the previous example of the wire size selection for the fridge compressor (see page 53), the cable resistance over the 15m (49ft) run was estimated to be 0.108Ω. The worst-case short circuit current (from Ohm's Law) for a fully

Left Main battery systems benefit from fuses that can be re-set if they trip, as this is much easier than having to replace a blown device.

Below Equipment often has its own internal fuse, so it is worth remembering this when fault finding.

TYPICAL 5 AMP FUSE

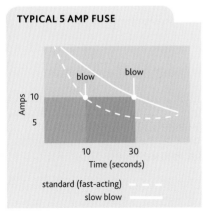

standard (fast-acting) – – –
slow blow ———

Above This graph shows the length of time a fuse will handle a particular current before 'blowing'. A 5A fast-acting fuse will allow an overload of 10A for around 10 seconds (but 100A would only survive for 0.001 seconds). The 'slow blow' version would allow the 10A to survive for up to 30 seconds. Both types will continuously allow 5A, plus a margin for good measure.

Above It may be worthwhile fitting a fuse in the main battery cable. Any electrical problem that results in this fuse blowing would almost certainly have caused a fire.

RANGE OF CIRCUIT BREAKERS

There are many different types of fuses and protection devices. The re-settable type (with the push button) act as both a switch and circuit breaker/fuse. There are also versions which are just re-settable circuit breakers, requiring an external switch and indicator. These circuit breakers are simple to re-set if they 'pop' out but that does not resolve the reason why they 'popped' out in the first place – that must be investigated.

standard automotive type spade fuse

main battery cable fuse

cartridge fuse (rating marked on the end)

selection of commonly used types

charged battery is (12.7V/0.108Ω), or 117A. A 50A protection device rating would be a safe (absolute maximum) value for this wiring.

- **Minimum rating:** As the fridge current is only 3.7A (assuming it is the only equipment on this circuit), 50A is excessive. However, to avoid false or nuisance blowing or tripping of the device, the minimum rating should be 150 per cent of the equipment running current. This allows for device tolerances and the effects of ambient temperature. For the fridge in this example, it equates to 5.55A, so the next highest standard size of fuse should be fitted, which is 8A.

Type of fuse

There are two types of fusing device – 'fast acting' and 'slow blow', with the choice governed by the type of equipment on the circuit.

- **Fast acting** fusing devices are the standard type used. They blow (or trip) very quickly and are suitable for items such as cabin lighting, electronic equipment, small pumps, radios and so on.
- **Slow blow** devices are used for equipment with high levels of 'start-up' or 'inrush' current at switch-on. These fuse devices react more slowly, allowing for this (normal) start up condition, while still protecting the circuit against prolonged fault currents. They are recommended for powerful incandescent lamps, which have an inrush current up to ten times the running current, and for motors driving large pumps, bow thrusters, winches and so on.

You may find the equipment manual for your device will recommend the type and rating you should use to save you making the decision.

Adding new systems

When adding electrical equipment, you need to consider wiring, circuit protection and switching. You may be able to use a spare switch/fuse position on the main DC panel, or to add new positions to it, or you may need to install a new small panel elsewhere.

Deciding what you need to achieve, and drawing a wiring diagram, are the first steps for adding in more electrical equipment. If the main DC panel has no spare positions, it's worth considering whether it's easier to locate a small additional switch panel elsewhere. As well as reducing work, this may keep wiring runs to a minimum and provide scope for adding more equipment later.

A complete installation of a new distribution panel will require a 12V feed from the battery switch (position 2) to a new positive bus bar. However, first the main battery cable to the battery switch needs to be checked to ensure it has sufficient capacity for the extra current that it will carry.

The negative (0V) wiring returns can also be collected together on a 0V bus bar, with a single cable going back to a spare point on the battery negative (0V) terminal. Wiring for the new equipment can then be easily routed from the bus bars with the positive wire going via the switches and protection devices on the new panel.

PLANNING THE INSTALLATION

	Current (A)	Total wire length (m)	Wire AWG (3%)	Wire mm² (3%)	Fuse rating A
Autopilot	5	6	12*	1.4	10*
Fridge	4	8	14	1.5	8
Cockpit lights	0.6	2	18	0.1	3
Anchor light	0.8	20	16	1.0	3
Spare	5 (max)				8
12V supply	15.4	3	12	2.9	
OV return	15.4	11	12	2.9	

* These values are recommended in the manual.

Right **A wiring diagram is the best planning aid but it may take you several attempts. For this one, as it is in the engine bay, extra margin was allowed on the wiring and fuse ratings because of the warm environment.**

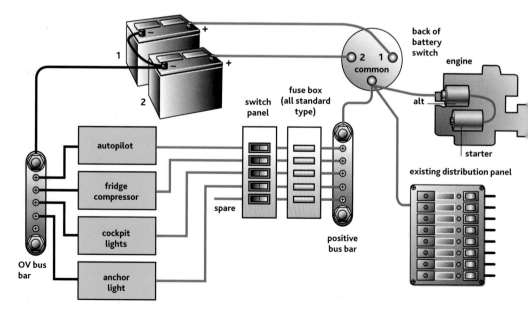

Wire sizing

We can use an example of installing five items: an autopilot with a drive motor requiring maximum current of 5A, plus another 500mA for the control unit itself, a 4A fridge compressor and 1A cockpit lighting, plus two further 5A-rated positions on the new panel for future expansion:

- ❂ If the positive feed from the battery switch must handle a maximum of 20A over a distance of 3m (10ft), the table of wire size (3 per cent) in Appendix 1 shows that 10AWG ($3.1–4.6mm^2$) is suitable.
- ❂ If the negative (0V) return to the battery terminal that handles the same current, is much shorter, at just 1m (3ft) in length, 12AWG ($2.9mm^2$) can be used.
- ❂ If the autopilot supply wires need to handle 5.5A over a total cable length (there and back)

of 6m (20ft), the installation manual recommends 14–12AWG ($2.5mm^2$).

- ❂ Given a 6m (20ft) total length of wiring carrying 4A for the fridge compressor, 14AWG ($1.7mm^2$) is needed.
- ❂ Finally, if the lighting circuit is also a 6m (20ft) round trip, this only requires 18AWG ($0.8mm^2$).

Switching, indication and fusing

For the switch, the choice is whether to go for combined switch/circuit breakers or a separate 'toggle' switch and a multi-way spade fuse box. All three circuits can use fast-acting (standard) fusing. The protection ratings will be:

- ❂ 10A for the autopilot, which is recommended by the manufacturer in the installation manual. The control unit also has a 10A fuse fitted internally, but

the external fuse is to protect the wiring.

- ❂ 8A or 10A will be sufficient for the fridge compressor.
- ❂ 3A or 5A for the lighting circuit.
- ❂ A maximum of 10A rating for the two spare circuits, as each one will be limited to 5A continuous current.

Indication for toggle switches can be achieved by marking the panel with the 'ON' position. If combined switch/circuit breakers are used, the buttons stand proud when in the 'OFF' position, making it easy to tell which circuits are active.

If visible indication is wanted, there are several models of toggle switches with LED indicators conveniently built in.

Below It's often worth making provision for future expansion with extra bus bars.

Right Individual wires are then fed to the back of the new panel which has a separate fuse and switch for each function.

Installing permanent voltmeters and ammeters

The object of meters mounted on the switch panel is to check all is well with the system at a quick glance. With a quality voltmeter in the panel, you can check the batteries' state of charge, or see if charging is taking place for each battery bank. Similarly, an ammeter can provide net current flow data at strategic points.

Voltmeters

Voltmeters come in two styles – with an analogue dial or a digital readout. There are a few considerations for both types:

- Analogue dial meters that are suitable for boats have an expanded scale from 8V to 16V (or 18V to 32V for a 24V system). Values below these are irrelevant and the expanded scale makes it possible to get readings that are accurate to one decimal place. As discussed on pages 42–43, a terminal voltage range of 12.1–12.7V for 'rested' batteries,

represents battery charge of between 50 and 100 per cent.
- Digital readout voltmeters will cover 0–32V in a single meter and again only one decimal place is needed. A separate supply is required for the meter electronics and backlight.
- The choice may just be down to whether you have an analogue or digital feel to your boat.

Below **A voltmeter on the panel can be switched between each battery bank.**

Installation

A connection from the meter '+' terminal to the battery positive (+) terminal is needed, with a one amp in-line fuse at the battery end. The meter '-' terminal is connected to any one of the battery negative (-) terminals. The wires can be thin gauge and the meter itself positioned where you like.

If you have several battery banks, the positive connection to each bank should have its own in-line fuse at the battery end, with the other end of the wire going to a selector switch by the meter.

Ammeters

Again, analogue and digital versions are available but, more importantly, there are three types, depending on how large the current is and how it is measured (see pages 90–92):

- **Current passing directly through the meter.** As the current of the circuit being measured has to go through the meter itself, cable runs and size realistically limit this approach to a maximum of around 30A. This is suitable for measuring solar panel, wind generator and possibly mains charger currents.
- **Current measured via a resistive current shunt.** Shunts are connected into the negative battery cable, next to the battery. The ammeter (which is actually a voltmeter), measures the voltage

bank 1

rotary
switch

bank 2

fuse

1
3

2

fuse

bank 3

fuse

+

–

0V

Note:
1. The selector switch must be a 'break before make' type.
2. A 1 amp fuse should be included in each wire to the batteries and be positioned near the batteries themselves.

across the shunt and the scale is suitably calibrated to read amps. Remotely positioned ammeters capable of measuring +/-150A (using the appropriate shunt) are readily available. As with a voltmeter, a single meter can be switched between several shunts. The main limitation of this approach is that standard ammeters cannot measure current in positive cables, such as the alternator output.

⚙ **Current measured using a Hall effect sensor.** This is essentially the same as the resistive shunt, but current can be measured in any cable which passes through the centre of the sensor. The sensor itself needs a power supply (usually between 10V and 32V) and two other thin (signal) wires are led to the ammeter. Again, a single ammeter can be switched between several sensors, and no modifications to the cables being measured are required.

Above As with all instruments, a quick scan of the voltmeter and ammeter readings will tell you if all is well with the electrical system.

TIP

Both the ammeter dial and the sensors will have a 'full scale voltage' quoted and the sensor must match the dial otherwise the reading will be inaccurate. Full scale voltage is the value that represents the maximum current, for example, the Hall effect sensor gives a voltage of +/- 60mV when +/- 60A is passing through it, ie a calibration of 1mV/amp. The dial must be the same.

RANGE OF AMMETERS AND SENSORS

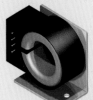

The style of panel meter very much depends on the style of your boat. Digital meters may look out of place on traditional boats.

The sensors 'send' a voltage signal to the ammeter dial for display. Both positive and negative current are displayed, illustrating the direction of current flow.

Either the Hall effect sensors or the current shunts can be used as the means of measuring the actual current.

Data recording over long periods

Monitoring and recording key voltages and currents can give you a better understanding of how batteries are used over an extended period, without resorting to a full power management system. Data loggers are used to sample the data measured and store the result in memory for later analysis.

Voltage data loggers

In their simplest form, these are standalone, battery-operated measuring devices, with internal memory, connected to the source of the voltage being recorded. They take a sample of the voltage at regular intervals and store it. At some point in the future, you plug the device into a computer, download the recorded data and plot a graph of the voltage over the period.

The length of time over which data can be recorded depends on the total memory capacity and the rate at which samples are taken. Low-cost examples with up to 130,000 memory locations can sample from once per second to once every 12 hours, giving periods of 9 hours to more than 2 years. They can measure voltage changes down to 50mV over a maximum voltage range of 0–30V. Plugging it into your computer's USB port, the device set-up software allows you to select the sample rate and calibrate the output data.

Current measuring loggers

These are essentially the same as the voltage logging versions, but with a much smaller input voltage range.

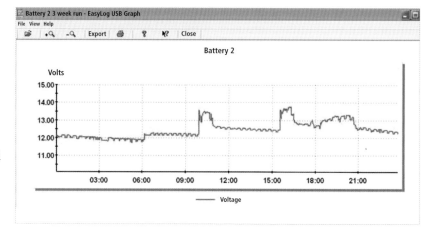

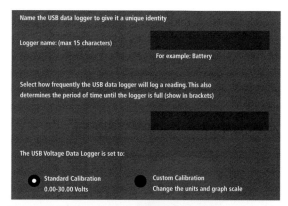

Above The data log can run for long periods, giving clear daily trends of battery voltage. The small steps in battery voltage are because of the fridge cutting in and out on its thermostat.

Right and below Once the voltage data logger is set up and calibrated via the computer software, it is connected to the battery terminals.

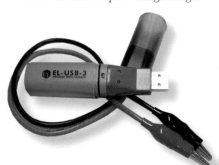

They are designed to be used with resistive current shunts or Hall effect sensors. They have the added advantage of being able to record positive and negative voltage, showing current in both directions. Typically they are calibrated to +/- 1mV per amp (up to 1,000A with the appropriate current shunt or sensor) although this is often programmable by the user.

What can be gained?

Over each 24-hour period, you will see the starting and finishing battery voltages and any overall change.

- This approach is particularly useful to see the impact of running the engine on a daily basis. If you normally do this for a set period, you can see whether it is too long compared to the time actually needed. Some boats rely on a diesel generator as the primary source of power and, again, the timing can be established a little more scientifically. If you run a four-stage mains charger off the generator (a likely scenario), you will see the benefit of allowing extra float charging time to get the batteries nearer 100 per cent charged.

- If you have a fridge, you can compare running it continuously (letting the thermostat turn it on and off) to having it on for a set period each day. Similarly a temperature data logger placed in the fridge will show the effect on its temperature by running it in the ways described above.

- The performance of solar panels and wind generators can easily be monitored. The smaller 30A or 60A shunts can be used for this as the currents are smaller.

- Overall, you can gain valuable experience about how the way you use your boat impacts on the battery system, which will enable you to make changes to optimise performance if necessary.

Below **The current data logger measures the voltage drop across the resistive current shunt or it can use an external Hall effect current measuring device (as shown here). The calibration for either option is taken care of in the set-up software.**

Right **Occasional, apparently random, faults can be picked up by monitoring the system over longer periods. Here, a glitch in the alternator regulator gave rise to a period of over-charging. Zooming in on the data plot showed this lasted for over an hour. It also appeared that the regulator was delivering 14.5V, which is a bit high and may be over-charging the batteries.**

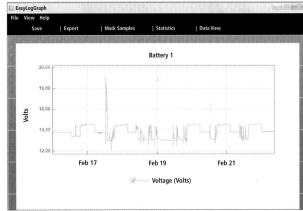

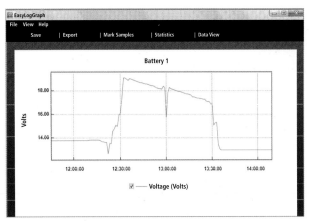

The engine and its electrics

Most small boats have straightforward diesel engines with mechanical fuel pumps and injectors that do not need electrics to function. However, a starter motor instead of a starting handle makes life easier, and sensors to monitor temperatures and pressures are useful. Ultimately, this becomes one of the most important electrical sub-systems on the boat.

Breaking the system down into its main elements, the starting circuits and sequence (for most common engines) comprises:

- **Injector pre-heaters or 'glow plugs'** (only used on more recent and larger indirect injected engines). The injector is in a small chamber off the cylinder bore and to improve starting, a small, quite powerful heater element surrounds the injector nozzle, making the atomised diesel ignite more readily. To energise the pre-heaters, the ignition switch is turned to the left against a spring for 10–15 seconds.

Below **The complexity of engine electrics grows exponentially with engine size.**

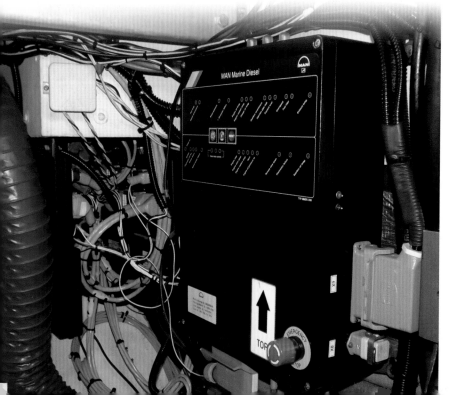

- **The starter motor solenoid** (piggybacked onto the starter motor) is then engaged by turning the key clockwise, through the 'OFF' then 'ON' position to 'START', again, against a spring. Engaging the solenoid rams two large switch contacts together, connecting the engine start battery (positive terminal) to the starter motor. On some engines, the start switch engages an intermediate relay that, in turn, activates the starter solenoid. This further reduces the current which the start button or key switch has to carry. Once the

engine starts, the key is released and the spring returns the switch to the 'ON' position, disengaging the starter solenoid but leaving all instruments and lights powered up.

- **The starter motor** is a very powerful electric motor requiring a substantial amount of current, up to 100A even on smaller engines. Its function is to drive the engine round until ignition takes place. A large diameter cable, able to handle the starter current, goes directly from the engine start battery positive terminal, to the starter solenoid terminal. The connection from the other side of the solenoid to the motor is done internally, so is not visible.

- **The negative, 0V return path** is, for the majority of boats (other than metal hulls), back to the battery through the engine block itself. This accounts for there being only one (red) wire between the starter motor and alternator. Somewhere on the engine there is a strap connecting it, electrically, to the battery negative terminal, so completing the return path of the circuit.

- **The alternator** starts producing power once the engine fires up. Its positive cable usually goes to the same stud contact on the starter solenoid as the battery to starter cable. This is how the alternator charging power gets back to the battery.

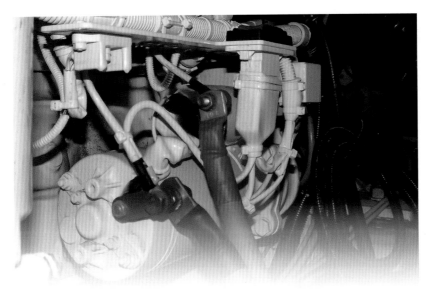

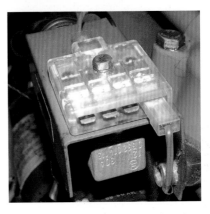

Stopping the engine requires the fuel supply to be cut off. This is achieved by activating a shut-off lever on the fuel pump, either by pulling a 'stop' handle (linked to the lever) or by pressing a 'stop' button that energises a solenoid which, in turn, operates the same lever.

Monitoring equipment

The second part of the engine's electrical system consists of alarms, sensors, indication lights and gauges. The complexity varies from a few indicators and an alarm to something akin to an aircraft cockpit. The heart of any monitoring system is the sensors, which fall into two types:

- **Alarm senders** are on/off switches triggered by the feature they are sensing. Being screwed into the engine block, they switch their spade connector (to which the wire from the engine panel circuit is connected) to 0V through the engine block. Oil pressure (switch closed for insufficient pressure) and cooling water temperature (switch closed

Above The correct cable size is vital for the starter motor. It's likely to consume the highest current on board and needs all the voltage it can get, so cable losses must be minimised.

when water temperature too high) are common to all engines. These operate the indicator lights and an audible alarm.

- **Pressure and temperature gauge senders** are variable resistors altered by changes in oil pressure and water temperature and form part of the gauge circuit. Again, they are screwed into the engine block. They normally also incorporate the 'alarm sender' function, which means you get an audible warning from the panel in the event of a problem.
- **Rev counter (tachometer)** is normally driven from the alternator. On the Valeo versions, it is from the 'W' terminal.

Top To start the engine you press the power 'ON' followed by the injector pre-heaters for five seconds (not fitted on this panel) and, finally, the 'START' button.

Above middle The 0V (negative) return path is just as important as the positive side. This cable carries the same current as the positive cable to the starter motor.

Above On some engines the ignition switch drives an interim relay which then provides power to the starter solenoid. The feed from the ignition switch is fused and the plastic housing has four fuses in, one in use and three spares. The relay is visible below the housing.

Engine data monitoring

Many vessels have either a set of engine instruments showing, at a glance, the engine's vital signs or just indicator lights and an alarm, alerting you to a problem once it has occurred. Recent multi-function displays (chart plotters) and multi-page instruments are capable of displaying engine data but first, it must be converted to NMEA2000 format.

Three key areas have to be addressed to enable cooling water temperature, oil pressures and a host of other information loosely related to the engine to be displayed on a chart plotter.

- The raw data is obtained at the engine, batteries and so on by either senders (for pressures, temperatures and levels), direct connection in the case of battery voltages and via an intermediate amplifier for current measurement and some other temperature measurements. Each type of sender (or sensor) converts the parameter being measured into an electrical signal.
- An electronic conversion module (often referred to as an 'analogue to NMEA2000' converter) collects these raw analogue signals from the senders and converts them into digital form, effectively a

discrete number that represents the value of the parameter. The converter then assembles the data into NMEA2000 format with the correct 'Parameter Group Number' (PGN), denoting what the data represents. Once the data is available on the network, the chart plotter can decode the PGN and display the associated data.

- Because of the variety of senders and parameters being measured, the electronic module has to be fairly generic and requires each input to be configured and each sender to be calibrated.

The typical parameters you might want are:

- Cooling water temperature (actual value)
- Cooling water over temperature alarm switch

- Oil pressure (actual value)
- Loss of oil pressure alarm switch
- Engine speed (revs)
- Battery volts (each bank)
- Battery terminal temperature (each bank) to warn of over-charging
- Alternator charging current
- Current consumption from the domestic battery bank
- Fuel tank level
- Fuel flow rate (allowing consumption, range and other calculations to be made by the chart plotter)

Using existing gauges

Where you already have a full system with gauges and alarms, the inputs to the conversion module are piggybacked off the back of the gauges. The only set up required is to enter the calibration data into the conversion module. All that data will then be available on the NMEA2000 network.

Systems without instrument dials and gauges

Simpler systems usually only have a rev counter and temperature/oil alarm switch units fitted. It is possible to purchase combined sender/switch units to replace the existing switch, but you will have to consult your engine dealer for the correct part number. It is very important to leave the existing alarm system intact; simply piggyback off the alarm switch terminal with a second wire to the converter module.

Below **A very comprehensive engine data converter. This unit may have too many inputs for smaller, single-engine vessels but illustrates what can be measured.**

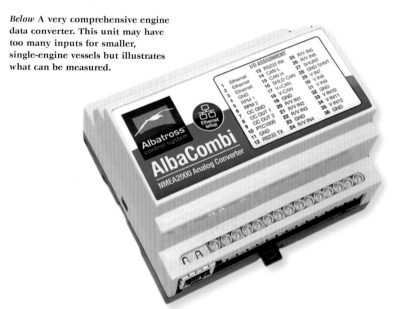

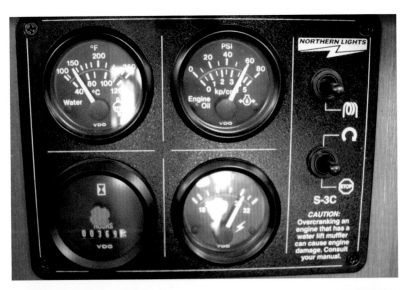

Left If your vessel already has instruments then all the required senders are available. The analogue to NMEA2000 converter will make the same data available elsewhere on the vessel, at the chart table for instance.

Below left The most convenient place to pick up the analogue signals is on the back of the gauges themselves.

The conversion unit

The analogue to NMEA2000 conversion unit typically has an array of inputs and outputs grouped into three main types:

- The gauge inputs accept a voltage signal from resistive senders such as the water temperature, tank level and oil pressure senders.
- Alarm inputs connect to the over-temperature and loss of oil pressure switches to activate an alarm.
- Tach (or pulse counter) inputs accept a signal in the form of a train of pulses, typically from the tacho (rev counter) or from flow meters measuring the flow of, say, fuel to the engine.

To facilitate calibration of the senders and other inputs to the conversion module, set-up software is included which allows each individual input or output to be characterised and allocated to the correct PGN, so the data is correctly decoded and displayed by your chart plotter.

Left The engine speed (RPM) can be picked up from the back of the alternator, typically terminal 'W'.

Middle A combined oil pressure sender and switch. The threaded end screws into the engine block and a small hole allows oil to pass inside the sender unit under pressure.

Bottom This is a replacement temperature sender and switch (in the one unit). The tip protrudes into the waterway inside the engine and is immersed in the cooling water so picking up its temperature.

Engine data monitoring
– set up and calibration

Engine information can be displayed on multi-function displays through the use of multi-input, analogue to NMEA converters. Each input will have a sender or other signal source associated with it that requires calibrating, for instance with a temperature sender, this will be how many mV/°C, or for the rev counter it will be the number of pulses per revolution.

Several types of senders or sensors can be used for engine monitoring, but each needs to be considered from the set up point of view.

Measuring temperature, pressure and fluid level

The most common senders are resistive, where the resistance changes depending on the actual value of the parameter being measured. The temperature sender may have a range of resistance from 700Ω, representing the low temperature limit (say 40°C), to 22Ω (120°C) for the highest. Oil pressure and tank level senders behave in a similar fashion.

To derive a voltage from resistive senders it is necessary to pass a constant current through them, supplied (when enabled) from the Gauge Input Channel on the conversion module. From Ohm's Law, the sender terminal voltage = the constant current x the resistance at any point in time. Assuming that at 90°C water temperature the sender resistance is 275Ω, for a constant current of 10mA, the sender output voltage would be 2.75V. Similarly, for 40°C (700Ω), the output voltage would be 7V. This sender terminal voltage is connected to the converter input.

Warning alarm switches

If the switch operates, due to loss of oil pressure for instance, the switch's terminal is connected to 0V through the engine block. In the existing engine electrics, this completes the circuit to 0V and results in the warning light and alarm sounder

Above Senders have a resistive element inside, the value of which changes according to the actual value of the parameter being measured.

coming on. Only the Actisense converter has inputs specifically allocated for this function.

Rev counters and flow meters

These send out a train of pulses depending on the speed of the rotation. Normally these can be fed straight into the converter's RPM/Flow inputs.

Battery terminal volts

These form a connection directly from the battery terminal to one of the gauge inputs.

Temperature measurement by thermocouples

Thermocouples can be used to measure other temperatures around the boat, for example battery terminals. They need a separate amplifier to make the output suitable for the converter.

Current measurement via current shunts or Hall effect sensors

The voltage from the shunt or Hall effect sensor is so small that it needs to be amplified by a 'differential

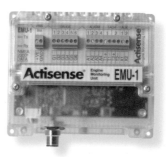

Left and above Noland and Actisense analogue to NMEA2000 converters operate in a similar way, but with slightly different functions.

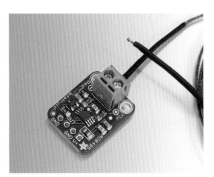

Far left **Thermocouple amplifiers are available from electronic hobby shops. They may need protection from moisture by using circuit board varnish.**

Left **These differential amplifiers are suitable for marine use.**

amplifier' before sending to the converter gauge input. A 1mΩ resistive shunt will only produce a voltage of 10mV when 10A are flowing through it – this is too small for the converter and therefore needs to be amplified. The Alba-Combi unit has an input that is dedicated to this task with an integrated amplifier.

Differential amplifier

A differential amplifier amplifies only the difference between the voltages on both of its inputs. From the illustration, the difference between the measured voltage at each terminal of the current shunt is 12.715V – 12.700V = 0.015V. This is amplified 50 times to give 0.75V representing 15A of current flow. By the same calculation, 50A would result in 2.5V at the amplifier output.

Analogue to NMEA2000 converter inputs

These fall into three categories and can accept signals from any source that meets their criteria.

○ Gauge inputs accept a voltage signal, typically between 0 and 30V. Some, if not all of these inputs can also be configured as a 'constant current source' for use with resistive senders as described above.

○ Alarm inputs are specially designed to accept the switch type sensor.
○ RPM/Flow inputs accept a train of pulses from the alternator or flow meters.

Below **The differential amplifier multiplies the voltage drop across the current shunt to a larger value suitable for the converter.**

Calibration and configuration routines

The software that comes with the converter will allow you configure each input and to set up the calibration of each sender or signal being monitored. This can be done in a practical way by logging a number of actual readings; the converter will work out a calibration curve for the sender.

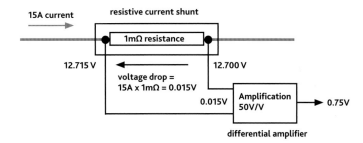

	Actisense EMU-1	Noland RS11	Albatross Alba-Combi
COMPARISON TABLE BETWEEN THREE CONVERTER MANUFACTURERS			
Unit supply voltage	9–35V	10–30V	10–32V
Gauge input:			
Number available	6	6	12
With constant current o/p	6	6	6
Input voltage range	0–35V	0–20 & 0–30V	0–32V
RPM/Flow	2	2	2
Alarm	4		
Thermocouple			1
Relay driver output			2

Starter motors

Starting the engine is possibly the most important function on the boat, which puts the starter motor in the spotlight. They are intrinsically simple and reliable, but still give problems very occasionally. Usually the electrics side of the starter system is the first place to look.

The starter motor consumes an enormous amount of current. Its job is to turn the engine over and get it started. If you have ever tried to do that by hand, you will realise how much power is required.

In order to switch this high current remotely, an intermediate switch is needed to do the hard work. This is the first job of the starter solenoid, a device which is usually piggybacked onto the starter motor casing. The other function of the solenoid, once energised, is to mesh a drive gear or pinion, driven by the starter, into the flywheel of the engine.

Electric circuit

As the most likely cause of a problem will be electrical, it is useful to understand this part of the system.

- The battery, whether a dedicated starter battery or a single bank system, will need to be sufficiently charged.
- The positive side of the starter circuit will be a cable from the battery to the battery switch, possibly via a main fuse. From there it will go to the main terminal on the starter solenoid.
- The second main terminal on the solenoid has a cable (usually a braided type) going into the motor casing. This is the feed to the motor itself.
- There will be one more, thinner wire, onto a smaller terminal that provides the much lower current to activate the solenoid. This comes from the ignition switch or start button.
- If the ignition switch is a long distance from the solenoid, a second, intermediate relay is used. This in turn provides the higher solenoid energising current (anything up to 30A on large engines).

All these connections need to be inspected for being loose or corroded. If there is not enough voltage getting to the starter motor to turn the engine over, you get a characteristic clunk as the solenoid operates, and then – nothing... For the return path back to the battery negative terminal, the starter is bolted to the engine block and all the associated currents flow through the metal of the engine to a large cable, also bolted to the block, and back to the battery negative. This side is less likely to give problems.

Left The starter motor (right circle) and starter solenoid (left circle) are seen behind the alternator. Even on a brand-new engine, access to the bolts for removal is quite difficult.

Mechanical system

The starter motor and solenoid can be removed as a unit. Only two or three bolts are involved, but access to them may not be easy. There are only two parts that can be accessed for inspection or maintenance:

- The brushes, reached by removing a cover plate at the back end. These wear down over time and as they shorten the springs may not press them hard enough against the rotor to transfer the high current. Again, large voltage drops can occur here due to bad connections.
- If the pinion is stuck on the shaft it will not engage with the flywheel. The secondary function of the solenoid is to operate a lever that pushes the pinion forward into the flywheel. Because this section is not sealed from the outside world, dust and grease can build up over time. Removal of the front cover gives access to this area.

Left The cable from the engine start battery switch goes directly to the starter solenoid and then to the alternator.

Below Many electrical installers advocate main fuses in the battery cables. While this is a safety feature, it introduces yet more connections.

Bottom Even on smaller engines the starter current is in excess of 120A. Any resistance in the cable connections will result in significant voltage drop, making it difficult to turn over the engine.

Below Sectional view of a starter and solenoid assembly.

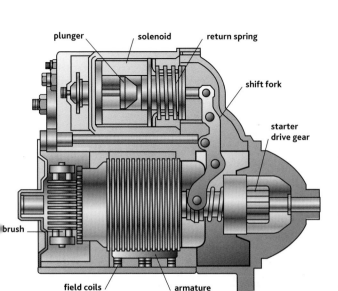

plunger   solenoid   return spring

shift fork

starter drive gear

brush

field coils   armature

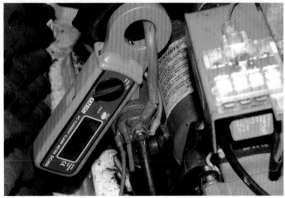

Digital switching

Digital switching has been around for many years and offers incredible flexibility, enabling systems to be controlled solely through electronics. In the boating environment, these systems can mimic and extend the functionality of the distribution panel, as well as many other aspects of vessel management. The interface is via the chart plotter, touch-sensitive switch panels or even a mobile phone data link.

The output switch

A powerful transistor is used to switch power to the vessel's equipment. This device (a 'Metal Oxide Semiconductor Field Effect Transistor' or MOSFET) takes the place of the mechanical switch on the distribution panel.

As with the panel, these transistor switches are fed from the DC positive bus bar (or return to a 0V bus bar). One remarkable feature of this type of device is that the drive or input mechanism is a simple voltage level; generally 0V equals 'OFF', 10–12V equals 'ON'. This makes the interface between the processor part and the real world of volts and amps seem relatively straightforward.

Behind the switch

Digital switching systems are invariably split into a number of channels, each of which can have its own output switch, or input signal conditioning circuitry. The tremendous flexibility of these systems starts with channel configuration, each being set up and tailored to a specific task. Some of the many examples are:

- Output channels have the option to measure their own current and therefore incorporate the fuse function, protecting against over-current and short circuits.
- In the same way, under-current detection gives feedback that the equipment is not working. For instance, if a navigation light bulb has broken, the system will detect this as soon as you turn the lights on.
- The channel's output status is fed back to provide indication.
- Voltages, currents and other vessel information, such as fuel and various water levels, can be monitored through input configured channels and fed back for display. Acceptable limits can be set to initiate further actions through different channels, such as turning on a pump.
- Channels dedicated to LED or halogen lighting can incorporate extras such as dimming, mood and effects controls.
- Channels can be combined to give bi-directional motor speed control, such as required for windscreen wipers.

Left The digital control unit (DCU) has a positive feed directly from the battery switch and a 0V return to the battery bank. Power to individual equipment is then switched from the DCU under the control of an NMEA communication link (see page 144).

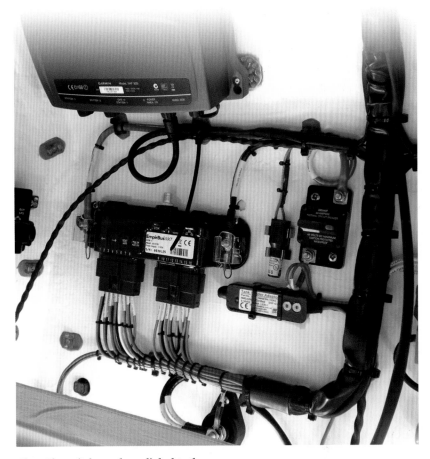

One limitation is the maximum current handling capability of each channel. Realistically, because of the nature of semiconductors used, this is likely to be around 20A. However, items that require more current can be driven via a relay.

A good example is the VSR (voltage sensing relay) to direct charging current to a particular battery bank. The command signal for this would originate from the digital switching system.

Main control unit

This unit, which is given different names by different manufactures, houses the microprocessor that is the real heart of the system. Some of its many functions are:

- The ability to connect with a computer that has software to aid setting up and configuration.
- Two-way communications with its own modules to allow control of the system and receive data from it.
- At some point there will be a human interface for the digital switching system to receive its orders and to enable the data that is fed back to be displayed. The most likely scenario on a boat is communication to chart plotters, switch panels and instruments all via a common network, on which the digital switching system also sits.

Above The switch panels are linked to the master control unit by a communication link using the NMEA2000 protocol, which greatly simplifies wiring. There can be several located around the boat.

Below The boat's systems can be controlled and monitored from the multi-function display.

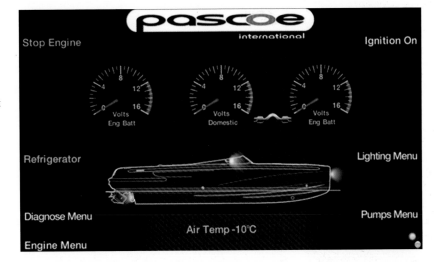

AC mains on board

Shore power

Mains power opens up a whole new arena of on-board comforts. Around 3kW is available at most berths, while some marinas offer up to 12kW supplies on selected berths for large yachts. However, mains power is especially dangerous when surrounded by water, so great attention must be paid to preventative maintenance of the system and any equipment plugged into it.

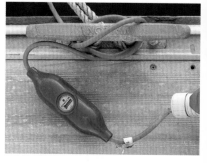

Above **The extension cable is a potential weak link – it's worth investing in a good quality one.**

Terminology

Slightly different terminology is used in the AC mains environment:

- ☼ **Earth or ground** is the wire or conductor that is (literally) sunk into the earth or ground somewhere near to the sub-station for the marina's main incoming supply.
- ☼ **Hot or live wire** is the one with the high voltage (typically 110V or 220/240V). Whilst all mains is potentially harmful, this is the most dangerous one.
- ☼ **Neutral wire** is the wire providing the return path for current flowing in the hot or live wire.

Below **The marina's protection ends here with a residual current device (RCD) and over-current trip (not shown here). Beyond this point, protection is down to each boat.**

The earth wire is particularly important from a safety point of view. Any equipment with exposed metal surfaces accessible to people will have an earth wire connection. In certain fault conditions, current will flow down the earth wire (known as earth leakage) and a detection device will trip the supply off.

Protection devices

There are two aspects to protection:

- ☼ Over-current fuses or circuit breakers, as with the DC system, will blow or trip to disconnect the hot or live wire if the current exceeds the rating. One level of protection is at your AC panel, where a circuit breaker will protect a complete circuit, while fuses in the individual items provide another level of protection.

- ☼ Residual current devices (RCDs) monitor the current flowing in the live and neutral wires, which should be equal. If some current is leaking to earth (even as little as 30mA), the RCD will trip a switch in both wires, disconnecting the mains supply. The RCD unit has a test button, allowing you to check the function is working.

Bringing mains on board

An extension cable is needed to take the power supply from the pontoon to the boat. This is the most vulnerable part of the system as it is regularly wrapped, rolled and flexed. From a safety point of view it is essential that this is in good condition and has quality watertight plugs and sockets. The most crucial of the three wires is the earth, which may save your life one day.

- ☼ Even a temporary extension lead, used with power tools for example, should be protected. Use a portable RCD at the boat end of the lead to plug the tools into.
- ☼ A professionally installed mains system on board will start with the RCD unit. From there a cable will go to your circuit breaker unit, or panel-mounted circuit breakers, and out to the different circuits.

Above **Reverse polarity indication is often included in the vessel's mains distribution panel.**

❂ Normally pontoon outlets are limited to 3kW but if you need more, there may be 'superyacht' pedestals with up to 12kW. The sockets will be different to the standard type because of the extra power and the cable will be thicker to take the extra current.

Below **A reverse polarity tester will tell you immediately if there is an issue.**

Polarity testing the supply

There is no guarantee that the wiring in some marinas is the same way round as on your vessel (particularly between Europe and the UK). It is possible that the live and neutral on the pontoon are reversed. Although this will not affect the operation of on-board equipment, it has a significant safety implication.

❂ Where polarity reversal exists, your live wire will be connected to the marina's neutral wire. More significantly, what you think is your neutral wire is now, in fact, live and of course dangerous.

❂ Polarity testers are built into many boats in the AC panel, otherwise you can buy a portable one, plugging it into any of your sockets to do the test.

❂ If the marina supply is reversed, use a plug/socket lead that re-reverses the connection – two wrongs make a right in this case.

INCORRECT OR 'REVERSED' POLARITY

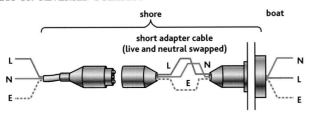

CORRECT POLARITY

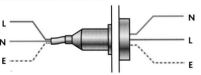

INCORRECT POLARITY

TIP

Many boat owners are very capable of doing mains wiring, certainly small modifications. It is worth contacting your insurance company to see if they are satisfied with your level of competence. And it is definitely worth having a professional electrician do a safety test once the work is complete.

INCREASING POWER

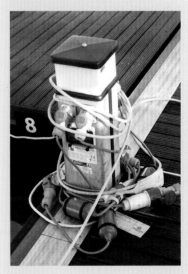

There is always a high demand for electricity with just about every boat in the marina wanting shore power, often resulting in a messy 'spaghetti' of cables (top picture). Some will need more than the standard 3kW and there may be a few berths with higher rated outputs available, but they will often need reserving in advance.

System installation

Marine AC mains systems are broadly similar to domestic ones, particularly in terms of safety devices. It is possible to have multiple sources of AC power on board, which may be linked to common outlets, or kept separate. As with DC systems, a means of distribution, protection and indication is needed, as well as measuring and monitoring equipment.

All boat AC system installations should be certified by a qualified and licensed electrician, ideally one accustomed to the marine environment. Failure to do this may, in extreme circumstances, invalidate your insurance.

System layout
Irrespective of the source of the AC supply, there will be a system on the boat. Overall the mains wiring should use multi-strand cables rather than the solid core type used in housing. The first element is the RCD protection device, followed by a master switch and circuit breaker. From this point, the system will break out to individual sub-circuits,

each with their own switch and fusing device in the live/hot wire (usually a circuit breaker) and an indicator. Typical circuits might include:

- Outlet sockets arranged in a ring just as in the household system – this spreads the current evenly throughout the wiring
- Mains heater element in the calorifier/water heater
- Battery charger
- Mains lighting ring
- A couple of spares.

As with DC systems, it makes sense to collect switching, fusing and indication together on one panel, along with the polarity tester,

voltmeter and mains ammeter. As there is a limit on the amount of power available, the ammeter indicates how close you are to the maximum available current.

Calculating or measuring power in AC systems
Essentially this is the same as for DC systems in that power = volts x amps.

- The power is measured in watts (or kW).
- The volts correspond to the mains voltage supply, depending where in the world you are (120V, 220V or 240V).
- Amps can be measured by the mains ammeter.

Alternatively, you can buy a power meter that measures both the voltage and total current being used, multiplies the two and displays it as power.

Power audit
For different reasons, just as for the DC system you will have to limit AC power consumption. An audit of the mains equipment you want to use will enable you to stay below the

Left The RCD is the first level of protection on the boat. It should be placed close to the point at which the mains supply comes on board. The selector switch will 'break' the connection from one source before 'making' the connection to the alternative source. This is an essential requirement when switching between AC sources (including an inverter).

Right Many boats have both DC and AC switches on the same distribution panel – take extra care when working behind it. Here the left-hand board is AC and the right-hand one is DC.

power limit, even if it means choosing which items can be used simultaneously. A label somewhere on the equipment will tell you the power consumption in watts. Typical values are:

- Fan heaters typically have settings at 500W, 1kW or 2kW.
- A calorifier element is usually around 700W.
- A mains battery charger will be up to 320W when supplying 20A at 14V DC (allowing for some efficiency losses).
- A dehumidifier will consume around 200W.
- Microwave oven, toaster, hair dryer, steam iron, coffee maker and kettle are each around 1kW.
- Washing machines are nearer 2kW and air conditioners can be over 3kW.

Multiple AC sources

Shore power, diesel generators and voltage inverters can all be used to produce an AC power supply. If they are all linked into the AC system at the RCD, enabling you to choose which source to use, they must not be allowed to supply power simultaneously. A master selector switch must be fitted to ensure one source is switched 'OFF' before an alternative source is switched 'ON'. This switch must operate on both the live (hot) and neutral wires so each source is completely removed. This switch will be a 'break before make, double pole' type.

Right The power meter system measures voltage and current and multiplies them together to display the power. This will tell you how close your consumption is to the marina berth's maximum output.

Below There are several switching configurations; here all the mains equipment can be powered by one of three sources – shore power, on-board generator or battery-powered inverter. High power consumers such as water heaters and washing machines will often be restricted to use only with the on-board generator, as even the shore power may have insufficient capacity.

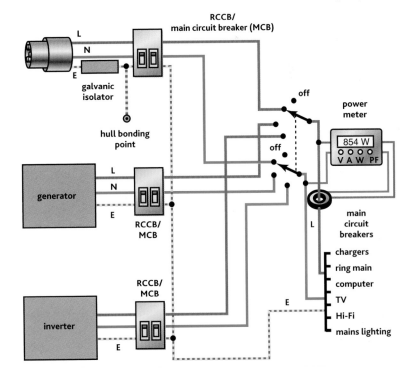

Mains protection

Marinas have multiple layers of protection, building in magnitude until the whole facility is covered. An earth plate is buried in the ground to which every metal part of the marina that is in contact with water must be bonded. Your connection to this is made via your extension lead and pontoon pedestal. Away from shore, diesel generators and inverters must also provide an earth path.

Starting at the marina

The marina receives its supply from the electricity company via the national distribution grid. Those voltages are much too high for our use so they are transformed down to more manageable levels. In the USA and Canada this is 115V (three wire) and 230V (four wire) and in Europe, three wire 220/240V. This is also where the earth wire is finally connected to the neutral and grounded through the earth plate.

In the same way as your boat is protected, the marina has a master incoming switch bank and gradually splits the power out into different sections, one of which will include your pontoon pedestal. Each section is protected against the accumulated power in terms of over-current and earth leakage faults. Even mid-sized marinas will have to cope with currents of thousands of amps resulting from consumption of hundreds of kilowatts of electricity.

Each standard pedestal outlet will be protected by a 15A (Europe) or a 15A/30A option in the USA and Canada, depending on whether you are using one or two phases. There will also be an appropriate RCD for earth leakage detection. The marina's responsibility ends where you plug in: from there it's up to you.

From pontoon to boat

The extension cable is one of the main sources of faults. It needs to be marine-quality cable and have plugs and sockets with relevant approval and certification for use in the marine environment.

The most vulnerable points are where the cable enters the plug and socket at either end. The cable clamps can start to wear through the insulation due to repeated flexing, so this should be checked periodically. Chafing along the length of the cable should be looked for on a very regular basis as the insulation can become worn through.

Above and left **The marina sub-station basically has an 'ON/OFF' switch and a couple of circuit breakers in case of problems. This marina has around 200 berths and has the capability to supply up to 1 million watts (1MW) of electricity. Each pontoon then has a smaller set of protection switches and breakers.**

On board

Once the cable is plugged in to the boat, you bring into play the boat's own protection devices. The first is the RCD, followed by a master circuit breaker (MCB) – these are often combined in one unit.

- The RCD looks for leakage and fault currents flowing in the earth wire (for instance a metal case becoming live or hot due to a chafed wire).

- In normal circumstances there will be no current flowing in the earth wire. If the RCD detects more than 30mA in this wire (a fault condition) it will trip and switch off the supply (live/hot and neutral wires) to the rest of your vessel.

- The MCB reacts to excessive or overload currents, including a short circuit between live (hot) and neutral.

- The MCB may also be the manually operated master switch to pass power through to the rest of the system.

- Both devices are so-called 'double pole' in that they will switch off both the live (hot) and neutral wires, thereby totally isolating the mains supply.

The next feature is the reverse polarity tester before the power finally arrives at the individual circuit breakers. These will be one of two types:

- Single pole devices, when tripped, will only disconnect the live (hot) wire. This is fine providing you are not plugged into a marina supply of reverse polarity to your own vessel (see pages 122–123).

- Double pole circuit breakers isolate both wires, completely

isolating the supply and protecting you even where a reverse polarity situation exists.

- The final level of protection is a fuse in the plug of each item of equipment.

Above The pontoon pedestal has an RCD and over-current trip to protect each pontoon.

Above The extension cable should be checked each season. Your safety really does depend on it.

Above Mains power is safe provided it is correctly installed and the protection devices all work. Test the RCD occasionally by pressing the test button.

TIP

Don't overtighten the main cable clamp; it should be just tight enough to prevent the cable pulling through without crushing the wires. Open up the clamp when you check the plug to ensure there is no evidence of damage before re-closing it and assembling the plug again.

The earth system

The earth or (electrical) grounding of your boat is a mini-electrical system in its own right. For AC mains, safety is the overriding consideration, while for DC systems minimising the corrosion of metalwork immersed in sea water is the objective. When both systems are present, these requirements remain essential, but there's also an interaction between the two systems to consider.

Safety regulations

Recommendations issued in the USA by the American Boat and Yacht Council (ABYC), in the UK by the British Marine Electronics Association (BMEA) and in Europe by the European Recreational Craft Directive (RCD, not to be confused with residual current device) advise:

- Bonding together, or electrically connecting, the boat's major metalwork (engine, prop shaft, sea cocks and so on) that is in contact with the water.
- Joining the mains EARTH wire and the DC system's GROUND point (battery negative terminals) AND attaching both to the bonded metalwork.
- The maximum resistance between any two points in the earth system should be 1Ω.

This improves the safety on board vessels using mains power. The bonding of earth, ground and metalwork together ensures that everything is connected to the sea water's electrical potential (virtually earth in reality). If you don't have these connected, this can be serious if you also have:

- A badly corroded or resistive earth wire through the shore power connection.
- A piece of equipment that develops a wiring fault causing its case to become live.

In these situations, it is possible that you could find yourself completing the circuit between the (now live) case and a route back to earth via your body. Although this constitutes a leakage current, it only requires about 30mA passing through the heart to be potentially fatal.

Below and right **Bonding applies to metalwork in water. Metallic hull fittings should be bonded if your boat regularly has water in the bilge.**

A mains earth loop

With the recommendations being accepted, an earth loop now exists. This goes from your boat through the water via the metalwork (because of the AC and DC earth/ground connection) to your neighbour's boat. It comes back via their equivalent route to the pontoon pedestal, where it returns onto your vessel through the extension cable.

Although this is not a safety issue, one of the boats will be more 'anodic' than the other resulting in erosion, first of your sacrificial anode, then the other metalwork.

Breaking or blocking this loop

You can remove the earth loop and its potential consequences in one of two ways:

An isolation transformer

- This has the same voltage on its output terminals as its input ones. However, the terminals are

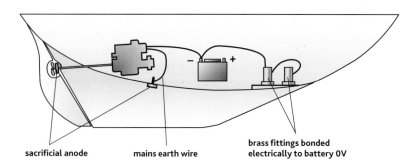

sacrificial anode   mains earth wire   brass fittings bonded electrically to battery 0V

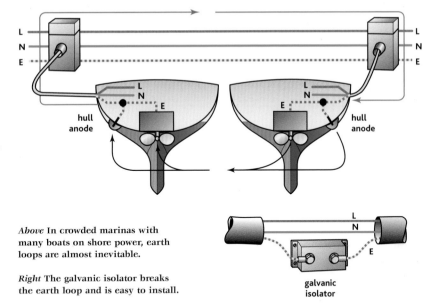

Above **In crowded marinas with many boats on shore power, earth loops are almost inevitable.**

Right **The galvanic isolator breaks the earth loop and is easy to install.**

galvanic
isolator

electrically isolated from each other, which makes the output, or boat side, appear as if it were not connected to shore power at all, hence there can be no earth loop.

☼ Your AC system's neutral and earth can now be connected on board at the transformer output's neutral wire. This in turn means your earth safety system no longer depends on the marina.

☼ The polarity of the shore system is no longer relevant as the transformer input can accept current in either polarity.

☼ On the down side, the transformers are heavy, bulky and quite expensive but, in some environments there is considerable overall benefit.

Galvanic isolator

☼ This device is a simple pair of high current diodes in parallel but connected the opposite way round (discussed in more detail

on pages 126–127). It is installed in the earth wire.

☼ The main requirement of the galvanic isolator is that it must never fail, as that would effectively disconnect the earth wire, the vessel's primary protection against faults. It

Below and left **The isolation transformer provides a complete break in a mains earth loop, so avoids the problem completely.**

therefore must be able to handle considerably more current than the on-board over-current trip or fuse device ratings so that, in a major fault, the trip reacts first, preventing damage to the isolator.

☼ Under normal circumstances, the voltage producing the earth loop current is so small it is unable to force its way through either of the diodes, so it is blocked, effectively breaking the loop.

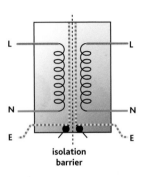

isolation
barrier

TIP

Fitting a galvanic isolator is highly recommended if you have mains on board. Make sure it is certified by one of the three marine associations, the BMEA for the UK, RCD for Europe and the ABYC for the USA and other nations. Their standards require the highest quality so safety is not compromised.

Galvanic and electrolytic corrosion

If two different metals in sea water (an electrolyte) are wired together, current will flow between them. The metal the current flows from, called the anode, dissolves over time in a process called galvanic corrosion. By contrast, if current is made to flow between two metals in, for example, an earth loop, the metal that the current flows from becomes the anode and will dissolve. This process is electrolytic corrosion.

Metals and their galvanic relationship

If a metal is placed in flowing sea water, it will 'sit' at a particular voltage potential with respect to ground. A second metal, different from the first, will sit at a different potential and, if they are bonded together, as advised by the ABYC, BMEA and the RCD, a simple battery is created and a current will flow between them.

- On board the boat, the current will flow from the cathode, the galvanically more positive metal, to the more negative anode, just as in a battery. The current will

then return through the sea water from the anode back to the cathode, corroding the anode.
- To protect the important bits of metalwork in contact with the sea water, including the propeller, shaft and sea cocks, another much more anodic (galvanically negative) metal is introduced below the waterline and bonded through the hull to the earth system. Because of its more negative position on the galvanic scale, this becomes the anode in the system and is eaten away. This so-called sacrificial anode is usually made of zinc. Once the

sacrificial anode is depleted it must be replaced. If not, its sacrificial role will be taken by a more important part – perhaps the propeller or a sea cock.
- Metalwork not electrically bonded to the earth system will not suffer from galvanic corrosion.

The Galvanic scale and how it applies

Zinc has an electropotential of around -1.1V. Compared to copper, various brass and bronze alloys and types of stainless steel, which sit at between -0.1V to -0.4V, it is much more negative and so offers itself as a natural anode.

Without this the other different metals attached to the hull would set up smaller, but no less destructive, currents between them because of the guidance (for mains safety reasons) to bond them all together.

One combination common on boats is aluminium plates with stainless bolts. There is about 0.8V between them in favour of the stainless, so the aluminium will become the corroding anode if it is regularly being covered by sea water.

Left Zinc is the most commonly used material for the sacrificial anode as, apart from magnesium, it is the most anodic material in the galvanic series. Magnesium is better suited to fresh-water boating and aluminium is a good compromise if your vessel is in both fresh and sea water throughout the season.

ADDITIONAL ANODES

Greater protection can be gained by suspending additional anodes into the water, ensuring a good connection via the wire to some point on the hull. Aluminium boats in particular are naturally prone to galvanic corrosion and will benefit from the extra anode. It is easy to check the state of the anode on the wire, to gain an indication of the state of the main anodes.

Above Anodes clamped to a propeller shaft will help protect the shaft and propeller from galvanic corrosion.

Electrolytic corrosion

Again this relates to all the metalwork bonded to the earth system. Electrolytic corrosion results from an external current being imposed or introduced into the system.

The outcome, in terms of corrosion, depends on which fitting becomes the anode because of the imposed direction of current flow. Currents will typically result from:

- The earth loop current, discussed on pages 126–127. If not blocked by a galvanic isolator, it will increase the natural corrosion of the sacrificial zinc anode quite significantly.
- Stray leakage currents from both the DC and AC system will find a path to earth (or back onto the boat) through the sea water via the zinc anode.

- An external voltage field already present in the water, particularly around marinas, will induce a current inside the hull, entering via a sea cock, passing through the bonding wire or strap (since it offers less resistance than the water) and exiting via the prop shaft, or its anode.

TIP

Aluminium and steel-hulled boats need plenty of sacrificial anode protection. Extra anodes, apart from those fitted on the hull, can be wired in to the grounding point and hung over the side. These are worth considering on fibre glass boats as well. They are low cost and, of course, very easy to check!

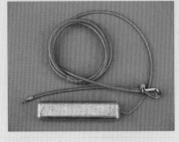

Installing a galvanic isolator

Electrically bonding all underwater metalwork, engine, internal metal tanks and the DC ground together improves safety when on-board AC mains is fitted. The addition of an inexpensive device, called a galvanic isolator, will both block any earth loop current that results from bonding this metalwork together, and improve protection from a fault in any mains voltage equipment.

A galvanic isolator is a pair of high current diodes connected together and encapsulated. They are attached to an aluminium casting, called a heatsink, to dissipate heat away from the assembly. Under normal operation there is no current flowing in the device, and therefore no heat is generated.

Diodes have been mentioned already, particularly in terms of battery switching circuits. The adverse characteristics of diodes are an advantage for this purpose. The diodes in galvanic isolators are connected in parallel, but the opposite way round, and are installed in the earth wire. The first function of this arrangement is very useful and the second, for safety reasons, is vital.

⚙ The diode is a semiconductor device with two terminals, the input being the anode and the output the cathode.

⚙ It will only pass current, the 'forward current', in one direction, from anode to cathode. If the cathode is at a higher voltage than the anode, ('reversed biased'), no current will flow.

⚙ The potential difference from anode to cathode must exceed the 'forward voltage drop' value, typically 0.7V, for forward current to flow.

⚙ This characteristic blocks earth loop leakage current because the loop voltage is so small it will never reach this value, so no earth leakage current can flow.

The device achieves this without compromising the earth wire's safety function. However, to install the galvanic isolator you have to cut the earth wire and connect each end to its two terminals.

⚙ By having the two diodes the opposite way round, the isolator allows DC leakage in either direction. AC leakage currents will pass through alternate diodes because AC current flows alternately in each direction.

⚙ An earth leakage current (as opposed to the earth loop current) will pass through once the voltage exceeds 0.7V in either direction. Once this current flows, the RCD will trip.

Protection from excess currents, including short circuit faults, requires a little more consideration. As these currents are AC, the pair of diodes will allow the fault current to pass through. The problem is that if the diodes fail they blow themselves apart, breaking the earth wire. This would remove the most important protection we have from the mains.

The solution is to have diodes capable of handling more current than would occur in a fault condition. Even in the worst-case scenario, the earth wire should melt before the diodes fail. In practice they are rated between 135 and 150 per cent above the main circuit breaker and can pass this level of current continuously, the heat generated being dissipated by the heatsink.

ABYC's latest guidelines mean manufacturers have to guarantee that the isolator is failsafe, the design

Below **Galvanic isolators are worth fitting if you have mains power on board.**

having been tested and certified as such. If the isolator meets this requirement, the monitoring circuits that were previously required are no longer needed and the unit becomes a fit and forget device.

Installation is essentially a simple process, but do follow the manufacturer's instructions:

- Disconnect the shore power completely before starting.
- Cut the earth wire close to where it enters the boat.
- With the appropriate connectors, join each end of the earth wire to a terminal on the isolator. It can go either way round.
- Mount in an area with reasonable air space such as a large locker, rather than a small cupboard.
- If advised, orientate the isolator so that the fins of the heatsink are vertical to improve airflow.

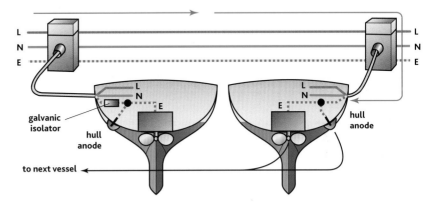

Above The galvanic isolator blocks any earth loop current from entering (or leaving) your vessel.

Below left As there are two back-to-back diodes in the basic isolator, it does not matter which way round the isolator is connected. Having said that, always read the installation instructions to check mounting orientation. The position of the isolator can be either side of the RCD, but again, check the installation instructions.

Below The isolator must be rugged enough to take the maximum short circuit current for the time it takes the main fuses to blow, without being damaged. In reality, provided the RCD works, current through the isolator will never reach this figure.

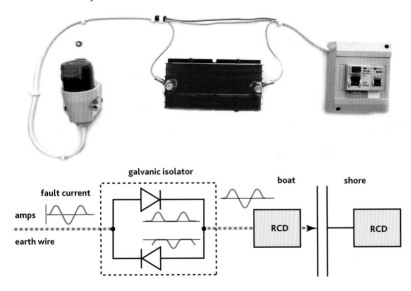

Voltage inverters

Away from shore power there are other ways to generate AC mains power. Voltage inverters generate mains voltage from a boat's batteries by inverting the supply from DC to AC and stepping up the voltage to the mains level. They are useful for low-power equipment such as phone and laptop chargers and some power tools, although with enough battery capacity there is technically no limit.

While most equipment installed on your boat will be designed to connect to the vessel's batteries, there will be other bits you bring with you from home such as mobile phones, computers and power tools. Because these were designed for the domestic environment, they rely on AC mains for their direct power source, or internal battery charging.

Voltage inverters will provide you with a ready source of mains and, at the lower power levels, they can be plugged in to a cigar lighter type socket as and when required.

Power ratings from about 300W up to as many kilowatts as you need are common at 110V, 220V or 240V AC.

Whilst they are electronically very complex inside their box, from an installation and use point of view, they are straightforward. There is a wide choice of quality, styles and capabilities ranging from simple standalone units, to high-power combined charger/inverter systems which require more permanent installation.

Types of inverters

Household mains voltage is a pure sine wave because of the way it is generated and so that all types of equipment will function correctly. Inverters recreate the mains voltage, but in practice there are three types according to how close their output wave form matches the ideal sine wave:

- **Square wave** output is the easiest to produce electronically, therefore the cheapest. It is a bit rudimentary, although items like phone chargers will work perfectly well. They will cause interference in other nearby equipment, particularly radios, so are not a good choice for the boating environment.

Left **The top of the range 'sine wave' inverters can power all types of mains equipment and have very high conversion efficiency.**

- **Modified square wave** (or quasi sine wave) inverters soften the edges of the output waveform and reduce interference considerably. They struggle driving electric motors but offer useful and good value inverters for most other equipment.
- **Sine wave** inverters are at the top end of the market and mimic the household type of mains very well, sometimes better. These will run anything without a problem and cause virtually no interference to other equipment. They are also more than 90 per cent efficient overall.
- **Combined charger/inverters** are probably the ultimate in both cost and performance, providing a fully automated and integrated system. With shore power available they switch to being a battery charger, while allowing the shore power through to your mains outlet sockets. Away from shore, they revert to being an inverter, providing AC mains voltages from the batteries.

Can the batteries cope?

The inverter power is derived from your batteries and it is essential to appreciate the impact their use will have. Generally inverters are 85 to 90 per cent efficient in terms of power conversion, but the biggest factor to appreciate is the current drawn from the batteries. To illustrate this, consider powering a small electric kettle with a 1kW element. The output power provided by the inverter, plus the efficiency losses will be taken from the batteries, equating in this example to around 1175W.

As power equals volts x amps then to provide 1175W of power for the kettle the inverter will need to draw around 50A from a 24V battery bank (1175W/24V) and a massive 98A from a 12V bank. As a result, battery capacity, cable sizing and connectors are all important factors in delivering this amount of power. For power boats, power consumption will be less of an issue, as the engines will be running when underway and the alternators doing the work, but the impact on sail boats is significant.

The inverters themselves also consume a small but appreciable current if left switched on in standby mode. Even for the smallest 300W units this can be up to 0.4A.

TIP

Take care when using a cigar lighter socket to plug in the inverter. The wire thickness from the inverter to the plug will be a suitable diameter for the maximum current it has to handle, but don't assume the same is true for the wire to your cigar lighter socket.

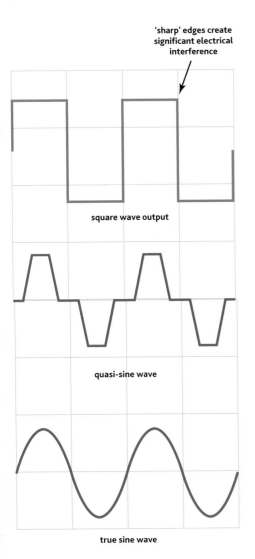

'sharp' edges create significant electrical interference

square wave output

quasi-sine wave

true sine wave

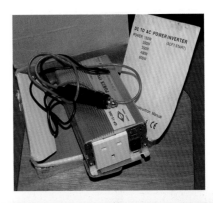

Right There are a number of low-power inverters on the market, which are ideal for powering chargers for mobile phones and other equipment.

Left The three output waveforms: square, quasi-sine and sine wave.

Bottom Small inverters are very useful but beware of the current pulled from the batteries (6.4A at 12V), even for a laptop.

Voltage inverters 2

You can choose between a simple set up where AC outlet sockets powered from the inverter are totally separate from those powered from the shore power system. If you want to link the inverter into your existing shore power system a special switch is needed to absolutely ensure the mains is provided by either the inverter OR the shore power, but never both.

Installation

Deciding the type and power output of the inverter is the first step so, as with the DC system, a power audit of the equipment is necessary. As regards the output side, remember this is mains power and is just as dangerous as in a household environment. You may need to have this part installed by an approved marine electrician, and you must ensure that you are protected from the inverter output by circuit breakers and an RCCB in the earth wire, just as with a shore power supply.

All units have some degree of overload protection, but that is current-related and does not protect you from the high voltage.

Wiring considerations

For permanent installations, the instruction manual will indicate the wire size required for the battery connection and this must be adhered to. The wire and its connections must be able to cope with the

Below **With enough battery power and a generator, a fully integrated inverter system will power all the domestic appliances on board.**

inverter running continuously at full power, plus a safety margin for overload conditions. On the mains side, the electrical installation standards for the country in which your boat is located or registered will need to be observed, and you may need certification of the work for insurance purposes.

Integrated or independent?

A fully integrated system allows all mains equipment to be supplied either from shore power or from the inverter. The two systems (and even a third AC source from a generator) will be combined before the consumer unit in which the circuit breakers are located. A special switch will allow selection between the sources, ensuring that only one supply is providing the power at any time. The switch (typically a rotary type) is a 'break before make, double pole' type which, as you rotate the selector, disconnects or breaks the source currently being used before connecting or making contact to the new source.

The double pole means that both the hot (live) and neutral wires are switched by the same action.

In larger power systems, suppression capacitor banks may be needed to prevent arching (or sparks flying) as the switching action is made, because of the sudden interruption of power.

In an independent system, the equipment using shore power is kept separate. The high-power consumers

such as the immersion heater in the calorifier, electric kettles and space heaters are in the shore power system with their own direct connections. The lower-power kit such as radios, televisions and laptop chargers can be plugged into the mains outlet sockets on the inverter side. This approach removes the need for the selector switch, but both systems will need their own residual current device (RCD) protection and consumer unit.

Locating the inverter

Once fitted, you do not need routine access to the inverter, so it can be fitted behind a panel, out of the way with just the controls accessible. Having said that:

- ✪ It must be in a dry environment, away from the warmth and direct vibration of the engine(s).
- ✪ Inverters can be quite heavy so the mounting position must be strong enough.
- ✪ Good ventilation is essential; when working hard, a fair amount of heat will be generated. A 2KW, 90 per cent efficient inverter will generate up to 200W of excess heat at full power. Even with a fan blowing, this heat needs somewhere to go.
- ✪ Inverters should be positioned away from other direct sources of heat and direct sunlight.

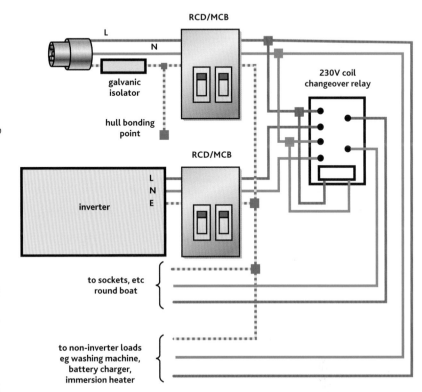

Below The charger/inverter automatically switches from the ship's batteries to shore power when available. Either way, the on-board mains supply is maintained.

Above In a fully integrated system the changeover switch is automatic, detecting the presence of shore power. When it is available, more power-hungry equipment can be used.

TIP

When considering purchasing an inverter, be very realistic and 'generous' in terms of the amount of power you will want to draw from it. Probably add 50 per cent to your estimate to allow for expansion of its use. They are so good that you will think of all sorts of other equipment you can bring on board once it is fitted.

Generators

Petrol and diesel generators have been around for a long time and offer immediate access to large amounts of power. In recent years, perhaps because of competition from alternative power sources, they have improved considerably, particularly in noise reduction. Transatlantic and world rallies have put them in the spotlight with regard to long-term reliability and repair and maintenance issues.

The first decision is whether you want a full system supplying mains-quality AC to your outlet sockets, or a DC system for topping up the batteries. In this case, more batteries and a good inverter keep the peace in the evening and a smaller, cheaper generator recharges your batteries later.

A generator is a diesel or petrol engine driving an alternator to produce the DC or AC output. Generators producing AC mains need to do so at the correct frequency (50Hz or 60Hz), which is achieved by running the engine at a constant speed. More electrical loading means that more fuel is therefore needed to maintain the constant speed.

Permanently installed generators usually need to be supplied with water for cooling, a fuel supply and an exit for the exhaust. A 4kW diesel generator consumes around 1 litre of diesel per hour and provides more than enough power for small to medium-sized boats.

Generator ratings

Generators are rated in VA, volts x amps (or KVA), known as 'apparent power', rather than watts or kW. This is because the 'real' power (watts) that produces useful work is adjusted by a multiplier, called the 'Power Factor', or PF.

$$\text{Real power (kW)} = \text{Apparent power (KVA)} \times \text{PF}$$

The PF depends entirely on the type of equipment being powered. A motor, for example, would have a PF of around 0.8 whereas a water heater element would be nearer 1.

How much power?

After an audit of your likely power needs, you also have to consider extra capability for equipment with motors (such as fridges, freezers and air conditioning units) as they have high start-up currents which will activate overload trips if the generator is running near full capacity. As a rule, add 10 per cent to your total power requirement for that and divide by an average power factor of 0.9 to arrive at the KVA requirement. Finally, consider the next size up to allow for future enhancements to your boat and home comforts on board.

Left Larger generators are permanently installed and are often the primary source of the boat's electrical power. Here, the total power system has its own space next to the engine compartment.

Types of generator

The first decision is whether you want it to be portable or permanent, and the second is fuel.

- **Petrol-powered portable** generators are small and fully enclosed in a case. These are quieter than their diesel counterparts, but you need to carry petrol. They are constant speed, four stroke engines driving the alternator. The primary power output is AC mains, but there is often a 12V DC charging output as well. Power ratings are between 600VA and 2KVA.

- **Diesel-powered** generators will always be heavier so will probably be permanently installed and of higher power. They can then take fuel from your main diesel tank and have a cooling water supply installed along with a fitted exhaust outlet.

- **Gen-Sets** are another name for diesel generators but traditionally these are used for larger installations, often in the engine room. They are intended for more or less constant use, providing power for a full array of domestic appliances and other electrical comforts.

- **Gen-Verters** are an alternative approach, with a diesel engine driving a DC generator outputting (normally) 24V or 48VDC. This is fed directly to an inverter, converting it to AC for mains equipment, including a mains charger to charge the batteries. The advantage is greater efficiency as the engine speed does not have to be constant, and it is run at a speed to achieve maximum fuel efficiency for the given electrical loading. The AC inverter synthesises the sine wave output, at the correct frequency and 'power factor corrected'. This maintains a PF of very near 1 irrespective of the type of equipment being powered – again, an improvement in efficiency.

Left **In this generator, most of what you need access to for daily checks has been designed to be at or near the front.**

Right **The Gen-Verter is a compact solution for providing large amounts of mains power.**

Left **Whilst this small generator looks highly accessible in the showroom, once installed in a locker it may be a different story!**

Generators 2

A permanent installation is a major undertaking, with the boat needing to be ashore to fit the skin fittings. Generators need to be housed with access to key points for servicing and maintenance, have sufficient airflow and have access to an external starter battery. Larger vessels will have room in the engine area, otherwise a locker may be a suitable location.

The installation

Diesel generators will need all the same considerations as your main engine(s) in terms of air, fuel and water supplies, along with exhaust disposal. The generator manufacturers have gone to great lengths to place important components together for ease of access and servicing. Don't forget the case has to go back on once you have finished. They are usually split down the middle, but you still have to feed half of it round the back of the unit and get at the latches. Professional installers estimate three to four days from start to finish to install a diesel generator.

Routine checks are the same as for the main engine. The oil dipstick, fuel pump and water impeller housing all need to be accessible for daily inspections and routine maintenance. A good location for all these services may not be close to the starter battery, but the starter current will be a lot less than the main engine so this should not be a major issue.

Mounting plate

There will be slight vibration from the generator, so the base needs to be very rigid so as not to act as a sounding board, amplifying any noise. Thin bulkheads nearby may also resonate once the generator is running, so again, these may need stiffening. Of course, you will not discover this problem until you have finished the installation and started it up for the first time.

Air intake

The air supply is crucial for diesel engines. The volume available and the temperature both have a significant effect on performance. The air intake must not become obstructed by fenders or sail covers

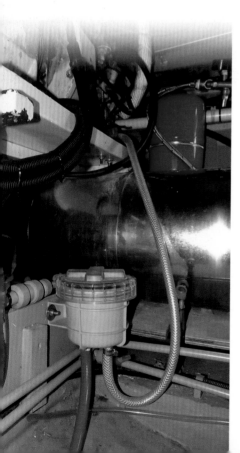

Left The water inlet filter is easily accessible. If the engine and generator primary fuel filters are also accessible, fuel could be supplied from either source via a transfer valve should one filter become blocked.

and the incoming air temperature must be below 40°C. This may be an issue if locating it in the engine bay, in which case, an air feed from outside will be necessary.

Cooling water

A completely separate system from the engine is always recommended for cooling water, hence the need for two skin fittings. Smaller generators are direct cooled, while others have a heat exchanger between the sea water and the closed cooling systems. If the unit is installed below the waterline an anti-syphon valve, high up, needs to be included along with an inlet filter, also above the waterline. Generators have an impeller pump, just as your main engine, and the same care and maintenance needs to be afforded to this.

Exhaust

The cooling water exits via the exhaust elbow and the exhaust hose should go to the outside via a water trap and silencer box (or combined unit). The outlet skin fitting is usually underwater to further reduce the noise.

Fuel system

Again, ideally, the generator should have its own system. Clean fuel is essential, so filters are an important part of the system, which includes:
- Fuel pick-up pipe into the main tank (or dedicated tank on larger vessels).

- An additional low pressure electric fuel pump is recommended by some manufacturers.
- Coarse fuel filter and water trap followed by a shut-off valve.
- Fine fuel filter nearer the generator position, ideally with a one-way valve included in the housing.
- Second shut-off valve at the input point on the generator.
- Return feed and shut-off valve back to the tank.

Electrics

An external starter battery is required. If you do not install a dedicated one, it is common to take the generator starting power from the domestic batteries. If you use the main engine starter battery you could run a new, separate, low-power mains charger from the generator output to top it up while the unit is running.

Control unit

The shore power changeover switch and starter controls are usually positioned near the navigation area. Finally, the mains output is fed into the consumer unit and the earth wire to a separate RCCB.

Right **The exhaust water trap is the final element before the skin fitting.**

Below right **Ideally the fine fuel filter will be easy to change. This is the one that dirty fuel will block.**

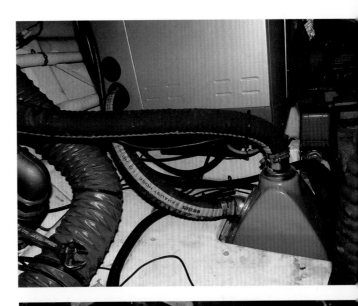

Below left **Large rubber mounts reduce the generator noise considerably and prevent resonance in the adjacent panels.**

Below right **The control panel has a 'break before make' changeover switch.**

TIP

There is a growing tendency to have the generators produce a suitable battery charging voltage rather than mains as greater overall efficiency can be achieved. The mains is then produced by a voltage inverter.

Networks

Marine networks – NMEA0183

Enabling instruments to talk to each other via a network opens up lots of opportunities to expand on the data acquired by individual sensors. While this is relatively easy for individual manufacturers to achieve, a brilliant move in the 1980s saw manufacturers creating an industry standard, so that any item could talk to any other.

Above One of the main driving forces behind establishing an industry wide communication standard was to enable position to be transferred from the GPS to the radio. DSC/VHF radios can then transmit the vessel's position in a distress situation.

Before the standard

It was always useful to have additional displays at another location on the boat repeating the data acquired by an instrument. But depth, boat speed and wind information for example, could only be repeated if additional displays were directly wired to each instrument. The introduction of a network greatly simplifies the wiring and allows different information from several instruments to be displayed on one repeater unit.

NMEA0183

The National Maritime Electronics Association's common protocol developed in the 1980s is known as NMEA0183. It became adopted across the industry and marked the start of systems integration.

In simplistic terms, data is assembled in a standard format by the instrument and given an identifying tag dependent on what the data is (boat speed, GPS position, depth and so on). The packet of data, known as a sentence, is transmitted repeatedly onto the network. Other instruments can then read the data as appropriate. A depth gauge, for instance, will only display data contained in a 'depth sentence' and will ignore all other sentences.

The protocol is limited in several different ways:

- ⚙ **Only one 'talker'** is allowed on the network. A 'talker' is an instrument that transmits data. A GPS, for instance, can send data

Below NMEA0183 is effectively a 'one direction' star network with one transmitter, or 'talker' sending out a range of data. The receivers, or 'listeners', pick out the data they want by looking for the correct sentence 'tag'.

including position, speed over ground (SOG), course over ground (COG) and cross track error (XTE) for other instruments to read and use or display. Because NMEA0183 is an unsynchronised system, there is no control over the timing of when data is sent. Data from multiple 'talkers' would inevitably clash, hence the limitation to only one 'talker'.

- ⚙ **Up to three 'listeners'** can be connected to the one 'talker'. A 'listener' is an instrument that will

BAUD RATE

Digital data, in its most basic form, is represented either by a '1' or an '0', known as a 'bit'. This could be that a voltage signal is present, representing a '1', or not present, representing a '0'; more commonly, a higher level is a '1' and a lower level is a '0'. However it is achieved electronically, it ends up as a stream of '1' or '0' bits being sent down the wire or through the air by Wi-Fi, Bluetooth etc. The 'Baud rate' is the number of 'bits' transmitted per second.

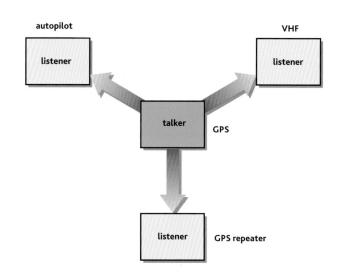

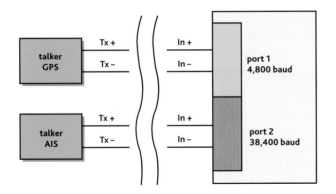

Left Additional ports, on a multi-function display for instance, allow more talkers. Each port can be set to the appropriate baud rate according to the equipment manual. AIS will need 38,400 baud, other instruments 4,800.

Below The 'baud rate' setting is found in the menu structure.

Bottom If the NMEA0183 network becomes overloaded, unused 'sentences' can be turned off.

receive the sentences. A VHF/DSC radio becomes a 'listener' when connected to a GPS and will accept position and time data sent by the GPS. This will be updated every few seconds as the GPS repeatedly sends the same sentence with the latest data.

⚙ **One or more 'NMEA ports'** are often included in instruments and displays to expand the basic capability; these are configured in software via the menu. Each port can have a different baud rate set (number of digital 'bits' per second, typically 4,800 and 38,400). Unwanted sentences can also be removed to declutter the network.

Below Don't be daunted by the random looking wires sprouting from the power cable. Each one has a function and is described in the manual.

Which wire is which?

As there is no connector detailed in the NMEA specification, there may be up to ten differently coloured wires in the system. Most, if not all, of these will be for the NMEA ports, with a pair of wires associated with each port function. The approach for a 'bi-directional' port capable of transmitting or receiving data is as follows:

⚙ **Two wires for transmit.** Data being sent to the network (by a 'talker') will be transmitted down a wire labelled 'Tx +' (or 'NMEA out +') and the return path is labelled 'Tx-' (or 'NMEA out-').

⚙ **Two wires for receive.** Similarly, incoming data will be received from the network by a 'listener' via wires labelled 'Rx +' (or 'NMEA in +') and 'Rx -' (or 'NMEA in -').

⚙ **A second bi-directional port,** if included will have the same arrangement, using another pair of wires.

⚙ **Occasionally, a third port,** usually configurable only as an input or output, will have the last two remaining wires. They will become transmit '+' and '–' or receive '+' and '–' as appropriate.

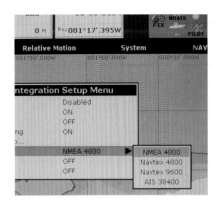

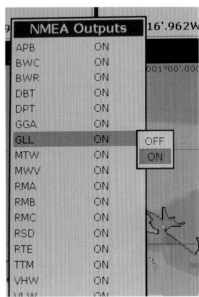

Talking to each other

In standard form NMEA0183 can achieve excellent results, despite its limitations. In this example four pieces of equipment from three manufacturers handle networked data. The wire connections are simple and are detailed in the respective manuals, along with the sentences that will be used. If anything, the most difficult aspect is finding a suitable connector for the thin wires.

The only set-up required once the connections are made is to check that the baud rate from the GPS is set to 4,800, the rate specified for the 'listeners':

○ In this case the Garmin GPS128 is the 'talker', sending position, time, date, waypoint (WPT) information and cross track error (XTE) out onto the network every few seconds.

○ The Raymarine autopilot takes in XTE once a 'GOTO waypoint' or 'ROUTE' is initiated. XTE is the distance your current position is from the line joining your start point to the waypoint and is the only information the autopilot needs to steer by. It alters course so as to keep XTE to a minimum.

○ The Nasa VHF/DSC radio reads position, time and date. This will be available in the event of receiving a DSC position request or sending a distress alert, which will include your position and the time you were at that position.

○ The Nasa GPS repeater reads position, time, WPT and XTE information. It is able to display latitude and longitude, or a rolling road image, along with waypoint distance, bearing and time to go (TTG) information.

Connecting up

○ The Garmin GPS128 is slightly unusual as it uses the ground (black) wire for its power supply 0V and the NMEA 'out -'. The NMEA 'out +' is shown as the blue wire. A connector block is arranged so that each of these can be joined to the three pairs coming from the autopilot, radio and repeater.

○ The autopilot computer has clearly labelled screw terminals on the edge of the unit. A multi-core signal cable is routed from the connector block to the pilot control unit location. Two of the cores are chosen and the colours noted on the wiring diagram.

○ The autopilot control unit is remote from the cockpit mounted pilot head (the human interface).

Below **The GPS sends out the data needed by the other equipment. Even with this basic unit, waypoints and routes can easily be set.**

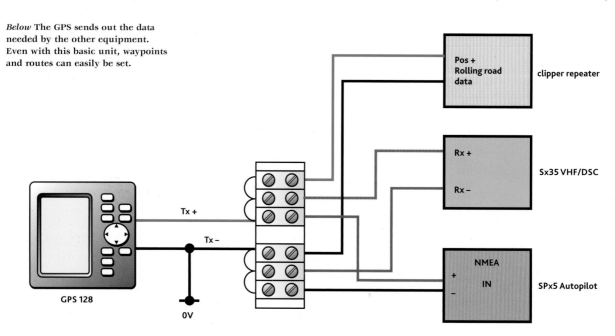

These are linked by Raymarine's own SeaTalk1 interface. The control unit will 'bridge' the NMEA data to the pilot head via the SeaTalk1 interface.

○ The VHF/DSC radio has a brown wire for 'Rx+' and a thin red wire for 'Rx-' (not the red 12V supply wire). This unit is close enough to the connector block to be wired in directly.

○ The GPS repeater in the cockpit needs another multi-core signal cable to be routed. Again, the chosen colours are noted on the wiring diagram.

NMEA sentences

The GPS sends the following NMEA sentences (see the list in Appendix 5 pages 182–183):

○ GGA, GLL, GSA, GSV, RMB, RMC, RTE, WPL and BOD. It also sends some Garmin proprietary sentences which are not recognised or used by other manufacturers.

○ The radio reads RMC.

○ GPS repeater reads RMB, RMC and GSA.

○ The autopilot reads GGA, GLL, RMB (which contains the XTE data) and RMC. It also transmits HDG, heading information from the fluxgate compass, but only over the SeaTalk1 network to the pilot head where it can be displayed.

Setting baud rate in the GPS

This can be found in the interface menu on the main page. Provided RTCM/NMEA is selected, you have the option to change the NMEA baud rate if it is not already set to 4,800.

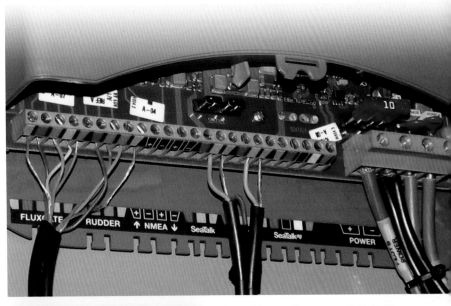

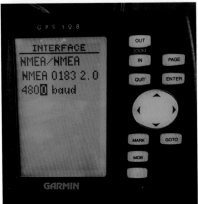

Above This autopilot accepts NMEA0183 or 2000 (see pages 144–145). The 0183 connector is clearly visible and the link to the pilot head is via the SeaTalk network.

Left Check that the talker is set to the correct data (baud) rate. As this is an older unit, it only goes up to 9,600 baud, but that is not an issue in this system.

Below left The GPS repeater unit can display position information or progress to the waypoint data once a 'GOTO Waypoint' is activated.

TIP

Before adding more instruments, decide where you spend most of your time when at sea and put them there. In my case, sitting in the companion way is my favourite spot (I am a great believer in self-steering kit!) so the chart plotter, autopilot head and instrument repeaters are in a panel there.

Multiplexers and converters

To overcome the limitations of NMEA0183, there is now a small but astute after-market industry which provides products to enhance the basic system. These include multiplexers, converters, buffers, boosters and many more. While some manufacturers retain proprietary standards for their own products, they or a third party provide converters to NMEA and other widely used networks including Wi-Fi and Bluetooth.

Multiplexers allow more 'talkers'

Multiplexers combine several inputs into a single output, allowing a number of 'talker' instruments to share one resource, in this case the NMEA0183 network. The electronics and software in the multiplexer collates the data from individual instruments and sends it to a single output for transmission onto the 0183 network. Multiplexers solve the two main limitations of NMEA0183 by increasing the number of 'talkers' and allowing different baud rates.

⚙ **Four-way multiplexers** have four inputs and one output. Each of the multiplexer inputs is a 'listener' and has a 'talker' instrument connected to it.

Below and right Data from four talkers can be combined into a single data stream.

The data from each input is temporarily stored in a buffer and the multiplexer combines all the buffered data and sends it as a single data stream to the output. This output is the only talker directly connected to the network.

⚙ **Data rates** for each of the four inputs and the one output are configurable. The inputs can be set to different baud rates to cope with different 'talker'

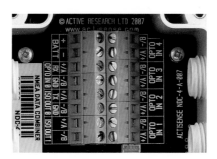

requirements. Typical rates are 4,800 and 38,400 but others are available. The output would normally be set to the higher baud rate to ensure no data is lost.

Who is a talker and who needs to listen?

Most marine instruments are talkers. In the previous example of a basic network the autopilot, if set in wind steer mode, would have been capable of maintaining the boat's angle to the wind had wind data been available. However, the GPS was the only talker allowed, so that was not possible. Introducing a multiplexer would enable both the GPS and the wind instrument to provide data. The pilot could then use the MVW sentence (transferring

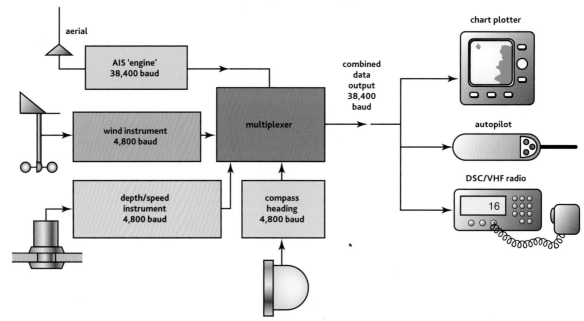

Apparent Wind Angle and Speed data) generated by the wind instrument to maintain wind angle, or steer to a waypoint using the cross track error sentence from the GPS, depending on the mode selected.

One relatively recent type of marine electronics that still largely uses NMEA0183 is the Automatic Identification System (AIS). Data transmitted from other vessels, such as position, speed and heading, can be displayed relative to your own. Because of the amount of data, AIS needs 38,400 baud to get the full benefit. The multiplexer is ideal for combining this with 4,800 baud data from instruments.

Multi-function displays can show

Right **The buffer increases the signal strength to allow up to six listeners from one talker.**

Below **Once the NMEA0183 data is processed by the multiplexer, the format can be converted into NMEA2000 format or standard, and connected into that network.**

THIRD PARTY CONVERTERS

The converter itself works with all manufacturers' equipment but you may need a cable adapter for some. This adapter allows the NMEA2000 output to plug into Raymarine's STNG socket.

just about anything you choose. They often help the NMEA0183 situation by having two, and sometimes three, ports. One can be set to 38,400 baud specifically for AIS, with the second set to receive the output of the multiplexer, containing the data from four other instruments.

Converters

A large range of converters is available – some made by major marine electronics manufacturers, others by third party vendors. Manufacturers occasionally find the limitations of NMEA0183 too great, so they retain proprietary network

protocols between their own instruments and displays to get maximum performance. A small amount of capability will be lost after conversion to NMEA.

Other types of converters will convert data from one network protocol to another, for instance, NMEA0183 to NMEA2000. Converters allow you to retain existing equipment (using NMEA0183) and convert their data to NMEA2000 to communicate with new devices using the newer network protocol. For example, a brand-new chart plotter can still display wind, speed and depth data from older instruments.

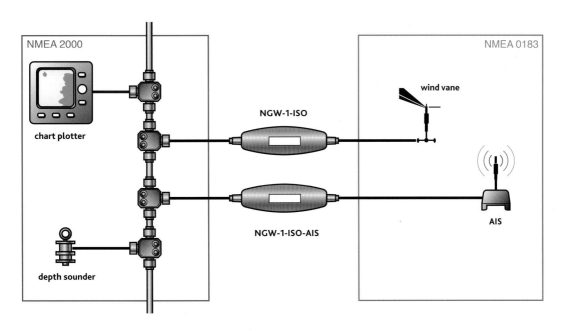

Marine networks – NMEA2000

NMEA2000 is vastly superior to 0183, with different architecture and performance, allowing each unit to be both a talker and listener. Data transfer is fully synchronised, with a baud rate of 250,000 bits per second, so several orders of magnitude more data can be handled. However, 0183 is still incorporated in the latest multi-function displays.

NMEA2000 (often referred to as NMEA2K or N2K) is based on a Controller Area Network (CAN) principle. It is a bi-directional, fully synchronised protocol giving enormous flexibility. Data is structured in a pre-determined way and attached to a parameter group number (PGN). Data packets are error checked, with delivery confirmed to ensure a high level of reliability. Each PGN is given a priority between 0 and 7 so that rapidly-changing parameters get priority and are assigned a higher transmit repetition rate.

In terms of the connector style, the DeviceNet Micro-C M12 5-pin is the favourite, but is not universal. Several manufacturers have developed their own designs but there is always an adapter cable available to link units from different producers into the network. The network cable structure has two parts, a backbone and drop cables.

The backbone

The backbone cable can be considered as the data and power highway. All data gets to and from the instruments, displays, transducers and other units via the backbone, which also supplies 12V power to the system, greatly simplifying installation.

- **Access to the backbone** is achieved by breaking it and introducing a 'T' connector or a multi-way socket block. Both retain the backbone integrity and enable 'drop cables' from individual items of equipment to be plugged in.
- **Power** has to be provided to the backbone, also via a 'T' piece connector. This is from a 12V supply only (9–16V) and should be fused at 5A. The limit of 12V is to protect equipment not designed to take 24V.
- **The maximum length** of the backbone is 200m (650ft),

depending on how much equipment is attached.
- **Terminator resistors** are required at each end of the backbone. These can be inserted into the last 'T' piece at either end and are one of the standard parts available from the manufacturers.

Drop (spur) cables

A variety of these are available, all plugging in to the backbone via a 'T' piece or connector block. You will need:
- **Power spur.** This is from your 12V DC distribution panel via a switch and 5A fuse or circuit breaker.
- **Equipment connection spurs.** These plug into a socket on the back of the equipment. Spurs with open wires at one end are also available.
- **Adaptors to other networks.** The manufacturer's proprietary connector at one end and DeviceNet connector at the other.

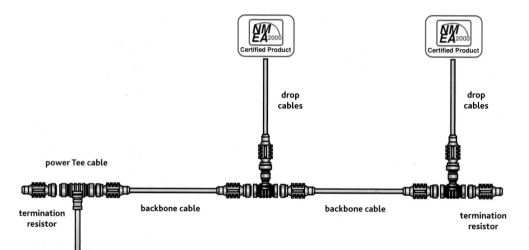

Left **The backbone structure of NMEA2000 makes wiring complex systems straightforward, especially as it includes the power supply for all but the largest, relatively power-hungry equipment.**

images courtesy of NMEA

Power consumption – the LEN number

As the backbone supplies power to the units on the network, you have to bear in mind the total power consumption of all the equipment. To help, each item quotes a load equivalency number (LEN). One LEN equates to 50mA so an instrument quoting 3LEN draws around 150mA.

Because of voltage drops in the backbone, the total length is determined to a large extent by the total LEN. For example, a 60m (197ft) backbone can supply 100LEN, longer backbones less. Relatively power-hungry units like chart plotters will have their own power supply arrangements so their LEN is usually just one.

Balancing the backbone

Ideally the power should enter the backbone in the middle of the equipment run. While this is not essential, if power enters at one end, the instrument at the other end may not get enough volts from the supply because of the voltage drop along the backbone length.

CONNECTING IN TO THE BACKBONE

1: Generic view of the DeviceNet 'T' piece.
2: Raymarine's version (single 'T').
3: Backbone and a three-way drop down connector block.
4: Multiple DeviceNet 'T' pieces. One has the yellow power supply cable for the whole backbone.

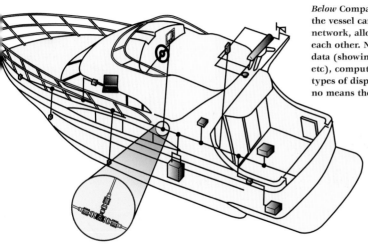

Below Compatible equipment all around the vessel can be linked via the NMEA2000 network, allowing them to communicate with each other. Navigation instruments, engine data (showing temperatures, pressures, speeds etc), computers, autopilot control and many types of displays are the more typical but by no means the only types of equipment.

Below Each end of the backbone will require a terminator resistor. The Raymarine and DeviceNet versions are shown here.

High speed data networks

The data rate demanded by radars, fishfinders and high-resolution cameras requires a network with speeds way above NMEA2000. The industry has turned to Ethernet (Local Area Network or LAN) for this, with data rates of up to 1 Gigabaud. While some marine manufacturers have stayed with marinised versions of the standard RJ45 connector, others have developed their own connectors.

Protocol

Data is assembled in packets called 'frames' in this context. As with most networks, each unit is given a specific address; however, there are two main differences from NMEA2000:

- ✪ Ethernet is a star configuration, with each piece of equipment connected directly to a 'switch' that functions as the data distribution controller. This virtually eliminates the chance of data collision even when the network is heavily loaded.
- ✪ You cannot mix and match manufacturers. Although Ethernet is a standard protocol, equipment that requires Ethernet is so sophisticated that it is manufacturer specific. The radar, for instance, and any displays have to be supplied by the same company.

Why the speed?

Multi-function displays (MFDs) have become the central hub for information on the boat. Their capabilities are quite staggering, especially if more than one is fitted. With a fully loaded system, the MFD will be managing a huge amount of data, hence the need for speed.

On Ethernet:

- ✪ Radar
- ✪ Fishfinders (digital sounder modules, or DSM)
- ✪ Standard, thermal or infra red cameras
- ✪ Weather data
- ✪ Second or more MFDs
- ✪ Chart data.

Below The data network 'switches' collect inputs from radar, fishfinders and other equipment requiring the high data rates, and distribute to multi-function displays.

In addition via NMEA0183 and 2000:

- ✪ Large array of standard instruments and other data
- ✪ Autopilot
- ✪ Differential GPS
- ✪ Digital switching modules
- ✪ AIS
- ✪ Navtex
- ✪ VHF/DSC radio.

Wi-Fi and Bluetooth:

- ✪ Links to tablets and mobiles
- ✪ Music systems.

Crossover couplers and network switches

A single source of Ethernet-based data, for example a radar, will plug straight into the MFD's Ethernet socket. There is often a second Ethernet socket, so if you have a second MFD on board you can daisy chain it from the first. As this involves connecting two Ethernet devices directly this needs to be done via a crossover coupler (unless a special cable is available).

The crossover coupler ensures the transmit pair of wires from one MFD go to the receive pair of the other and vice versa. Once the two displays are connected, you can share radar and chart data between them. You will probably have to set one as a master MFD but, other than that, the two displays share the radar and chart resources.

A system of three or more devices will need a network switch, with

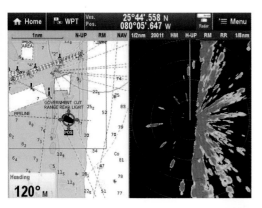

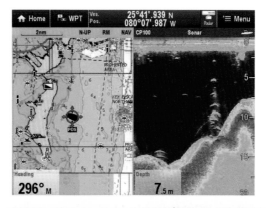

Below The multi-function display needs to handle all the different networks if it is to display instrument data (older NMEA0183 and newer NMEA2000) and images from radar, fishfinders and cameras.

Above and above right Each MFD can have its own screen set-up, pulling in the data from the network switches.

each piece of equipment plugged in to it. Network switches receive data from one network device, then transmit the message only to the device for which the message is intended. This makes the switch more intelligent than a hub, which transmits the message to every device in the network.

It also means data collision can only happen between the individual device and the switch, which the switch will sort out. It cannot happen between devices, as with the backbone approach of NMEA2000, because they all communicate via the switch.

It is possible to daisy chain the network switches if you don't have enough ports for all your kit. Irrespective of how many units are plugged in, there is no set up required (apart from choosing a master MFD, which is retained until you make a change) as the system is completely plug-and-play. All peripherals are automatically detected and readily accessible once they are connected.

Left Information is distributed around the vessel to each helm position and at the navigation station down below. Each display can be set up as required.

Capturing what's left

Multi-function displays (MFD) are set up to handle all manner of data, given the right NMEA PGN or sentence. You can capture other useful data from around the boat with appropriate sensors and conversion electronics. There are also excellent instrument-style displays with multi-page capability if you want to save the cost of an MFD.

Capturing engine data

To collect engine data for sending on to the network, the appropriate sensors have to be in place to feed a usable signal to the conversion electronics. The output will then be NMEA0183 or 2000 compliant. Four typical measurements to keep tabs on are:

⊛ **Engine cooling temperature.** The sensor needs to be a gauge sender rather than an alarm sender (see pages 108–109). Your engine dealer should be able to source one to fit in the same position on the engine if you need to swap. The NMEA converter will take a connection from the sender's 'gauge' terminal (picked up on the sender itself or at the gauge, if you fit that as well). A '0V' wire from the engine block or gauge will also be required as appropriate. The alarm function should also be in the new sender (the second terminal) so that can be wired into the existing system as before, still retaining the audible warning.

Above The multi-function display and some multi-screen instruments have an impressive appearance when displaying data.

⊛ **Engine oil pressure.** This is the same scenario.
⊛ **Exhaust temperature.** Generally this needs a separate sender and converter. There are several on the market with NMEA output.
⊛ **Engine revs.** These are taken off the 'W' terminal either at the rev counter (tachometer) or at the alternator.

Above and below Analogue data from engine sensors needs converting first to digital, and then formatting into network compatible data.

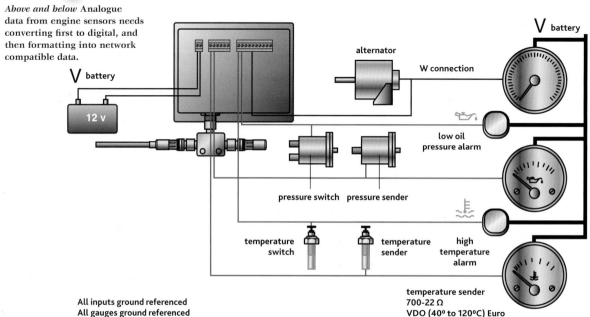

All inputs ground referenced
All gauges ground referenced

Fuel and water tank levels

If you already have gauges, on older boats it is likely that the senders fitted to the tanks are the resistive type and these can still be used. You just have to connect a wire from the sender to the conversion module, along with a 0V connection. For new installations, there is a choice:

- A resistive sender installed in each tank with wires going to the conversion module.
- A smart sender, which has the NMEA conversion built in. These are very convenient as the sender cable plugs straight in to the network and, assuming it is an NMEA2000 sender, the 12V supply is also provided from the backbone. Costwise, this may be a slightly cheaper overall option.

Battery voltage and current data

Engine data modules often include at least one battery voltage input taken from the alternator. If you want more, specific modules cater for several battery banks and at least one current measurement from a current shunt or Hall effect sensor (see pages 110–112).

Automatic Identification System (AIS)

AIS needs a display and a GPS input to function, but your system may already have these, particularly GPS. If you have (or are intending to install) an MFD, you will be able to overlay AIS on top of the chart and/or radar – an ideal solution.

Without an MFD, several multi-page instrument displays include an AIS display page. In these situations, all you need to buy is an AIS receiver module (or transmit and receive module in a transceiver version), which puts the data onto the network, making it available for your existing display. Both NMEA0183 or 2000 systems work just as well.

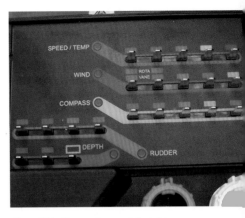

Above This Raymarine module takes in six transducers (wind, speed, temperature, heading, depth and rudder angle) and presents their data onto the NMEA2000 backbone.

Right A smaller module accepts speed, depth and temperature transducers.

Above and right Fuel flow is monitored by the transducer, and the interface module converts the data to NMEA2000 format and plugs into the backbone.

Bringing it all together

If you are starting a system from scratch it is probably better to go for an NMEA2000 approach, as the backbone makes individual unit installation much easier. If you already have NMEA0183-based equipment, a multi-plexer and converter (to NMEA2000) will keep it compatible with the new kit. The addition of radar will require an Ethernet-type network as well for the high data rates involved.

Cable routing

Introducing networks onto your boat greatly simplifies installation procedures. Start by putting together a quick plan of where the various bits of equipment will be located, including scope for any future expansion. This will dictate which type of cable and connectors are required. Network cables come in set lengths, so you will end up with lots of coils, but this is not a problem as they are all screened to stop interference.

If you need to cut off a pre-made connector to help cable routing, there are 'field attachable connectors' for the generic DeviceNet type that are usable with any manufacturer's cables. For Raymarine cables, you will have to strip the wires and re-solder the connector back on – it is not ideal but it works. Having said that, the Raymarine connectors are not much larger in diameter than the cable itself.

Ethernet

Once the switch is positioned, the cables are individually routed from the radar, fishfinder and other equipment requiring this type of network, so there is not much flexibility here.

NMEA2000

Think of every conceivable place you may want an instrument or display and run the backbone there with a 'T' piece or connector block installed. The cabling is relatively cheap and, as you will have removed ceiling and floor panels even for a short run, you may as well use the opportunity to do the whole boat. Don't forget to run connections near to all the tanks, as well as the engine and its control panel. Insert blanks into the spare drop cable sockets to prevent moisture and water ingress.

Below **All three networks run simultaneously to provide as much data as you need at the helm.**

Once the backbone is in, fitting a new instrument is much easier. A single 'multi-page' instrument in the skipper's suite (or bunk) is a real asset as it can display AIS data along with most other vessel information on the various 'pages'.

Where to start and finish

Starting at the base of the mast gives the option to extend the backbone cable from the masthead in the future.

⚙ Any masthead sensors, such as ultrasonic weather stations, with short drop cables can plug into the backbone at the top.

● The backbone terminator must always be at either end (start and finish) of the backbone cable.

● The backbone cable end coming out of the base of the mast joins to your original start point through a 'T' piece.

The other end of the backbone can be anywhere you like – don't forget, you have 200m (650ft) to play with.

NMEA2000 apparent 'daisy chaining'

It is common for new-style instruments to have two NMEA2000 sockets on the back, allowing several instruments to be 'daisy chained' together with drop cables. The last one in the chain has the drop cable into the backbone. This further simplifies the installation as it also includes the power supply for the chain.

Choice of backbone

Several manufacturers offer backbone and drop cables along with an array of 'T' or multi-way connectors and terminators. It really doesn't matter – there are so many adaptor cables and attachable connectors it is possible to mix and match as much as you like. This is the real beauty of the standardisation of NMEA2000 but your choice may well be down to the overall costs.

NMEA0183

Older NMEA0183-compatible instruments and equipment can still be used; there is a good second-hand market with many types still available and they will give long service if in good condition. You may need a multiplexer in addition to the NMEA0183 to 2000 converter (or SeaTalk 1 to SeaTalkNG converter in the case of Raymarine) but their data will then be available across the whole system.

Left Fix drop down points liberally around the boat like mains sockets – you will end up using all of them and probably need more.

Below and bottom For the backbone, it is best to stay with one manufacturer and use drop down cable adapters where necessary.

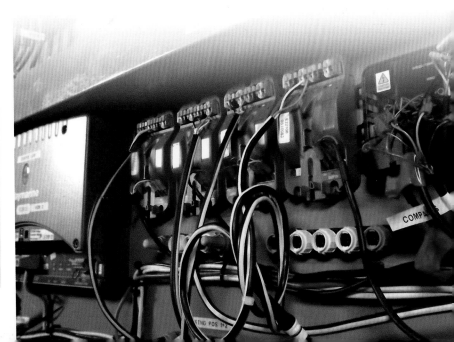

TIP

The 'DeviceNet' connectors come in 'male' and 'female' versions so look carefully at which type you need to make the connection; it is infuriating to have bought the wrong type. If you have to use a 'T' piece to resolve the situation, they take up quite bit of space so allow for that when positioning the equipment.

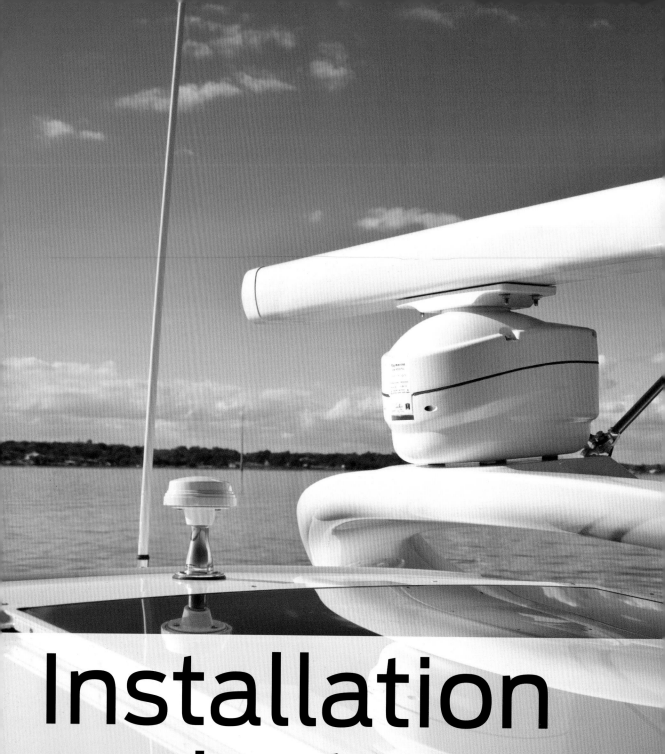

Installation
projects

9

Installing an AIS unit

AIS (Automatic Identification System) is a system for transmitting and receiving real time data about individual vessels. It requires a GPS input, an aerial the same as that of a DSC/VHF radio, a box of electronics and a display. There are some excellent products that make both new installations and upgrades straightforward.

AIS classification

AIS equipment is split into two categories, Class A and Class B. Class A type is the International Maritime Organisation (IMO)-approved unit which commercial vessels over 300 gross registered tonnes and passenger-carrying vessels are required to install. These are transceivers in that they transmit both static and dynamic data about the vessel and receive data transmitted from other vessels within range.

Class B equipment is lower cost (not being IMO-type approved) and is available either as a transceiver, similar to the class A unit, or as a receiver only version. Class B sets will receive (and display) data from both class A and class B transmitting units. If your vessel is capable of speeds in excess of 15–20 knots, you may want to consider a class A set, as the data transmission rate is far higher than class B, giving other vessels a more accurate track of your rapidly changing position.

Dual channel AIS

AIS uses two exclusive channels within the marine VHF radio frequency band and, as such, range is limited by the aerial height in the same manner as for a VHF radio. The two channels are used alternately for the transmission of updated data. All modern AIS units now receive data on both channels and are known as dual channel – some older units were single channel.

Installation of a Class B transceiver unit

There are four elements to an AIS system:

⚙ A separate, independent GPS source is required for the transceiver type AIS (unlike the receive-only versions) and is usually supplied with the equipment. If this is the only GPS on the boat, position data can be put onto the NMEA bus (default is off); otherwise, this remains separate from the GPS used for the rest of the boat's navigation systems.

⚙ A VHF aerial mounted as high as possible for best range. If you already have a VHF aerial, you can use an aerial splitter device so the same aerial can be used for both functions.

⚙ The AIS unit itself contains the electronics and can be installed anywhere below decks. Many models will accept 12 or 24V, but do check if you have a 24V system. Versions supplied without their own display are often referred to as an AIS engine.

⚙ A display is required to present the information to the user. Some models come with their own display, whereas AIS engines rely on using an existing chart plotter or multi-function instruments.

Interfacing to an existing display

If using a chart plotter as the display, the AIS data will need to be added to the network. An NMEA2000-compatible AIS will have a drop down cable which is plugged into the NMEA backbone. Alternatively you can use NMEA0183 and connect the appropriate wires together between

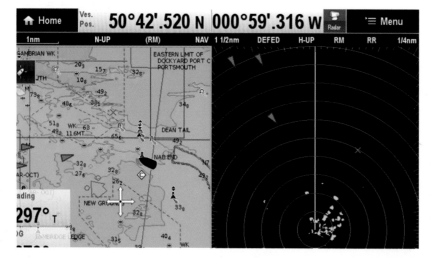

Left **AIS is very useful for tracking nearby vessels in confined waters but is particularly useful in open water where the AIS 'target' will appear on the display screen before you actually see it by eye. Only vessels transmitting data are displayed, so you must never rely solely on AIS for collision avoidance.**

CONNECTING AIS AND AERIAL SPLITTER

A separate aerial splitter unit simplifies the installation. The existing aerial connection is removed from the VHF and plugged into the aerial socket on the splitter. New cables are then taken from the splitter to the VHF and AIS units.

	AIS 650
WIRE COLOUR	FUNCTION
RED	power supply + (5 amp fuse)
BLACK	power supply -
NMEA 0183 Low band rate (4800)	
YELLOW	IN -
GREY	IN +
PINK	OUT -
PURPLE	OUT +
NMEA 0183 High band rate (38400)	
GREEN	IN -
WHITE	IN +
BLUE	OUT - ⎱ To IN +/- on
BROWN	OUT + ⎰ chart plotter
AIS SILENT MODE **	
ORANGE	AIS silent +
LIGHT GREEN	AIS silent -

** Switching off the transmit function (silent mode) can be done via the chart plotter or, by connecting a switch between the orange and light green wires for external operation.

With everything powered up and operational, the USB lead is plugged in and the ProAIS software run.

the AIS and the chart plotter, then set up the NMEA port on the plotter to receive the AIS data, ideally at 38,400 baud. Finally, enable the AIS overlay through the chart plotter or radar menus on the display.

Fitting the AIS GPS aerial

Ideally this should be installed externally to get the best reception, but they will often work just as well mounted in the cabin, high up under the coach roof or deck. The other end plugs onto the appropriate connector on the AIS unit.

Verifying the installation

Several manufacturers provide free software and USB drivers to enable full performance interrogation of the installation. A cable from your computer plugs into a USB socket on the AIS unit, also allowing the static

data settings to be entered. Bear in mind that data transmission can take up to six minutes to occur.

Below The best location for the GPS aerial was selected by watching the signal strength on the ProAIS software, as various positions were tried. Under the side deck, behind the distribution panel was perfectly acceptable in this case, making installation very easy.

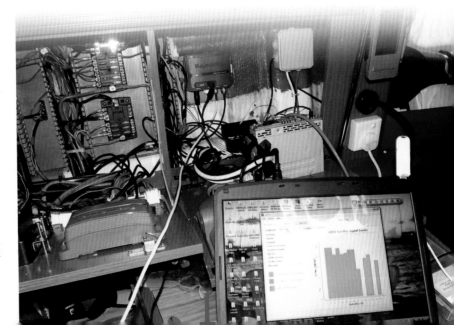

Radar

Radar is an asset on board if you understand how to use it and how to interpret the information on the display. Installing a system is electrically quite straightforward; the difficulty is mounting the hardware and routing the cable. The cable for newer digital radars is less bulky than in the past, and extending it is perfectly possible without compromising performance.

Standalone systems are still available, comprising a radar scanner, cabling and display. However, if you already have a compatible multi-function display (MFD), you only need to add a scanner and cable from the same manufacturer as the MFD.

Radome, open array and scanner length

Sailing yachts tend to use radomes which have an all-round case protecting the scanner from the sails, while large powerboats can opt for larger open arrays. The scanner length determines the horizontal beam width: the longer the scanner, the narrower the beam width and the better the target separation. Radomes typically have 46cm (18in) and 61cm (24in) scanners (4.9 and 3.9 degree beam width) whereas open arrays tend to be 122cm (48in) and 183cm (72in) (1.9 and 1.2 degrees respectively).

Positioning the scanner

Radar range, as with VHF and AIS, is inextricably linked to the height of the scanner. For sailing yachts, typically a position two-thirds up the mast or on a pole at the transom are recommended. The scanner must be above head height to avoid exposing those on board to the electro-magnetic energy being radiated, although this is not so critical for broadband radar units.

The mounting position should be as near as possible to the vessel's centreline, with the arrow (marked on the case) pointing to the bow. Fine alignment adjustment is done in the display menu. The vertical beam width is around 25 degrees,

Below and top **Radar scanners are essentially the same whether they are open arrays or enclosed in radomes. A self-levelling mount allows the unit to remain horizontal when the boat heels.**

so accurate vertical alignment is not crucial, although powerboats that have a pronounced bows-up trim may need the scanner to have a slight forward-down attitude.

Routing the cable

It is difficult to generalise on the best approach for feeding the cable up the mast, as the internal structure of the spar will vary depending on its make and age. Radar manufacturers have made this task easier as end connectors are now as small as possible, and power and data cables have been separated to reduce the bulk. There are many deck and bulkhead glands available and video advice on manufacturers' websites.

Power connection and grounding

As with most equipment, the radar will obtain its power from the distribution panel via a switch and fuse. Most open array radars require a separate power control module to step up the voltage needed by the radar. If a separate grounding wire is included in the power cable it should be connected to the boat's common ground point or, failing that, the battery negative terminal.

Follow the installation manual as regards fuse protection and wire diameters, but 46cm (18in) radomes generally take around 40W (20W in

standby) and 61cm (24in) models need 60W (25W in standby). Open arrays are 70W and above. Don't forget, the 4–6 kW that may be mentioned in the specification is not a constant power level – it's transmitted as a very short pulse so the average power for the radar will be as indicated above.

The display

Older analogue radars used to send weak analogue voltages along the full length of the cable to the display for processing before appearing on the screen. Cable lengths were therefore limited and could not be extended. Digital radars process the radar signals at the scanner and send digital data down the cable, which is much more resilient to interference.

Depending on the manufacturer you may have to plug the data cable into an Ethernet crossover coupler, then to a second cable leading to the display.

To display on multiple MFDs an Ethernet switch will be required, usually as a separate unit, although this is integrated into some MFDs. Due to the current lack of an international standard for these highspeed data networks, you will have to buy each element from the same manufacturer. In time this is likely to change.

TARGET SEPARATION

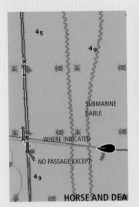

A 61cm (24in) scanner would show them as separate targets earlier because of the narrower beam width.

The two posts ahead merge into a single apparent radar target with an 46cm (18in) scanner, separating only as you get closer.

Fine adjustment of the scanner bearing alignment to the ship's head is done via the display menu. Without a chart overlay, take an accurate bearing of the object and adjust the radar bearing to bring them into line, having applied variation if the radar is in true bearing mode.

Below right An Ethernet crossover switch may be required to link the radar's digital data cable to the display socket via a more rugged cable and waterproof plug and socket.

Below left Most manufacturers are designing better connections to ease installation and removal. This is partly made possible as digital data cables are much less bulky than the older analogue ones.

Right To split out to multiple displays, or combine with other high data rate equipment like fishfinders, the radar is plugged into an Ethernet switch. These can be daisy chained to increase the amount of equipment and displays on the high speed network.

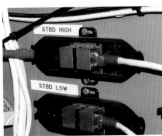

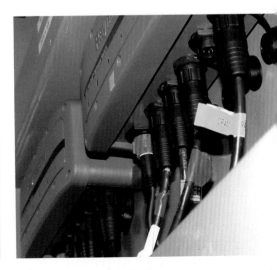

Navtex and SSB receivers

When near land we are awash with weather data, but out at sea this changes. Two easily installed receivers give access to weather, navigation and safety information when some way offshore. Navtex uses two medium wave frequencies to receive information sent by authorities such as the world's coastguards, while SSB gives access to similar information from a wider range of sources and over longer distances.

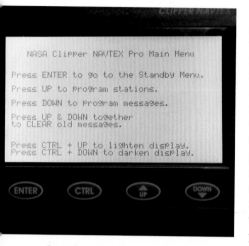

Above **The Navtex home screen shows how to access menu options. Information is in text form with the latest data visible on the screen. Scrolling up gives access to earlier broadcasts.**

Receiving Navtex information

An array of specific information is transmitted by coast radio stations in text form, in English, on an international frequency of 518KHz. This can be printed out (a requirement for commercial vessels), presented on its own display, or transferred to a chart plotter via NMEA. The world's coastlines are split into sectors and the relevant information is transmitted at set times in each one, with details published in almanacs, pilot books and so on.

If you leave the Navtex unit switched on continuously it will receive broadcasts, storing them in memory for later inspection. The unit can be programmed to filter out messages you deem irrelevant, for example ice warnings if you are in lower latitudes.

Although Navtex is considered a coastal service, the range (because of the frequency and high-power transmitters used) is some 400–500 miles offshore. The equipment is low-cost, easy to use and the service so good that no vessel should be without it. Occasionally reception is poor in marinas or bays with high cliffs, but you are rarely without weather and navigational-related information at sea.

Local services

Many nations have augmented the international service with a local one, at different time slots, on a second frequency of 490KHz. This is often in local language and is more geared to inshore weather forecasts and local navigational information. The simpler units do not monitor both frequencies, so you have to check broadcast times and switch to the local frequency as needed.

Single side band (SSB)

There is a little mysticism attached to SSB radios, particularly their aerials, and a misapprehension that a separate licence is required to use

Left **Navtex and SSB receivers essentially receive similar information from different sources. The SSB receiver will require a computer and de-coding software, whereas Navtex is a standalone system.**

this long-range equipment. Both of these assertions are true for transmitting SSB equipment, but not for a receive-only model. Again, the installation is straightforward, although a little more involved than for Navtex.

The unit we installed for this example came with decoding software and a useful guide to get started. A long wire aerial was replaced by a separately purchased active antenna, which is more suited to marine use. The receiver spans a wide range of frequencies, from 30KHz to 30MHz and, by tuning into the right station at the right time, you can receive anything from Navtex data to full synoptic weather charts, including five to ten day weather forecasts, for just about anywhere in the world.

To decode the data, a 'mono jack plug to jack plug' cable links the audio output of the receiver to a computer's sound card. From there the software takes over, enabling automatic reception and storage of broadcasts if the computer is permanently up and running. Alternatively, the Admiralty List of Radio Signals and the NOAA Marine Service Charts give complete details of broadcast station names, frequencies and transmission times for stations throughout the world.

Installation

Both units are installed in the same way. As the radio frequencies used do not depend on line of sight for reception, aerial height is not important so they can be mounted on the pushpit. All that is then left to do is to install a 12V supply and route the aerial cables to where the receiver will be mounted.

MOUNTING AERIALS

Both aerials come with a bracket to clamp on to rails. This is a simple arrangement, but they are vulnerable to stumbling crew. The SSB aerial shown is longer than the Navtex one, but otherwise has the same mounting arrangement.

The SSB receiver audio output lead is connected to a jack plug socket giving access from the front of the panel. A jack-to-jack lead then connects the socket to the microphone input on the computer.

Tune in to the right frequency and at the right time, then the information trundles out at a beautifully slow speed, just like old-fashioned teletype.

Hall effect ammeter

Hall effect sensors detect the magnetic field generated by a current present in a wire. If the wire is passed through the middle of the sensor a small voltage will be generated. This is directly proportional to the magnitude of the current, with its polarity indicating the direction. An appropriately calibrated gauge connected to the sensor output displays the current in amps.

Above **The sensor is a ring of magnetic material, which focuses the magnetic field generated in the wire onto the Hall effect sensor that is mounted in the slot.**

Selecting the sensor

Sensors are specified by the maximum current they will measure. Their output is a small voltage sent to the gauge to be displayed as the value of the current in amps. Typically the maximum rated current for the sensor results in an output voltage of plus or minus 60mV (millivolts) with the direction of current flow described by its polarity. The sensors range from 30A to 200A maximum current and the choice depends on the highest current to which the sensor could be exposed. It is important not to expose the sensor to current beyond its range, as this will adversely affect performance over time.

Positioning the sensor

The sensor may be placed in the positive or negative (0V return) paths. The installation in this example measures everything going into and out of the domestic battery bank, in this case two 120Ah sealed batteries. In this situation, it was easier to put the sensor in the positive side to measure:

❂ Current consumption from the domestic equipment via the distribution panel. The supply to the panel comes from the batteries via the main battery cables, which are all joined at the battery switch.
❂ Diesel heater current. A separate supply cable taken directly from one of the batteries.
❂ Mains charger current. The two charger outputs go directly to each battery via separate wires.
❂ Charging currents from the alternator, towing generator, solar panels and hydrogen fuel cell all go to the battery switch and then to the batteries via the large battery cables.

A 60A sensor and gauge were chosen to cover the worst case scenario in terms of maximum expected current, given that the 120A starter motor current is not being measured as it comes from the engine start battery. To achieve this, five cables have to pass through the sensor aperture: two main battery cables, two charger wires and the diesel heater wire.

The convention chosen was that charging current flowing into the batteries would show as positive on the gauge and current flowing out (consumption), negative. There is an arrow on the sensor showing which direction of current flow results in a positive output voltage.

Sensor connections

The sensor contains a small amount of electronics, so needs a power

Left **Initially the project looked a little daunting, with instructions (in 12 languages) containing little useful information; however, it proved quite straightforward.**

MOUNTING THE SENSOR

Once the location is chosen, the mounting bracket can be fitted so the sensor is the right way round.

The four white wires are marked every few inches to identify them. The 12V and 0V connections are picked up from nearby bus bars and a 1A in-line fuse is added. The two signal wires will be joined to the appropriate wires coming from the gauge.

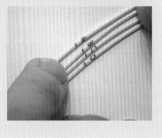

Finally the five wires of interest are passed through the sensor aperture and the resultant current flow can be measured.

TIP

You can measure several different currents around your boat's system by having more than one sensor linked to the same gauge via a switch. They will have to be the same rating though, otherwise the calibration will be incorrect.

supply (12V or 24V) and a 0V return. There are then two sensor output wires, which go to the gauge. The harness (purchased separately) had four white wires but on closer inspection, each wire had the letters A, B, C or D printed on them. Pin assignment is defined on the side of the sensor itself. A 1A fuse was installed in the positive supply wire.

The cables under scrutiny

The five cables have to be disconnected, passed through the sensor aperture the correct way and re-connected again so that the direction of current in each cable results in the correct reading on the gauge. The two charger wires, for instance, were passed through from right to left (conforming to the arrow mark), resulting in a positive output voltage when charger current was flowing into the batteries. The resultant, combined effect of all five currents (in and out) will therefore be measured and displayed as a single, net value.

Hall effect ammeter 2

The output voltage from the sensor needs to be displayed to show the correct magnitude and direction of the current flow, as this is the function of the gauge. The industry has standardised, to a large extent, so a wide range of sensors can be used.

Selecting the gauge

The gauge is chosen so that its input voltage range is matched with the output voltage range of the sensor (+/- 60mV in this installation), thereby achieving correct calibration and to show the corresponding maximum current range on the display.

The sensors mentioned above (30A–200A versions) all have the same maximum output voltage of +/- 60mV and most also have a backlight and an over-current indication. Other than that the choice of a specific model comes down to style and quality. These gauges can also display current passing through a resistive current shunt installed in the 0V return path, so they are not limited to Hall effect sensors.

Sensors and resistive current shunts

Gauges of this type (and their digital display versions) accept a pre-set range of voltages as their input, translating this into a needle movement across a dial (with a printed scale of 0 to +/- 60A), or a corresponding number on a digital display. The maximum input voltage (+/- 60mV) corresponds to the highest value of current shown on the dial (60A in this case). For the reading to be a correct reflection of the current, this requires the Hall effect sensor, used here, or a resistive current shunt, to also generate +/- 60mV at 60A, in other words, rated as 60A/60mV.

For measuring higher currents, up to 150A for example, both the gauge and sensor or shunt would have to be 150A/60mV versions. Two other

common ratings, particularly of resistive shunts, are +/- 50mV and +/- 100mV so the correspondingly rated gauge would have to be used.

The most important distinction between the Hall effect sensor and a resistive shunt is that the sensor can measure current in the positive cables (so-called 'high side' measurement), the 0V cables ('low side') or a combination of both. This makes it extremely versatile and simplifies the installation. The resistive shunt, on the other hand, can only be used to measure current in the 'low side' 0V return cables with gauges of this type. They must be collected together before connection to the shunt, so this may involve a fair bit of re-wiring.

Gauge connections

The gauge is supplied with a colour-coded eight wire plug-in harness. If the instructions do not define the wire colour/pin number relationship, this can be determined using a continuity tester (the VDO website provides a full data sheet). The pin number, wire colours and functions for the model in this installation are as follows:
1. V+ (8–32V), red. The supply to the gauge. This should come from a fused source, such as the instrument supply circuit.

Left The continuity tester was used to define the wire colour/pin function as the instructions for our unit omitted this. A full data sheet was available on the manufacturer's website.

2. Ground (0V), black. The 0V return.
3. To the sensor, blue/black. One of the two sensor inputs.
4. Battery switched (8–32V), brown. A positive supply to this wire will turn the gauge on. It can also be switched separately from the pin 1 supply, enabling the gauge to be turned on independently, or can be wired in with pin 1 so it comes on with the rest of the instruments.

5. To the sensor, green. The other sensor input.
6. Internal back light, blue/red. Again, 8–32V input, typically from the instrument lighting circuit.
7. Not connected.
8. Not connected.

Right **With several styles available, the gauge fits very neatly in the panel.**

INSTALLING THE METER

Connect up the gauge's wire harness first, including feeding the sensor input wires through to where the sensor is positioned. The gauge can be temporarily plugged in for testing.

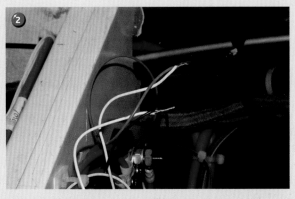

Temporarily twist together the sensor output wires (B and C) with the gauge's sensor input wires (blue/black and green). This allows you to check that the current direction is correctly reflected on the gauge. If not, swap them round.

Once everything is checked and working, the sensor connections can be soldered together and covered with heat-shrink tubing. Remember to slide the tubing on before soldering.

The gauge hole can be cut in the panel, the gauge secured and the harness plugged in. The harness includes the +12V and 0V connections for the gauge, the dial back light and the blue/black and green wires joined to the signal wires, B and C, from the Hall effect sensor.

Lightning protection

Lightning strikes to boats are relatively rare, and usually cause damage rather than injury. While lightning can't reliably be discouraged from striking your vessel, a few simple additions will help to guide it safely away from anything vital if it does.

The coast of Florida, USA, has the highest incidence of marine lightning strikes in the world, with an average of 1.5 hits per 1,000 motorboats, and 5 in every 1,000 yachts. Away from Florida's climate, the odds grow longer, but boats still remain vulnerable as they can act as a 'lead' for a ground charge, effectively shortening the distance a bolt has to travel to earth via the sea.

A great deal of research has been done over the years to protect ships and boats from the effects of a lightning strike, but there is still no perfect solution. Most defences involve providing the charge – which can be thousands of amps – with a safe route to ground. Unprotected boats could see the

Below Storm clouds gather across a Greek anchorage, emphasising the vulnerability of the yachts to a lightning strike.

charge flash sideways between the mast base and the chain plates, or exit through grounded seacocks, which are promptly blown out of the hull.

The most vulnerable vessels are yachts, mainly due to their tall masts, with multihulls being the most likely to be hit and damaged. This is due to their large surface area, which acts as a platform for the lightning to arc through. The safest vessels, oddly, are large steel ships, as there is so much metal in contact with the water that the charge usually dissipates safely.

Lightning prevention
You can't physically prevent a lightning strike, but you may be able to lessen the chances of being hit. Part of the problem of being offshore is that the water also

contains an electrical charge, and this literally climbs up your boat to the highest point and acts as a 'lead'. The opposing charge in the air above is drawn to this lead, and closes the circuit with a lightning bolt.

The usual culprit is the VHF aerial which is not only the highest part of the rig, but also tapers to a point, which focuses the charge. If this lead can be broken up, it is possible the boat will be less likely to be hit. One approach is a wire brush type arrangement that is put on a post very close to but higher than the tip of the VHF, and so makes the boat less attractive to a strike.

Lightning deflection
Another approach to limiting damage or injury from lightning is to create a Faraday cage (or Faraday shield) around the hull. In 1836, the

British scientist Michael Faraday observed that a metal enclosure would absorb electrostatic charges (and some kinds of electromagnetic radiation) and redistribute them around the external surface only. Anything inside the cage remains electrically neutral due to the physics of opposing electrical fields.

The large-scale Faraday cage systems designed to shield an entire yacht work on much the same principle. Highly conductive lightning rods at the top of the boat are connected to a series of thick cables that run outside the hull, and then run to earth on submerged copper grounding plates. Each system is custom designed and installed by specialists. Great care is taken to steer the cables away from vital systems.

Direct path

A further solution is to provide any lightning strike with a direct path to earth by grounding the mast to the keel. Other systems rely on a grounding plate of at least 930cm^2 (1ft^2) of copper connected without any sharp bends to the base of the mast to steer the charge to earth. Similarly, the bonding system that

links all the underwater components of a boat (propellers, stern gear, seacocks etc) is also connected to the grounding plate, and should steer the charge away from the crew while also preventing post-strike fires.

Unfortunately, lightning protection isn't an exact science and sceptics argue that any system designed to protect against lightning may also serve to attract it. Even so, a protection system should go some way to keeping the charge away from the crew by preventing dangerous side flashes.

Above left Lightning normally strikes the highest point on the vessel and the aerials and other equipment make easy targets without protection.

Above The top of the lightning rod is at the highest point and is splayed out to give it the best chance of being hit first.

Below These will almost certainly be the highest masts in the marina, much to the relief of the other yacht owners! Lightning protection is absolutely essential for this vessel.

> **TIP**
>
> A domestic oven offers protection from massive electromagnetic fields by acting like a Faraday cage. This means it is a good idea to put sensitive portable electronics in the boat's oven during a storm. Even a strike in the sea nearby can damage chip-based electronics if they are not protected. A customised metal box could also be used in the same way.

Underwater lights

If you want to light up the seabed, turn your rooster tail into a plume of 'fire', or just create your own underwater aquarium, submersible LEDs are the way to go. They are inexpensive to buy, easy to fit, low in power consumption and very durable. With a little imagination, they can turn your boat into a floating work of art.

Fitting underwater lights is proving increasingly popular, especially among motorboaters, and while there is some practical value in lighting up the surrounding sea, such as checking the seabed for obstructions or inspecting your stern gear, the main reasons are aesthetic. LEDs draw very little power, so are ideal for even the smallest craft, and

Below **LEDs are now available in a variety of colours, including some that can change on demand. This powerboat has chosen flame red for its rooster tail, but 'warp drive' blue is equally popular.**

by matching interior LED lights to the underwater lights, the whole boat and the surrounding water can be bathed in soft mood lighting. Better still, multicoloured lights are available that can be synchronised to music, allowing you to create your own underwater light show via a tablet computer.

At the heart of each underwater light is the hard-wearing and highly reliable LED, usually housed in a metal or polycarbonate fitting enclosed with a tough acrylic lens. These lights are invariably either 12V or 24V, and range from the

equivalent of 20W bulbs (producing 770 Lumen) to 250W (giving 12,000 Lumen). They draw anything from a few milliamps to an average of 0.2A each, so they won't drain the domestic power supply. Each unit emits a specific colour and intensity, while the top-end range can be multicoloured. The beams emitted can penetrate as far as 30m (98ft) in crystal-clear water, with different colours suited for specific areas.

Smaller units are available for tenders, and a remote control unit can be used to flick on the underwater (and deck) lights of

Far left The smallest lights are often the simplest to fit, as they only require a small hole for the wiring. The rest of the unit is simply bonded to the hull with a sealant.

Left Larger units such as these US-made Ocean LEDs will require a hole to be drilled in the hull, much the same as when fitting a seacock.

an anchored yacht to help identify it if you are approaching on a dark night after a run ashore.

Choosing the lights

Fitting underwater lights will involve drilling into the hull, although the holes themselves are not particularly large, usually around 9.5mm (approx.½in) for the smallest units to a maximum of 114mm (4½in) for superyachts. There are a few things to consider though before you start planning your system:

- **Location:** On motorboats the most usual location is on the transom/bathing platform area, although some owners ring the entire waterline with a halo of lights. As some bathing platforms extend a considerable distance from the transom, where the underwater lights will be mounted, allowances have to be made for the reach of the beams, and any shadows that may be cast by stern gear. The lights should be evenly spaced for best effect. If in doubt, use more lights. Larger yachts also run lights along the outer hull near the transom. Floodlights give a wash of colour whereas beam lights look more dramatic.

- **Colour:** The most popular colour is blue, as the shorter wavelength allows it to penetrate deep into the water. Apart from looking good, the blue light also excites natural phosphorescence in the sea, adding to the display.White is ideal in very clear seas,where it brings out the natural beauty of the seabed. The LEDs usually give a very pure whitelight, but in murky or brackishwater it will tend to look yellow or even brown. For these conditions, green is a much better choice, as it has excellent penetration and retains its colour the best, especially on lakes and rivers. Multicoloured LEDs are perfect for creating light shows, and for mixing and matching the colour to suit the mood. Red, for example, can be used to give an 'after burner' effect in a sportsboat's rooster tail.

Right top Green is the best choice in murky water.

Right middle White gives the best penetration in clear water.

Right bottom Blue is universally the most popular colour.

Underwater lights 2

Having established the location of each light, and ensuring there is nothing on the inside of the hull that will get in the way, fitting will involve drilling a single hole right through the hull. On smaller units, this will be just for a power cable, as the light is held in place by adhesive sealant, but larger units use a threaded stem with a flange sitting flush against the hull. The fitting is secured using a large nut tightened down on a flat washer from inside the hull, with generous amounts of underwater marine sealant to make it absolutely watertight.

Some units may also use stainless steel screws to lock the flange in place. After that, connection is easy. Unlike ordinary bulbs, LEDs have a positive and negative terminal, and won't work if these are reverse connected, so a clearly marked red (positive) and black (negative) wire protrude through the stem for connection to each side of the lighting circuit.

On the metal units, usually bronze, a grounding lug is included so the light can be connected into the boat's anti-galvanic bonding circuit, but this precaution is unnecessary on polycarbonate units. It is a good idea to antifoul the exterior flange of each light; they are usually supplied with a masking template to protect the lens during the painting process.

Once deployed, the lenses will need a quick clean with a soft brush every six weeks or so to keep them clear of slime, although some clear silicone antifoulings have been successfully used to deter any marine growth.

The LEDs should last for up to 50,000 hours of continuous use, and as they are highly resistant to vibration, shock and sudden changes in temperature, they can be used while under way at full speed with dramatic effects. Some designs allow the emitter unit to be withdrawn from inside the boat should the LEDs need replacing, although more usually the whole fitting will need to be changed.

Below **The lights on the transom of this Dutch-built motor yacht are spaced about a metre apart. Long bathing platforms may require more LEDs with a beam effect rather than a floodlight, to reach out from underneath.**

Complementing the lights

Most boats have, as standard, some kind of deck light. Many different lights are now available to fulfill both practical and aesthetic functions. All of the colour matching and mood lighting is available for above water locations such as spreaders, on the mast or gantry, and around the companionway. Whilst none of this lighting is actually necessary, there is no doubt that carefully thought out lighting adds a new dimension to a boat's appearance.

Up and down lighters fitted to the spreaders show a yacht at its best when in a marina but also have a more practical use of lighting up the sail. Whilst the skipper has an overriding responsibility not to interfere with the visibility of the vessel's navigation lights, you can make yourself more prominent to other vessels, especially if they are not taking the avoiding action you are expecting. Sail trimming is also easier if you can actually see the sail. It is also important, when at anchor, not to detract from the effectiveness of the anchor light by leaving the mood lighting on

overnight. The extra lighting, of course, makes the vessel more visible but it is essential that other vessels can establish your direction from the navigation lights so they must remain clearly obvious.

Personal watercraft and RIB/tenders, particularly on larger sailing and motor yachts, have become an opportunity to 'express oneself' with an array of underwater lighting and transom lights to illuminate the

Above left and right Placing LEDs on the spreaders of the mast is both attractive and practical, especially if they can be switched on wirelessly.

water plume. LEDs offer the best solution for this type of lighting because they can be fully sealed into the light fitting, making them truly waterproof. As they typically last in excess of 50,000 hours, it is more economic to replace the whole unit.

Below LEDs can be placed under the boom to illuminate the cockpit.

Upgrading mast electrics

Gone are the days when a masthead light and VHF aerial were the only electrics up the mast. There is a whole array of excellent products that benefit from being partway up, or at the top of the rig. Trunking space may be a limiting factor, but whatever you fit, make sure you use the best-quality cable, connectors and deck glands.

Installing new cables in the mast can be difficult, even with the mast out. Passing the wires through the deck is also an issue, so if this can be avoided without too much compromise a lot of effort can be spared.

Lighting
For sailboats, LEDs are a great benefit from the power consumption standpoint but beware of interference, especially when installed near an aerial. Some LED tricolour lights have been found to give out significant electro-magnetic interference noise, causing severe hissing on both VHF and SSB radio receivers.

LED bulb replacements can be used for all the lighting you want on the mast. The steaming, or masthead

Below **Six items of electrical equipment mounted at the top of the mast.**

light, is the only one required to be fitted partway up the mast, assuming your boat has an auxiliary engine. Before good-quality LED bulb replacements became commonplace, there was a significant power saving by also fitting a tricolour light at the top but, if you do not already have one, replace the bulbs of your separate port, starboard and stern lights with LED versions to get the power reduction, making sure they are the appropriate type for navigation lights.

The same applies to the anchor light, whether it is a temporarily hoisted type or a fitted masthead version. Deck lights can be fitted either on the spreaders or the mast – it may be worth using blue LEDs to maintain night vision. Blue LED uplighters also look good.

The benefit of height
The VHF aerial really does benefit from being at the top of the mast to get maximum range and is fitted as standard. If you subsequently install AIS, this also needs the same type of aerial and, again, the ideal is to fit it at the top. If you are unable to fit the AIS aerial at the top of the mast, you can use an aerial splitter on the existing VHF aerial or put the new AIS aerial on the pushpit. This is not ideal but it will still give a minimum range of around five miles – and a lot more for big ships because of the height of their aerials.

SSB active receiver and Navtex aerials don't need height, so a location around the transom is sufficient. SSB transmission aerials are a whole different ball game. Because the length rather than

height is the most important factor, they are added to or become part of the back stay. There are many other issues with full SSB implementation, outside the scope of this book.

Active radar reflectors again rely on height for maximum range, and as you want to be seen, you want the benefit of a mast top installation. TV reception aerials benefit a little from height, mainly to get them away from other metalwork. Lightning dispersers can only do their job if they are at the highest point on the boat.

Instrument transducers and sensors

Your wind vane needs to be at the top of the mast to have a clear wind flow for accurate readings. The relatively new solid-state weather stations have several advantages in that there are no moving parts. The top of the range versions generate the following data from a single unit:

- Wind speed
- Wind direction
- Air temperature
- Relative humidity
- Barometric pressure
- Compass heading
- 3 axis rate of turn gyro (for Class A AIS transponders)
- Pitch and roll accelerometer
- 10Hz GPS data
- Calculated true wind, speed and direction data (from apparent wind and SOG/COG data).

They are NMEA2000 compatible so you can start your backbone cable at the top of the mast and plug the weather station in at that point. It picks up its power and transmits all the data along the backbone cable.

Radar and hailer/foghorn

Typically mounted two thirds of the way up the mast, although not related, these tend to be on the same bracket. Most VHF/DSC manufacturers offer units that generate pre-programmed fog horn

Above Large yachts may also have hydraulic systems in the mast and boom to do the really hard work.

sounds, repeated at the correct intervals, and include a loud hailer option as well.

SITING NEW EQUIPMENT

1: An active radar reflector sited at the top of the mast gives the maximum range and therefore earliest warning.
2: Loud hailer/fog horn
3: A 'solid state' (no moving parts) multi-function transducer feeds its data into the NMEA2000 backbone.

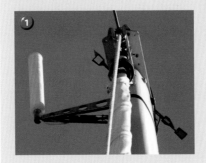

Appendix 1: Wire size matrix

The choice of wire diameter is governed by the losses deemed to be acceptable in a given circuit. Copper wire, like all conducting materials, has a finite resistance, and when current is flowing Ohm's Law dictates that the voltage drop (or loss) is a function of that current multiplied by the wire's resistance.

Acceptable losses

The battery terminal voltage is the maximum voltage available to a circuit. The voltage that actually appears at the terminals of the equipment in that circuit is the battery voltage minus the losses in the wire. In general, using a larger wire diameter resulting in a smaller 3 per cent loss is deemed acceptable for critical or sensitive equipment (chart plotters, autopilots and so on) and 10 per cent for lighting and other non-essential kit. In practice, however, the 3 per cent figure can be used throughout, unless there is a cost issue.

Using the tables

Wire resistance is calculated using a number of parameters:
- ρ – the resistivity constant of copper (0.0164 Ωm)
- L – the length of the wire (in metres), both out (positive wire) and return (back to 0V connection)
- A – cross-sectional area of the copper in mm^2.

The tables opposite calculate the cross-sectional area of copper required to achieve losses of 3 per cent and 10 per cent given the amount of current and length of wire required.

The cross-sectional areas are then grouped by colour into the nearest American Wire Gauge (AWG) value that corresponds to the calculated areas. (Note, it is not intended to be a direct conversion but a 'closest fit' solution.)

As the range of available wire cross-sectional areas is limited, go for the nearest size above the suggested one in the tables. This also allows for the fact that the calculation is based on a single solid wire, not the multi-strand wire that is used in practice, which has a tiny air gap between each strand.

An example

To illustrate using the tables, consider the example of installing a fridge compressor. From its installation manual, let's say, you find the power consumption quoted as 90W and it can run from 12 or 24V systems. From the equation amps = power/volts (see page 17), the current will be around 7.5A on a 12V system and 3.8A on a 24V system. Assume you estimate the cable length from the distribution panel to the compressor to be 8m (26ft) (4m/13ft to it with the positive cable and 4m/13ft back with the 0V cable) and you decide to opt for less than 3% losses in the cable run.

From the lower (3%) table, choose the 8m column and the 8A current row for the 12V, or 4A row for the 24V systems. This results in 12AWG and 14AWG respectively. Use these or the next sizes up (next lower AWG, remember) for extra margin. The table below summarises the choices.

WIRE SELECTION (SEE TABLES OPPOSITE)

Battery system voltage	12V	24V
3% voltage drop	0.36V max.	0.72V max.
Running current	7.5A	3.8A
Total cable run	8m (26ft)	8m (26ft)
Cross-sectional area	2.92mm² – use 3mm²	1.46mm² – use 2mm²
AWG	10AWG	12AWG

Use the 3% table to determine the wire size for critical equipment, where minimum voltage losses are important for correct functioning. For more general equipment, the 10% table will be acceptable. If the slight extra cost of the larger wire diameter is not an issue, then use the 3% table as your standard approach.

10% VOLTAGE DROP IN CABLE

Cable length (metres)

Current in amps	2	4	6	8	10	15	20	25	30	35	40	45	50
1	0.03	0.05	0.08	0.11	0.14	0.21	0.27	0.34	0.41	0.48	0.55	0.62	0.68
2	0.05	0.11	0.16	0.22	0.27	0.41	0.55	0.68	0.82	0.96	1.09	1.23	1.37
3	0.08	0.16	0.25	0.33	0.41	0.62	0.82	1.03	1.23	1.44	1.64	1.85	2.05
4	0.11	0.22	0.33	0.44	0.55	0.82	1.09	1.37	1.64	1.91	2.19	2.46	2.73
5	0.14	0.27	0.41	0.55	0.68	1.03	1.37	1.71	2.05	2.39	2.73	3.08	3.42
6	0.16	0.33	0.49	0.66	0.82	1.23	1.64	2.05	2.46	2.87	3.28	3.69	4.10
7	0.19	0.38	0.57	0.77	0.96	1.44	1.91	2.39	2.87	3.35	3.83	4.31	4.78
8	0.22	0.44	0.66	0.87	1.09	1.64	2.19	2.73	3.28	3.83	4.37	4.92	5.47
9	0.25	0.49	0.74	0.98	1.23	1.85	2.46	3.08	3.69	4.31	4.92	5.54	6.15
10	0.27	0.55	0.82	1.09	1.37	2.05	2.73	3.42	4.10	4.78	5.47	6.15	6.83
11	0.30	0.60	0.90	1.20	1.50	2.26	3.01	3.76	4.51	5.26	6.01	6.77	7.52
12	0.33	0.66	0.98	1.31	1.64	2.46	3.28	4.10	4.92	5.74	6.56	7.38	8.20
13	0.36	0.71	1.07	1.42	1.78	2.67	3.55	4.44	5.33	6.22	7.11	8.00	8.88
14	0.38	0.77	1.15	1.53	1.91	2.87	3.83	4.78	5.74	6.70	7.65	8.61	9.57
15	0.41	0.82	1.23	1.64	2.05	3.08	4.10	5.13	6.15	7.18	8.20	9.23	10.25
16	0.44	0.87	1.31	1.75	2.19	3.28	4.37	5.47	6.56	7.65	8.75	9.84	10.93
17	0.46	0.93	1.39	1.86	2.32	3.49	4.65	5.81	6.97	8.13	9.29	10.46	11.62
18	0.49	0.98	1.48	1.97	2.46	3.69	4.92	6.15	7.38	8.61	9.84	11.07	12.30
19	0.52	1.04	1.56	2.08	2.60	3.90	5.19	6.49	7.79	9.09	10.39	11.69	12.98
20	0.55	1.09	1.64	2.19	2.73	4.10	5.47	6.83	8.20	9.57	10.93	12.30	13.67
25	0.68	1.37	2.05	2.73	3.42	5.13	6.83	8.54	10.25	11.96	13.67	15.38	17.08
30	0.82	1.64	2.46	3.28	4.10	6.15	8.20	10.25	12.30	14.35	16.40	18.45	20.50
35	0.96	1.91	2.87	3.83	4.78	7.18	9.57	11.96	14.35	16.74	19.13	21.53	23.92
40	1.09	2.19	3.28	4.37	5.47	8.20	10.93	13.67	16.40	19.13	21.87	24.60	27.33
45	1.23	2.46	3.69	4.92	6.15	9.23	12.30	15.38	18.45	21.53	24.60	27.68	30.75
50	1.37	2.73	4.10	5.47	6.83	10.25	13.67	17.08	20.50	23.92	27.33	30.75	34.17
55	1.50	3.01	4.51	6.01	7.52	11.28	15.03	18.79	22.55	26.31	30.07	33.83	37.58
60	1.64	3.28	4.92	6.56	8.20	12.30	16.40	20.50	24.60	28.70	32.80	36.90	41.00
65	1.78	3.55	5.33	7.11	8.88	13.33	17.77	22.21	26.65	31.09	35.53	39.98	44.42
70	1.91	3.83	5.74	7.65	9.57	14.35	19.13	23.92	28.70	33.48	38.27	43.05	47.83
75	2.05	4.10	6.15	8.20	10.25	15.38	20.50	25.63	30.75	35.88	41.00	46.13	51.25
80	2.19	4.37	6.56	8.75	10.93	16.40	21.87	27.33	32.80	38.27	43.73	49.20	
85	2.32	4.65	6.97	9.29	11.62	17.43	23.23	29.04	34.85	40.66	46.47	52.28	
90	2.46	4.92	7.38	9.84	12.30	18.45	24.60	30.75	36.90	43.05	49.20		
95	2.60	5.19	7.79	10.39	12.98	19.48	25.97	32.46	38.95	45.44	51.93		
100	2.73	5.47	8.20	10.93	13.67	20.50	27.33	34.17	41.00	47.83			

3% VOLTAGE DROP IN CABLE

Cable length (metres)

Current in amps	2	4	6	8	10	15	20	25	30	35	40	45	50
1	0.09	0.18	0.27	0.36	0.46	0.68	0.91	1.14	1.37	1.59	1.82	2.05	2.28
2	0.18	0.36	0.55	0.73	0.91	1.37	1.82	2.28	2.73	3.19	3.64	4.10	4.56
3	0.27	0.55	0.82	1.09	1.37	2.05	2.73	3.42	4.10	4.78	5.47	6.15	6.83
4	0.36	0.73	1.09	1.46	1.82	2.73	3.64	4.56	5.47	6.38	7.29	8.20	9.11
5	0.46	0.91	1.37	1.82	2.28	3.42	4.56	5.69	6.83	7.97	9.11	10.25	11.39
6	0.55	1.09	1.64	2.19	2.73	4.10	5.47	6.83	8.20	9.57	10.93	12.30	13.67
7	0.64	1.28	1.91	2.55	3.19	4.78	6.38	7.97	9.57	11.16	12.76	14.35	15.94
8	0.73	1.46	2.19	2.92	3.64	5.47	7.29	9.11	10.93	12.76	14.58	16.40	18.22
9	0.82	1.64	2.46	3.28	4.10	6.15	8.20	10.25	12.30	14.35	16.40	18.45	20.50
10	0.91	1.82	2.73	3.64	4.56	6.83	9.11	11.39	13.67	15.94	18.22	20.50	22.78
11	1.00	2.00	3.01	4.01	5.01	7.52	10.02	12.53	15.03	17.54	20.04	22.55	25.06
12	1.09	2.19	3.28	4.37	5.47	8.20	10.93	13.67	16.40	19.13	21.87	24.60	27.33
13	1.18	2.37	3.55	4.74	5.92	8.88	11.84	14.81	17.77	20.73	23.69	26.65	29.61
14	1.28	2.55	3.83	5.10	6.38	9.57	12.76	15.94	19.13	22.32	25.51	28.70	31.89
15	1.37	2.73	4.10	5.47	6.83	10.25	13.67	17.08	20.50	23.92	27.33	30.75	34.17
16	1.46	2.92	4.37	5.83	7.29	10.93	14.58	18.22	21.87	25.51	29.16	32.80	36.44
17	1.55	3.10	4.65	6.20	7.74	11.62	15.49	19.36	23.23	27.11	30.98	34.85	38.72
18	1.64	3.28	4.92	6.56	8.20	12.30	16.40	20.50	24.60	28.70	32.80	36.90	41.00
19	1.73	3.46	5.19	6.92	8.66	12.98	17.31	21.64	25.97	30.29	34.62	38.95	43.28
20	1.82	3.64	5.47	7.29	9.11	13.67	18.22	22.78	27.33	31.89	36.44	41.00	45.56
25	2.28	4.56	6.83	9.11	11.39	17.08	22.78	28.47	34.17	39.86	45.56	51.25	
30	2.73	5.47	8.20	10.93	13.67	20.50	27.33	34.17	41.00	47.83			
35	3.19	6.38	9.57	12.76	15.94	23.92	31.89	39.86	47.83				
40	3.64	7.29	10.93	14.58	18.22	27.33	36.44	45.56					
45	4.10	8.20	12.30	16.40	20.50	30.75	41.00	51.25					
50	4.56	9.11	13.67	18.22	22.78	34.17	45.56						
55	5.01	10.02	15.03	20.04	25.06	37.58	50.11						
60	5.47	10.93	16.40	21.87	27.33	41.00							
65	10.47	15.93	21.40	26.87	32.33	46.00							
70	15.47	20.93	26.40	31.87	37.33	51.00							
75	20.47	25.93	31.40	36.87	42.33								
80	25.47	30.93	36.40	41.87	47.33								
85	30.47	35.93	41.40	46.87	52.33								
90	35.47	40.93	46.40	51.87									
95	40.47	45.93	51.40										
100	45.47	50.93	56.40										

AWG
18
16
14
12
10
8
6
4
2
1
1/0

2: Energy consumption analysis

For sailing vessels, accurately defining energy consumption is almost impossible as the nature in which the vessel is used on a day-to-day basis varies so much. It is however useful to list all your equipment and understand the current consumption in both standby (if applicable) and full running modes.

Grouping equipment into three categories – items that may be in use continuously, those mostly left in standby mode, plus those that are only turned on when required – will begin to build up a picture of the likely power consumption in a 24-hour period. Many powerboat owners will be able to ignore this appendix almost completely; even if you often spend nights at anchor, a quick run up the coast the following day will have all the batteries fully charged again.

Note that it is easy to overlook the impact of equipment considered fundamental to being underway. For the fridge, the average current over a day, when left on and controlled by the thermostat, is less than the full current as quoted in the manual, when the compressor is running continuously. Turning it on in short bursts reduces the total energy drawn from the batteries but at the expense of the temperature of the contents. Radar is often turned on when the chart plotter is initially powered up. It goes into standby but may get forgotten and its consumption overlooked. The multi-function display (chart plotter) itself is often left on even though it may not be being put to serious use.

The table opposite expresses the power consumption of each item, rather than current, as larger vessels may be running on 24V systems. From the fact that current = power / voltage, you can work out the current by dividing the power by the average battery voltage, say 12.5 for a 12V system and 25V for a 24V system.

Lastly, to enable direct comparison with the battery capacity, multiply the current by the number of hours each item is used during the day to get the amp hours value for the equipment. As the range of products is so wide, it is better if you fill in the actual power consumption for the equipment on your own vessel on the table.

EQUIPMENT NORMALLY RUNNING CONTINUOUSLY

Equipment typically left on continuously when underway	Typical running current	Amp hours (24 hours)
Automatic Identification System (AIS) with own display	0.1	2.4
Navtex	0.1	2.4
Wind / Log / Depth instruments	0.3	7.2
Instrument repeaters	0.1	2.4
Separate GPS receiver	0.1	2.4
Gas solenoid	0.1	2.4
Gas alarm	0.1	2.4
VHF/DSC radio	0.3	7
Fridge (average continuous current)	1.5	36
Power monitoring system	0.1	2.4
TOTAL		**67 Ah**
Chart plotter and radar		
Multi-function display (chart plotter) – latest model	0.75	18
Radar left in standby	1.5	36
TOTAL		**67-121 Ah**

POWER AUDIT GUIDE

Equipment in standby mode	Standby power (watts)	Running power (watts)	Amps (power/volts)	Amp hours
Navigational & ancillary equipment				
Multi-function display (chart plotter)				
2nd multi-function display				
Radar – radome				
Radar – open array				
Fishfinder				
Autopilot (vessels under 35 ft)				
Autopilot (vessels over 35 ft)				
Navigation lights				
Anchor light				
Deck lights				
Cockpit lights				
Additional sailing instruments				
Windlass				
Bow thruster				
Cabin and domestic equipment				
Cabin lighting				
Watermaker				
Stereo system				
Fans				
Diesel heater				
DC–AC inverter				
Water pumps				
TV				
Freezer				
MF DSC radio				
SSB receiver				
Laptop/computer				
Other equipment on board (not listed here)				

3: Battery configuration and switching

With two or more battery banks, it becomes necessary to introduce battery switching to control the charging and protect individual banks from being inadvertently discharged. The simplest switches are purely mechanical but depend on human operation. At the other extreme are fully integrated, electronically controlled automatic systems.

The objective

Most, if not all vessels have at least one battery and a means of recharging it. The standard approach on small to mid-sized vessels is to have two separate battery banks, and as the size of boat goes up, possibly a third bank for high-current equipment such as electric winches, anchor windlasses and bow/stern thrusters. Coupled with this, there may be multiple sources of charging. With this scenario, the system needs to be managed using battery switches. The main objectives are:

✪ To direct one or more sources of charging between the battery banks.
✪ With multiple banks, find a way of prioritising which bank gets charged first.
✪ Isolate the banks from each other when charging is not available to prevent inadvertent discharging.
✪ Isolate the banks completely when the vessel is not being used.

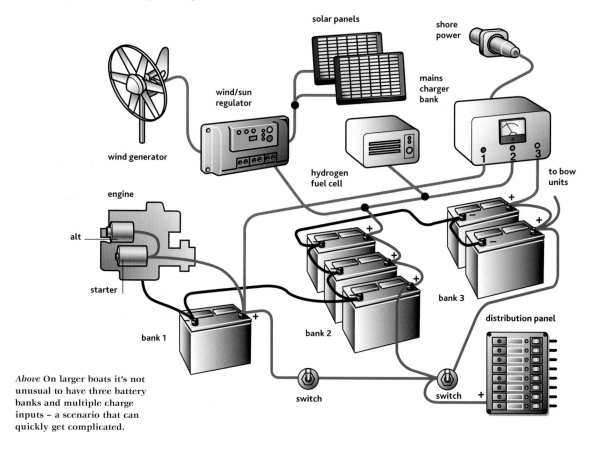

solar panels

shore power

wind/sun regulator

mains charger bank

wind generator

hydrogen fuel cell

1 2 3

to bow units

engine

alt

starter

bank 1

bank 2

bank 3

distribution panel

switch

switch

Above On larger boats it's not unusual to have three battery banks and multiple charge inputs – a scenario that can quickly get complicated.

BATTERY BANKS AND COMMONLY ALLOCATED SOURCES OF CHARGING

Battery bank	Source of charging
Engine (and diesel generator) start battery	Alternator Mains charger output 1
Domestic battery bank	Mains charger output 2 Solar panels Wind generator Water-powered generator Fuel cell
Thruster/windlass/winch battery bank	Mains charger output 3 Consider connecting the solar panels to this bank instead of bank 2.

BATTERY BANK CHARGE STATE SCENARIOS

A number of scenarios are possible with the various sources of charging.		Action
Engine off (no alternator power available)	Bank 2 getting ample charge from its sources.	Route excess power through to bank 1 (priority) and/or bank 3 once bank 2 is full.
	Bank 2 depleted with little charging from its sources taking place.	Need to ensure banks 1 and 3 are not dragged down to compensate.
	Bank 3 heavily depleted (after lots of anchor work).	Bank 3 must be isolated from 1 and 2. It will have to wait until excess power becomes available as it has the lowest priority. May have to run engine specifically for it.
Engine running, alternator providing power	Bank 1 gets priority.	Once bank 1 full, bank 2 starts receiving power.
Diesel generator running	Provides mains power to the mains charger.	All three banks get charged but the total output from the charger is split between the three banks. The most depleted will 'hog' most of the available current – probably bank 2 in reality. May have to run for several hours.
Fuel cell turned on	Can be left on overnight or longer to provide float current.	Bank 2 gets priority; once full banks 1 and 3 can get the benefit of the float charge.

3: Battery configuration and switching

The simplicity of manual switching between different battery banks and charging sources may be appealing, but it risks the possibility of running batteries flat due to human error. Automated switching systems are therefore preferable in most cases, although the simplest and most inexpensive suffer from significant voltage drops.

Right The four-way rotary switch is the most common manual approach for a two-battery bank system. Select 'Battery 1' prior to starting the engine, and switch to 'Both' after ten minutes or so to split the charging between both battery banks. Switch to 'Battery 2' once the engine has stopped to isolate the engine start battery. Each battery may have its own single isolator switch as well.

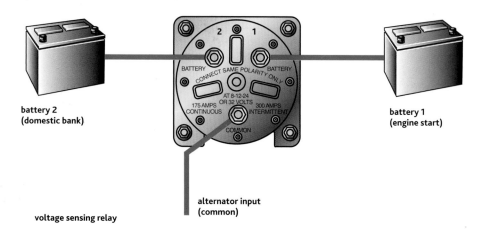

battery 2
(domestic bank)

battery 1
(engine start)

alternator input
(common)

voltage sensing relay

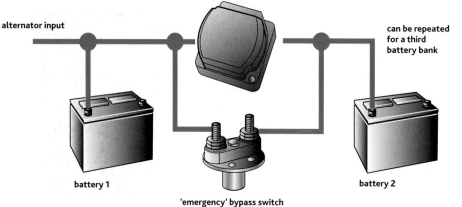

alternator input

can be repeated
for a third
battery bank

battery 1

battery 2

'emergency' bypass switch

Left A fully automated approach. The voltage sensitive relay monitors Battery 1 voltage and when that is charged, it closes its internal relay contacts and allows charge through to Battery 2. VSRs can be bi-directional so that if Battery 2 is full, excess charging current from solar panels or wind generators can be directed into Battery 1 (or through to Battery 3 if fitted). The optional emergency bypass switch would allow manual intervention if required.

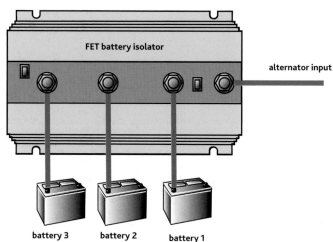

FET battery isolator

alternator input

Right A very neat solution automatically prioritising the available alternator charging current to the three battery banks. Again, emergency bypass switches could be added.

battery 3   battery 2   battery 1

PROS AND CONS OF SWITCHING SYSTEMS

	Advantages	Disadvantages
Manual switches	Purely mechanical, virtually zero voltage loss.	Rely on human operation.
Single	Ideal to use as an 'emergency bypass' around electronic switches and individual battery isolators.	
Four-way rotary	Minimum required for a basic two-battery bank system. Straightforward to use.	
Automatic switches	Pretty much 'fit and forget' devices.	Each type has its foibles but they are inherently reliable.
Diode splitters (or battery combiners)	Simple to install.	Loss of at least 1V across the diode, reducing the alternator voltage seen by the batteries.
Relay based automatic switches	Electronic control enables priority to be given to engine start battery.	Can suffer from 'contact chatter' unless steps are taken to reduce or eliminate this in the internal control electronics.
Battery separators (activated by the ignition switch)	Behave the same as the diode splitters but use relay contacts to carry the current, resulting in near zero voltage loss.	Limited 'intelligence' but basic and simple.
Voltage sensing relays	More 'intelligence' built in. Monitors battery voltages to determine which contacts are closed and therefore where the charging current is channelled.	
FET isolators *	Probably slightly more reliable than relay-based switches and allow more sophisticated electronic control.	More expensive than other types of switches. Can get warm when handling lots of current so require ventilation.
Integrated systems	Combine many functions into one unit.	Higher unit cost but may result in lower system cost.
Alternator to battery chargers	Get the best out of the alternator, provide multi-stage charging for the domestic bank and provide the intelligent battery switching.	

Note * Field Effect Transistors, or FETs are semi-conductor devices which can handle large amounts of current. They essentially exhibit a small resistance when conducting current and so will result in some losses (typically 0.1V – 0.2V at rated current). This is higher than the voltage loss of relays but much lower than diode splitters.

4: Engine electrics

The engine electrics are a major system on any vessel, yet they suffer a difficult environment, with vibration and high temperatures in the engine compartment, while exterior control panels are open to rain and salt spray. The system can be split into two parts: controls for starting and stopping the engine, and instrumentation to monitor engine behaviour.

Above Pull the stop cord until the engine stops, then you can turn the power to the engine electrics off.

Starting the engine

The diagram opposite outlines the basics of engine electrics. If the engine has injector pre-heaters (glow plugs) the control panel will be fitted with a four-position key switch. The first action is to turn the key to the 'Glow' position for about 10 seconds. This applies quite a high current to a heater element around each fuel injector to pre-heat the combustion chamber and improve starting.

At the end of this time, you then switch through 'Off' to 'On', which powers up all the engine electrics (including the alarm sounder (10)), apply some throttle and then turn the key against a spring to 'Start'. This energises the starter motor solenoid (12), engaging the starter motor (13). Once the engine starts, release the key and the spring will return it to the 'On' position.

The 'On' position feeds power to:

- ✿ All the instruments (6).
- ✿ The ignition or charge light (VR), oil pressure (15) and water temperature (14) warning lights. These go off as the engine starts and the alternator output voltage rises.
- ✿ Through the ignition light, power is supplied to the alternator's Voltage Regulator (wire 11) and then to the rotor winding. This creates a small amount of magnetic field in the rotor so that as it begins turning (as the engine starts) enough power is generated to kick the regulator into operation and control the alternator output correctly.
- ✿ The engine sensors (16) are also powered up with their return path via the engine block and strap cable (8) to the battery negative.

On engines without pre-heaters, the common procedure is to apply virtually full throttle, give one pull on the engine stop pull cord and then switch to engine start on the ignition switch. This is a mechanical action that feeds extra fuel within the high pressure pump to aid starting. As the engine fires up, then back off on the throttle to drop the revs.

Stopping the engine

To stop a diesel engine, you need to cut off the fuel supply. This is achieved by pulling a 'Stop Cord' until the engine stops, then you can turn the ignition switch to 'Off'. Alternatively there may be a 'Stop' button (17) which operates a stop solenoid (17) that does the same job. Again do not switch the ignition to 'Off' until the engine has stopped.

Sensors, gauges and alarms

If your engine has gauges, they are connected to sensors on the engine itself which perform two functions:

- ✿ A variable signal which gives an actual reading of cooling water temperature, oil pressure, voltages and currents and other features depending on the complexity.
- ✿ A switched signal connected to the alarm sounder (10) and the indicator lights showing when a parameter exceeds a safe value.

If there are no gauges then the sensors will be just the 'switch' type.

Left The four-position switch is used on engines with injector pre-heaters or glow plugs.

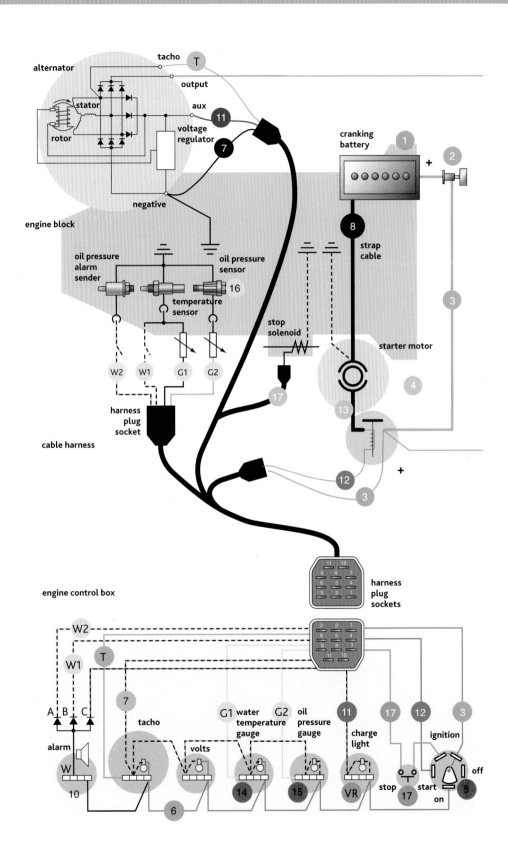

5: NMEA sentences

The table in this appendix lists the common NMEA0183 sentences. It is useful to understand which sentences are available from the 'talker' (or number of talkers if using a multiplexer) and which ones are needed by a listener, such as an autopilot. The other common requirement is to convert from 0183 to NMEA2000 and back.

Converting between standards

Converting from NMEA0183 to NMEA2000 may require an external module, often referred to as a gateway. There are many on the market. (NB: The majority of sentences are shown but, as the software is periodically upgraded, check on the manufacturer's website).

A very common upgrade to a vessel is to add an Automatic Identification System (AIS). Many AIS manufacturers, even now, still use NMEA0183 to output the data and if your vessel has a new chart plotter, it is likely to need the data in NMEA2000 format. Most, but not all chart plotters can accept NMEA0183 straight in via the wiring loom so you just have to check they request the sentences made available by the AIS.

Those that can't accept NMEA0183 will need an external gateway to do the conversion. The Actisense NGW-1-AIS is designed specifically for this (their NGW-1 is for more general conversion applications); the AMEC NK80 unit also has the required sentences.

Communicating between NMEA0183 equipment

The second issue is to understand which sentences are required by a listener to function correctly. Your system may have just one talker, for instance the GPS 128 from Garmin, and you can match up the sentences required by the autopilot, GPS repeater and the DSC/VHF radio. If you have expanded your 0183 system by multiplexing several talkers, then simply compile a single list of all the sentences as these will be available at the multiplexer output. As far as the listeners are concerned, the multiplexer output looks like a single talker.

Abbreviations(*)	
AIS	Automatic Identification System
COG	Course over ground
SOG	Speed over ground
GNSS	Global Navigation Satellite System
DOP	Dilution of position, a measure of GPS positional accuracy

COMMON NMEA0183 SENTENCES

Topic	Sentence	Definition
Waypoints & routes	AAM	Waypoint arrival alarm
	BOD	Bearing, waypoint to waypoint
	BEC	Bearing and distance to waypoint – dead reckoning
	BWC	Bearing and distance to waypoint – Great Circle
	BWR	Bearing and distance to waypoint – Rhumb Line
	DTM	Datum reference
	RTE	Routes RTE – Routes
	WCV	Waypoint closure velocity
	WPL	Waypoint location
	XTE	Cross track error (also included in RMB)
Depth	DBT	Depth below transducer
	DPT	Depth
Navigation/GPS	GGA	Global positioning system fix data
	GLL	Geographic position – Latitude/Longitude (no COG or SOG*)
	GNS	GNSS fix data *
	GSA	GNSS DOP and active satellites *
	GSV	GNSS satellites in view
	RMB	Recommended minimum navigation information
	RMC	Recommended minimum specific GNSS data (including COG
	VTG	Course and speed over ground
Heading	HDG	Heading, deviation and variation
	HDT	Heading, true
	ROT	Rate of turn
	RSA	Rudder sensor angle
Temperature	MTW	Water temperature
Wind	MWD	Wind direction and speed
	MWV	Wind speed and angle
	VWR	Relative apparent wind speed and angle
Engine	RPM	Revolutions per minute
Water speed	VDR	Sert and drift
	VHW	Water speed and heading
Time & date	ZDA	Time and date
AIS*	VDO	AIS VHF data link – own vessel report
	VDM	AIS VHF data link – messages
Radar	RSD	Radar system data
	TTM	Tracked target message
DSC/VHF radio	DSC	Data from DSC alert received by DSC/VHF radio

Explanation	Common recognised sentences						
	NMEA0183 - 2000 Gateways			Talking to each other			
	Actisense NGW-1	Actisense NGW-1-AIS	AMEC NK80	GPS 128	Autopilot	GPS repeater	DSC / VHF radio
Denotes waypoint arrival due to entry of waypoint arrival circle.							
Used in routes, describing the bearing and distance data on current leg between previous and next waypoint.					●		
Distance calculated based on speed through the water rather than GPS SOG.*							
Distance calculated as a Great Circle Route.					●		
Distance calculated as a Rhumb Line.					●		
Datum used for position eg., WGS84.							
Details the waypoints contained in an active route.					●		
Calculates the speed directly towards the waypoint regardless of the actual course.							
Waypoint name, latitude and longitude.					●		
Distance either side of the line joining the start point (or previous waypoint) to the next waypoint.	●	●	●		●		
Depth without keel or waterline offset values, ie., the 'raw' data from the transducer.	●		●				
Offset value introduced to display of depth below keel or waterline as required.	●		●				
Location data (including altitude!) along with positional accuracy information and number of satellites being tracked.	●	●	●	●	●		
An older variant of GGA.	●	●	●	●	●		
Comprehensive information regarding the GPS position fix being produced.							
Contains data on the quality of the GPS position fix.	●	●	●	●		●	
Data regarding the actual satellites being used in the positional fix.	●	●	●		●		
Navigational data relating to steering towards a waypoint including cross track error.	●				●	●	
Contains position, UTC time, date, SOG and COG along with variation.	●	●	●	●	●	●	●
The track over the ground (bearing and speed) made good.	●	●	●				
Data from a magnetic heading sensor (fluxgate compass) along with variation and deviation data.	●	●			●		
True heading after applying variation.	●				●		
Change in heading in degrees per minute due to the application of rudder.	●	●	●				
Degrees of rudder angle being applied.	●		●				
Sensor reading of water temperature. Often included in the water speed transducer.	●		●				
True wind speed and direction calculated from wind transducer data and adjusted for water speed and heading.	●		●				
Apparent wind direction and speed from wind transducer.	●	●	●		●		
Wind angle given relative to bow heading, ie., degrees off bow, port or starboard.	●						
Propellor shaft or engine revolutions per minute.	●						
Tide direction and speed calculated from the difference between GPS SOG/COG* data and boat heading and speed through water information. The assumption is that the difference equates to the tidal flow.	●		●				
Data taken from water speed transducer and heading sensor.	●					●	
Time data is UTC but sentence includes local time offset information as well.	●	●	●		●		
Own vessel data collated for use in plotting other vessels, aids to navigation etc., relative to your own current position. Speed and heading information is used for target tracking.		●	●				
AIS data extracted from the transmissions of other vessels, aids to navigation etc.		●	●				
Range and bearing of the cursor from ship's own position as displayed on the radar screen.							
Data related to a tracked target on radar from ship's own position. Target number, bearing and distance, speed etc.							
To enable a distress alert data to be displayed on a chart plotter. Range and bearing to vessel in distress can be calculated.			●				

Glossary

A

AC Stands for 'Alternating Current' but is generally used to describe a voltage or current that continually reverses in polarity. The number of times this occurs in a second is called its frequency, measured in 'Hertz'.

AGM batteries Absorbed Glass Mat battery technology is an improvement on the basic lead acid battery and has a number of advantages over sealed (wet) batteries.

AIS Automatic Identification System is a system that can transmit data regarding your own vessel and receive information about other vessels within range. It is a VHF system using two non-voice channels within the marine radio VHF band.

Alternator An electro-mechanical machine, mounted on the engine, that generates AC electricity. It then converts this to DC suitable for charging the batteries. It is usually driven from the main engine shaft by a drive belt.

Amplifier An electronic device that multiplies its analogue input voltage to produce a greater analogue voltage signal at its output.

Analogue (analog) signal A 'raw' signal voltage produced by a sensor.

Auto off A function that automatically turns a device off after a certain time, usually to conserve battery life.

B

Baud rate Digital signals are transmitted along a wire as either a '1' or '0'. The rate at which the 1s and 0s are transmitted in one second is known as the 'Baud Rate'.

Bonding A term referring to the connection together of all the metal parts of a vessel that come into contact with the water, in particular the sacrificial anode.

Boost chargers An electronic circuit that increases (or boosts) the voltage at its output to a higher value compared to the

voltage at its input. This technique is used in battery to battery chargers.

Bow thruster An electric (or hydraulic motor on larger vessels) driving a transverse propeller at the bow of a vessel. Electric versions consume large amounts of current and require special consideration within the vessel's electrical system.

Brushes Small carbon blocks that, in contact with a rotating shaft, conduct electric current into the shaft. They are held against the shaft by springs and are replaceable when worn. Found in alternators to pass current through to the rotor winding.

Bus bars A length of conducting material (typically copper) with a number of screws available to facilitate the connection of many wires together at one point.

C

Calibration value Setting up a meter or other measuring device so that it displays the parameter being measured correctly. For

example, the calibration value of a resistive current shunt is typically 1mV/A.

Charge acceptance rate The amount of current per hour that can safely be 'forced' back into batteries, by a charger, without causing overheating and the possibility of over-charging damage.

Charging current The value of current, in amps, that is being 'forced' back into the batteries by an external power source.

Circuit A collection of wires, connectors, switches, fuses and equipment starting and ending at the positive and negative battery terminals respectively.

Clamp meter A device for measuring current, that clamps over the wire carrying the current of interest. They can measure very high currents without any modification to the wiring itself.

Cold cranking The current required to engage and rotate the starter motor sufficiently to start the engine. Starter batteries quote a minimum cold cranking current (in amps) as part of their specification.

COM COM, short for COMMON, is the term given to the point of lowest voltage potential in a system. It is the zero reference voltage from which other voltages are measured. On a boat, it is the negative terminal of the batteries.

Conductors Metals or other materials with the ability to conduct electricity.

Continuity An uninterrupted length of wire, with no breaks in it is said to have 'continuity'.

Conversion of energy Energy cannot be created or destroyed, merely converted between different forms such as heat, light and motion.

Crimps A generic term for a connector where the wire is inserted in a tube which is then

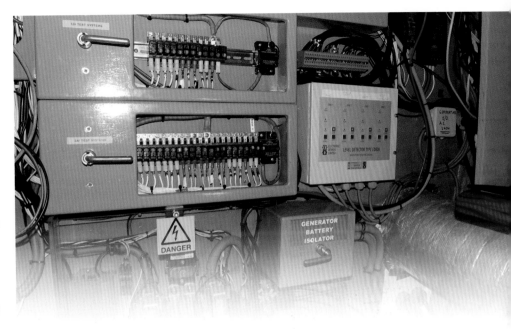

compressed with a crimping tool to clamp the wire in place.

Croc clips Croc (short for crocodile) clips are spring-loaded clips that have teeth to grip onto a wire.

D

Daisy chain Where instruments or elements of a system are connected to each other in a line.

DC Stands for 'Direct Current' but is generally used to describe voltages and currents that remain constant against time. A DC current of 4A remains at 4A so long as it is flowing, otherwise it is zero.

De-ionised water Purified and filtered water suitable for topping up un-sealed batteries, where access to the individual cells is possible.

DeviceNet An industry standard network including the specification of network cable connectors. Used as the standard connector for NMEA2000.

Differential amplifier An amplifier that only amplifies the difference between its two input terminals. Used in high side measurements, a differential amplifier removes the battery voltage element of the signal being measured.

Diode A semiconductor (electronic) device that acts as a one way valve to electric current, only allowing current flow in one direction.

Diode splitter A pair of diodes that allow sharing of the alternator's charging current between two battery banks, but prevent one bank discharging the other when the engine is not running.

Discharge current Current that is flowing out of the batteries, discharging them.

Discharge cycles The number of times a battery has been run down and recharged again. Deep cycle batteries can tolerate this

many hundreds of times so long as the depth of discharge does not exceed 50 per cent.

Domestic batteries The batteries associated with providing power for all the equipment other than the engine start and, possibly, the bow thruster or anchor windlass.

Drive belt A tough rubberised belt that enables the engine's main shaft to drive the alternator and water pump (on fresh-water cooled engines).

Dump resistors Large resistors that can handle reasonably high currents and convert that energy into heat. Typically used to 'dump' excess power from a wind generator that is not required for battery charging.

E

Earth The ultimate electrical reference point, the true zero. In household mains, earth really is earth, as a metal rod is sunk into the ground. In other systems, it refers to the point of lowest voltage potential, from which other voltages are measured. See *COM*.

Electrolyte A solution of salts dissolved in water. The salts are then available to interact in a chemical reaction. The electrolyte in a lead acid battery is sulphuric acid.

Emergency transfer switch A manual battery switch that bypasses an automatic one to allow manual intervention. The most common example is to allow the domestic batteries to start the engine, a situation normally prevented by the automatic system.

Energy balance The balance between energy consumption from the batteries and energy returned to them by any and all means of charging.

F

Filter (electronic) An electronic circuit that removes any unwanted signals.

Fishfinder A high performance depth sounder. Some versions are so accurate they can distinguish between different types of fish.

G

Gel batteries Batteries that have their electrolyte in gel form. They can be truly sealed and function at any angle without the risk of spillage.

Generators Devices that produce electrical power by various means.

GPS Global Positioning System, whereby a receiver can calculate its position with reference to three or more orbiting satellites.

H

Heat-shrink tubing Plastic tubing that shrinks in diameter when heated. Used to cover and seal some electrical wire joints.

Heatsink A piece of aluminium with fins that is designed to increase the surface area, improving heat dissipation from a piece of electrical equipment.

High side measurement Measurement of current in the positive (12V or 24V) cable. The best example on a vessel is the alternator output current.

Glossary

Horizontal axis drill An electric drill that has the drill bit axis at right angles to the main handle. They allow better access in confined spaces.

I

Idle revs The lowest engine running speed, typically when the gearbox is in neutral. It may be too low to generate any appreciable amount of electrical power from the alternator.

Inrush current The initial or 'start up' current of a bulb or motor. It is much higher than the normal running current but short lived.

Insulators Materials that do not conduct electricity.

Interlock A system that prevents one event from happening if another event has occurred. For example, an ignition

interlock would prevent a relay operating whilst the engine is being started.

K

Kilovolts Units to describe a very high voltage. 1kV is 1000 volts.

L

Lead acid A generic term for the battery technology typically used on boats.

Losses Losses in an electric circuit manifest themselves as voltage drops around the circuit, reducing the amount of battery voltage available at the equipment being powered by the circuit.

Low side measurement Measurement of current in the return path (0V) cable. See **High side measurement**.

M

Magnetic field The magnetic influence produced when an electric current passes through a conductor (or wire). If the wire is formed into a coil, as in a solenoid or alternator winding, the magnetic field is concentrated and becomes more intense.

Main contacts The high current handling contacts in a relay or switch.

Maintenance free Sealed batteries do not have access to the individual cells and you are therefore not able to top up the electrolyte levels, hence, you cannot do any maintenance.

Measurement hold A function on some models of multimeter. A button that allows you the retain the value of the last parameter measured (eg. voltage) once you

have removed the probes from the circuit.

Micro volts Units to describe a very small voltage; 1uV is one millionth of a volt.

Milli volts Units to describe a small voltage. 1 mV is one thousandths of a volt.

Multi-function display A display unit that performs multiple tasks. Principally acting as a chart plotter (using electronic charts), it can also display radar, video (from cameras around the vessel), Automatic Identification System data and many other parameters. Often referred to as a chart plotter.

Multi-pole switch A single switch lever which connects (internally) two or more independent pairs of contacts. Each pair is referred to as a 'pole' and is part of a different circuit. Multi-pole switches allow several circuits to be activated by the one switch.

Multimeter A meter capable of measuring several electrical parameters. Often known as a digital volt meter (DVM).

N

Node A connection of a number of wires or cables. The current into a node equals the sum of the currents leaving the node. More commonly called a bus bar.

O

Open circuit volts The voltage between two points when no current is flowing. For example, the output voltage of a solar panel may be 18–20V when not connected to a battery.

Over-charging Forcing too much current into a battery will result in a rise in temperature of the electrolyte, causing a consequent rise in pressure in a sealed battery or the evaporation of the water content of the electrolyte.

In either case, potential damage to the battery will result.

P

Parallel wired Elements connected in parallel are connected so that the same voltage is applied to each element. Batteries connected in parallel (within a battery bank) have the same output voltage as a single battery but add together the capacities of each battery.

Polarity The polarity of a voltage or current is described as positive or negative with respect to some other reference point. The '+' terminal of a battery is described as positive with respect to the '-' terminal; equally, the '-' terminal is described as negative with respect to the '+' terminal.

Potential difference The difference in potential, or measured voltage, between two points in a circuit, measured in volts. Often referred to as voltage drop or voltage difference.

Power audit A list of all the equipment on the vessel, its current consumption when in use and, an approximate (typical) number of hours used within a 24-hour period.

R

RCD/RCCB Residual Current Device/Residual Current Circuit Breaker. A safety device that detects a small current flowing in the mains earth wire (a fault condition) and activates an integral circuit breaker in both the live (hot) and neutral wires, so electrically disconnecting the mains supply.

Regulator An electronic circuit that controls the delivery of power from a generating source to the batteries.

Relay An electro-mechanical device which uses a solenoid to open and close main contacts capable of carrying very high current. The control current,

operating the solenoid, is very small (100s of milli amps).

Return path The path the current in a circuit takes to return to the battery negative terminal. It is normally a particular cable but may also include the metal structure of the engine in the case of the starter motor and alternator.

Reverse engineering The process of understanding and documenting the existing electrical circuits through tracing the wiring from the battery positive terminal, all the way around the circuit, to the battery negative terminal.

Reversible reaction A chemical reaction that can be reversed by the introduction of some outside influence, when required. Recharging a battery reverses the chemical reaction that produces the electricity in the first place.

S

Sacrificial anode Usually zinc or aluminium, the sacrificial anode dissolves (due to galvanic corrosion) before any other of the vessel's metal parts in contact with the water. They are replaced once spent.

Sealed batteries Batteries where the six individual cells are sealed, preventing electrolyte (sulphuric acid) spillage.

Sense wire A wire that is connected to a sensor at one end and an input terminal to a control unit at the other. It transfers the sensor signal to the controller.

Series wired Elements connected in series are connected along a single path, so the same current flows through each element. Batteries connected in series, in a bank, retain the same capacity of a single battery but add together the voltages. A 24V battery is made up of two 12V batteries in series.

Short circuit A direct connection between the positive and negative battery terminals. This may occur at the battery itself or within the wiring where a positive and negative wire become directly connected together accidentally. Either way, the resulting current will be dangerously high.

Side cutters Another common name for wire cutters.

Single pole switch When the lever of a switch is activated, it will connect (internally) two of its contacts together, allowing current to pass in via one terminal and out from the other (see *Multi-pole switches*).

Solenoid A electro-mechanical device consisting of two main parts. An outer coil of wire (with many hundreds or thousands of turns) producing a concentrated magnetic field when a current is passed through it. Secondly, a movable steel or iron 'plunger' (the armature) which moves as a reaction to the presence of the magnetic field. The movement can then be used to push electrical contacts together, completing a circuit, as in a relay.

T

Terminal voltage The difference in the measured voltage between two terminals. For example, a battery terminal voltage might be 12.7V between the positive and negative terminals.

Thermocouple A device consisting of two wires, of dissimilar metals, joined together at one end. The potential difference (voltage) measured between the other open ends of the wire is a function of the temperature being measured at the joined end.

U

Universal input A piece of mains-powered equipment that can accept mains input from anywhere in the world, without making any adjustment to the equipment.

V

Voltage drop The difference in (measured) voltage between two points in a circuit. For example, the voltage drop, or potential difference, between either end of a current sensing resistive shunt is directly proportional to the current flowing through it and is used to measure the current.

W

Winding A long length of wire that is wound around a former to produce a coil. Most commonly found in solenoids, relays and alternators, from a boating point of view.

Windlass A machine for lowering and raising the anchor. An electric windlass consumes large amounts of current and requires special consideration within the vessel's electrical system.

Wire chasers A flexible rod that can be pushed behind panels to help route wires and cables.

Wire gauge The diameter of a wire. Each time a wire is pulled through a 'draw plate' (in the manufacturing process) it becomes thinner; the wire gauge number describes the resultant diameter. The most commonly used is the American Wire Gauge (AWG) and the higher the number, the thinner the wire.

Index

Index

Acknowledgements

The publisher would like to thank the following agencies for their kind permission to reproduce photographs/artworks in this book.

Alamy 12, 36–37, 152–153
Peter Caplan 42
Corbis 40
istockphoto.com 2–3, 10–11, 20–21, 50–51, 62, 116, 164
Jake Kavanagh 166–169
The National Maritime Electronic Association (NMEA) 144–145
Rupert Holmes 86–87, 114–115
Shutterstock 58–59, 136–137

The author would like to thank the following companies and individuals for their kind permission to reproduce photographs and other material in this book.

Active Research Ltd. (Actisense), Advanced Yacht Systems, Airmar Technology Corporation, Ampair, Andrew Simpson (p173), Bardon Batteries, BOC (Linde Group) (p75), CC Marine, Eclectic Energy Ltd, Fuel Cell Systems Ltd, Furneaux Riddall, Marlec Engineering Ltd, Mastervolt, Merlin Power Systems, Murata Power Solutions, National Maritime Electronics Association, Optima Batteries UK, Richborough Consultants, Smart Gauge Electronics, Sterling Power Products Ltd, Victron Energy BV.

The author also appreciates the photographic opportunities that have been made available by: Aspire Boat Sales Ltd, Sarisbury Green; Hamble School of Yachting, Hamble Pascoe International, Sarisbury Green; Quintessence Sea School, Sarisbury Green; Raymarine Ltd, Fareham; Universal Marina, Sarisbury Green; Vortec Marine, Port Solent.

Additional technical input has also been provided by: Ampair Turbines, Northern Ireland; Noland Engineering in Florida, USA; Sterling Power Products, Droitwich, Worcestershire.

Also thanks to Sarah Doughty, Judith Chamberlain-Webber, Rupert Holmes and others at Ivy Group, the studio of Peters & Zabransky for the artworks and Andrew Simpson for acting as technical consultant. Finally I would like to express my appreciation to my wife Sue Johnson for her invaluable support and encouragement throughout the project.

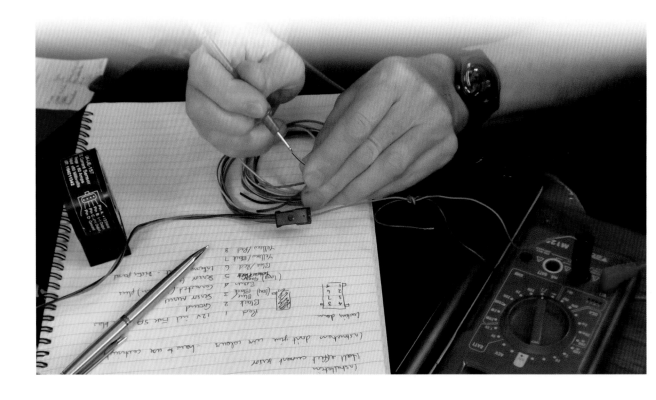

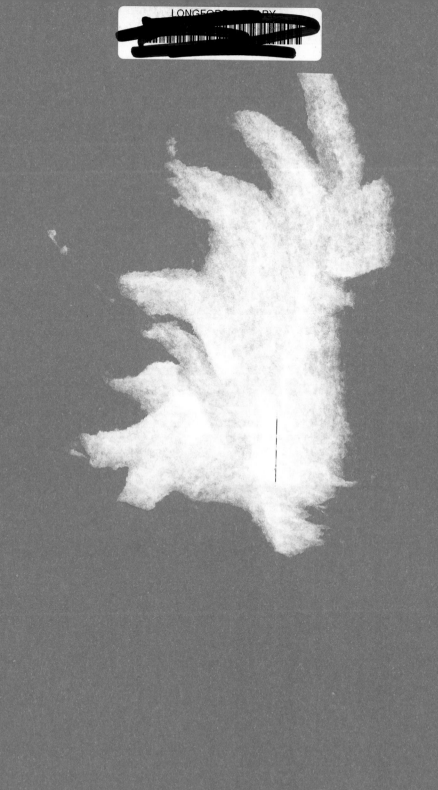